TUPOLEV TU-2
THE FORGOTTEN MEDIUM BOMBER

TUPOLEV TU-2

THE FORGOTTEN MEDIUM BOMBER

JASON NICHOLAS MOORE

FONTHILL

I dedicate this book to my nephews, Alexander and Nicholas.

Fonthill Media Language Policy

Fonthill Media publishes in the international English language market. One language edition is published worldwide. As there are minor differences in spelling and presentation, especially with regard to American English and British English, a policy is necessary to define which form of English to use. The Fonthill Policy is to use the form of English native to the author. Jason Nicholas Moore was born and educated in the United States but prefers to write in British English; therefore British English has been adopted in this publication.

Fonthill Media Limited
Fonthill Media LLC
www.fonthillmedia.com
office@fonthillmedia.com

First published in the United Kingdom and the United States of America 2016

British Library Cataloguing in Publication Data:
A catalogue record for this book is available from the British Library

ISBN 978-1-78155-532-3

Typeset in 10pt on 13pt Sabon
Printed and bound in England

Preface

As far as I am aware, this is the first reference book in English devoted solely to the Tupolev Tu-2. The Tu-2 bomber remains almost unknown in the west, or at best dimly known as a name, although it was one of the finest medium bombers of the Second World War and was produced and used for many years after the war by a number of different air forces. This lack of renown is due, I think, to the fact that the early version of the Tu-2, which participated in important operations like the Battle of Kursk, was used in small numbers only, due to the premature cancellation of its production in 1942 by Soviet Premier Josef Vissarionvich Stalin (1878–1953). By the time that the improved Tu-2S entered service in significant numbers (in the middle of 1944), the important early battles like the siege of Leningrad, the Battle of Moscow, and the Battle of Stalingrad had already been fought and won by the Soviets. Indeed, the Tu-2 saw more service (and production) after the Second World War.

It is my intention that this reference work will rectify the lack of knowledge on this nonetheless significant and interesting aeroplane. I will describe the Tu-2 from its development by Andrey Tupolev (while still in NKVD custody as a prisoner before the Great Patriotic War), its wartime service, and its long post-war history, including its usage in the Korean War (1950–53) and in the Tibetan uprising of the late 1950s and early 1960s. In addition, I will describe in some detail the many experimental versions of the Tu-2 and its experimental uses—much of it post-war.

Due to reasons of unavailability, I will not be able to go into as much depth on the actual combat usage of the Tu-2 as I would have liked. There is unfortunately little detailed information on the use of the Tu-2 in combat, especially its post-war use in Korea, despite the aircraft seeing action in the Second World War and in Korea, among other wars. There is little in either English or Russian on its use in combat missions. Its possibly substantial use in Tibet by the Chinese, during the Tibetan Uprising in the late 1950s and early 1960s is shrouded in mystery, and this is not likely to become clearer any time soon. Strangely enough, there is quite a bit of information on the various versions of the Tu-2, including its many post-war versions, so I will be able to cover these in considerable detail, although, even here, sources sometimes differ in the details.

Something that you will notice is my frequent usage of terms such as 'one source states', 'apparently', 'the record is unclear', 'it appears', etc. This is not due to any inherent indecisiveness on my part, but to the inconvenient fact that some questions and details regarding the Tu-2 are rather hard to be completely certain about. It is difficult to make comprehensive, all-inclusive statements about an aeroplane that was built at several different factories over a period of ten years, one that was produced in two completely distinct versions (separated by a year and a half), and one that featured many detail changes over these years—some minor and some major. It is difficult at times to be positive about certain details as the changes are not always well-attested in the record. Sometimes the sources are silent or contradictory on some matters, so I have had to examine all the available evidence and decide what I think is most likely.

The lack of exact information (as with its combat use) or conflicting information—for example, in the case of the production numbers for the Tu-2, where each source seems to have slightly different numbers—may be due to the almost privileged nature of the Tu-2. In its first incarnation, it was more of a pre-production aircraft than a mass-produced one, whose combat use at first was something of a closely guarded secret; in fact, it was so secret that Josef Stalin himself did not know of its success until the first official combat reports reached him, by which time he had already cancelled its production. In its second version (the Tu-2S), it was watched very closely by Josef Stalin. Josef Stalin was not exactly noted for his openness and he may have kept much of the combat information regarding the Tu-2 to himself. After the war, the cloak of Cold War secrecy descended on the Soviet military, but, nonetheless, a surprising amount of information about the post-war version has survived and is accessible. This may be due to the fact that, since there was no longer a war going on, with its attendant pressures on simply getting the production aircraft built, detail changes and prototypes could be better recorded and described. However, even here there are still gaps and contradictory information, especially concerning production figures (again), and even which variant was produced at which *zavod* (factory). When there is an unresolved question, or conflicting information from different sources, I will clearly state this.

A term you will not see me use in this book is 'Russia' to refer to the Soviet Union or 'Russians' to refer to the Soviets. Although this convention is still used in most English-language war histories and references, I consider it to be inaccurate and it will not be used in this reference work. Russia, or the Russian Soviet Federative Socialist Republic, was the largest and most populous constituent republic, but it was still just one of the republics that together made up the Soviet Union, or the Union of the Soviet Socialist Republics (to give its full name translated into English). Although ethnic Russians made up a majority of the military, both in the field and especially in the officer corps, millions of non-Russians also served (and died) in the Red Army during the Great Patriotic War, and it should be remembered that the head of the Soviet Union was himself a non-Russian, the Georgian named Josef Stalin. In addition, most of the Soviet civilian casualties occurred in the non-Russian republics of Byelorussia and the Ukraine. It is no more accurate to refer to the members of the Red Army (and more specifically the Red Air Force) as 'Russians' or to their country as 'Russia' than it is to refer to the British and Commonwealth forces of the Second World War as 'English', or to the UK as 'England'. When I use the term 'Russia' in this book, it is to refer to a specific geographic region in the Soviet Union, not to the Soviet Union as a whole, and 'Russian' will refer to an ethnic Russian, not just any Soviet citizen.

One interesting note about the Tu-2 is that it does not seem to have attracted the nicknames that most successful (and some not so successful) warplanes always seem to attract (especially with Western aircraft, where there are often official nicknames; in fact, after the Second World War, NATO gave the Tu-2 the nickname 'Bat'). The most widely used term for the production Tu-2 seems to have been simply the 'Tu-2' ('*Too-dvah*' in Russian). For this book, the first production version of the Tu-2, sometimes known as the 'Tu-2VS' (which designation I am not certain that the Soviets even used in the Great Patriotic War), will be referred to as the 'early Tu-2', or the 'early version of the Tu-2', or some such similar designation. The revised Tu-2 will be referred to as the 'Tu-2S'. In some instances, where the version is obvious from context, for example in the post-war period, where all production aircraft (save a few Tu-2Ts) were of the Tu-2S variety, I will simply use the term 'Tu-2'.

Perhaps the most important contribution to aviation history of the Tu-2 is a not so obvious one. If the first prototype had failed, Tupolev would almost certainly have been executed by the NKVD. That means no Tu-16 'Badger', no Tu-22M2 'Backfire', no Tu-95 'Bear', or any other of the large military and civilian aircraft that the Tupolev Bureau designed after the Second World War. The post-war aviation landscape, especially in the Soviet Union, would have been a very different one.

Jason Nicholas Moore
Seguin, Texas
1 November 2015

Acknowledgements

I gratefully acknowledge the kind assistance of Viktor Kulikov and Gennadiy Petrov for the fine photographs they have provided. Without the help of the aforementioned people, this book would have been much harder, even impossible to complete. I would like to give a special thank you as always to Mike Williams of Britmodeller.com (a fine site), who introduced me to the Fonthill Media editor Jay Slater (a special thank you goes out to you, Jay, also, and to all the fine folk at Fonthill for your hard work in turning this manuscript into a presentable book). I would also like especially to thank Michal Sekula. Without Michal's fine and accurate work on the colour profiles, this book would have been very much the poorer. Moreover, I would like to thank my family for their moral support, financial assistance, and forbearance as I pursued this literary work. As with all my humble efforts, I hope that I have made them proud with it. Finally, any mistakes and errors in this work are my own.

Contents

Preface 5
Acknowledgements 8
Glossary of Terms 10
Introduction 17

1 Tactical and Medium Bombers: A Definition 19
2 Soviet Bombers Before the Tu-2 21
3 Genesis of the Tu-2 28
4 First of the Breed: The 103 30
5 A New Beginning for the Tu-2: The Tu-2S 51
6 The Tu-2 *vs* other Medium Bombers of the Second World War 75
7 Post-war Development and Experimental Variants (Includes Projects) 85
8 The Jet Successors to the Tu-2 122
9 Post-war Service 130
10 The Tu-2 in Detail 136

Appendix I: Tu-2 Specifications 154
Appendix II: Survivors 158
Appendix III: Production Figures 160
Appendix IV: Plastic Scale Model Kits 165
Bibliography 167
Index 172

Glossary of Terms

AA: Anti-aircraft artillery, sometimes abbreviated to 'AAA' or referred to as 'triple-A'. Another name for this is *flak*, the German name for it (which is the name I will normally use throughout this book—see entry for flak further on). These were guns, ranging from rifle-calibre guns to large cannons that were used against aircraft.

ADD: *Aviatsiya Dal'nego Deiystviya*, or long-range aviation, which was under the direct control of the Stavka, the Soviet High Command. The ADD was dissolved in late 1944 and its aircraft absorbed into the Red Air Force as the 18th VA (*Vozdushnaya Armiya*—Air Army). It was reformed after the war as the DA, or *Dal'nyaya Aviatsiya*.

AVMF: *Aviatsionniy Voyenno Morskovo Flota*—the naval air forces. Tu-2s were used for anti-shipping duties, close air support, and as torpedo bombers.

BAD: *Bombardirovochnaya Aviatsionnaya Diviziya*—bomber division. This referred to bomber aircraft divisions. A Guards division would be referred to as a GvBAD (in this case the 'Gv' stood for *Gvardeyskaya*, the Russian adjectival variant of 'Guards').

BAK: *Bombardirovochniy Aviatsionniy Korpus*—bomber corps. This referred to bomber aircraft corps. A Guards bomber corps would be referred to as a GvBAK, with the 'Gv' standing for *Gvardeskiy*, the masculine equivalent of *Gvardeskaya*. This was the largest bomber unit, there being no named bomber air armies (although the 18th VA or 18th Air Army was formed from the bomber assets of the ADD in 1944).

BAP: *Bombardirovochniy Aviatsionniy Polk*—bomber regiment. This referred to bomber aircraft regiments. A Guards regiment would be referred to as a GvBAP, with the 'Gv' standing for *Gvardeskiy*, the masculine equivalent of *Gvardeskaya*.

Blitzkrieg: 'Lightning War' in German. This was the name given to the German method of war, whereby the enemy were to be overwhelmed by the speed of armoured columns striking deep through the enemy's lines, supported by infantry and the heavy use of aircraft, such as the dive bombing Ju 87. It was this method of warfare that worked so well initially against the Soviets during Operation Barbarossa.

Bort: Tactical or aircraft number. Most Tu-2s bore some sort of aircraft number—on the tail or fuselage or, much more rarely, both. The numbers were typically red, white, or blue, were normally one or two digits, and the style varied from regiment to regiment. These were not applied at the factory, but in the field by the regiments (*polks*—see entry further on). Although you may see it in colour profiles, yellow was rarely used during the Great Patriotic War, as this was the Axis identification colour.

CAS: Close air support, often referred to as ground attack; this was the main duty of the Il-2, but one in which the Tu-2 was also involved. This consisted of support for the Red Army ground troops and tank divisions, which involved attacking the German units that the Soviet troops were engaged with. Fighters were used for protecting the Tu-2s and Il-2s engaged in this activity. CAS, ground attack, and ground support are used interchangeably in this volume.

CMF: Black Sea Fleet. One of the Soviet naval fleets, based originally in Sevastopol. Although the Soviets did not have aircraft carriers during the Great Patriotic War, ground-based aircraft units, including Tu-2 units, were attached to all the fleets.

Construction Number: see Serial Number entry further on.

Design Bureau: see OKB entry further on.

Eskadrilya: A squadron.

Flak: A contraction of the German term *Flugzeugabwehrkanone*, or aircraft defence cannon. This is the same as anti-aircraft artillery (AAA) and is the term I will use throughout this book.

Frontal Aviation: Used to describe the aviation units that operated close to the front lines in support of the ground troops. This included fighter, ground attack, and bomber units, such as Tu-2 units.

Great Patriotic War: *Velikoiy Otechestvennoiy Voiyni* in Russian, or BOB in Cyrillic—the Soviet/Russian term for the war between Nazi Germany and the Soviet Union (22 June 1941–9 May 1945). This normally excludes the August 1945 campaign against the Japanese Kwantung Army in Manchuria (known by the Soviets as the 'Manchurian Strategic Offensive Operation'—see the entry for this further on).

Ground attack (support): see previous CAS entry. These terms will be used throughout the text, interchangeably.

Guards: A designation for units that had distinguished themselves in combat (*Gvardiya* in Russian). In addition to receiving higher pay than normal Red Army units, they also were the first units to receive new equipment. These were considered elite units. Some Tu-2 units were designated as Guards units.

Heer: The official name for the German Army under the Nazis. Seldom used, as the Wehrmacht has supplanted it in common usage.

Hero of the Soviet Union: Often abbreviated to 'HSU'. The highest military honour accorded to Soviet military personnel during the Great Patriotic War. Equivalent to being awarded the American Medal of Honour and the British Victoria Cross. The medal consisted of a simple golden star suspended from a small red rectangle.

Il-2: The main Soviet ground-attack aircraft of the war and the single most important aircraft in the Soviet inventory.

Istrebitel: Russian for 'destroyer', this was the Soviet term for a fighter aircraft.

Izdeliye: Russian for 'object'. Aircraft (and other products) were assigned an *Izdeliye* number by the appropriate design bureau or OKB; for example, the Tu-2 was initially the 103, with '103' being the *Izdeliye* number. Thus, the first Tu-2 was known as Object 103.

KBF: Red Banner Fleet (or Baltic Fleet). One of the Soviet naval fleets. Based in Leningrad, although during the siege of Leningrad its ships did not venture out into the Baltic Sea (other than submarines). The aircraft attached to the fleet did operate in the Baltic Sea against Axis shipping and Axis ports, as well as providing ground support for Red Army troops, with fighters providing protection for the ground attack and bomber aircraft.

Kriegsmarine: the German Navy. Although the war was fought mainly on land, the Kriegsmarine were very active in the Baltic and Black Seas during the Great Patriotic War. Along with the *Heer* (Army) and the Luftwaffe (Air Force), the Kriegsmarine formed the Wehrmacht.

Lavochkin, Semyon Sergeyevich: The chief designer of the Lavochkin design bureau, or OKB, and the designer of the Lavochkin fighters used during the Great Patriotic War, which along with the Yakovlev fighters were the main fighters used by the Soviet Union during the war.

Lavochkins: The term that I will use throughout the text to refer to the Lavochkin fighters of the Great Patriotic War. One of the main duties of these fighters was providing escort for bombers such as the Tu-2.

LII: *Lyotno Isslydovatel'skiy Institut*—'Flight Research Institute'. Based at Zhukovskiy, outside of Moscow.

Luftwaffe: the German Air Force. It officially came into existence in 1935, in defiance of the 1919 Treaty of Versailles. Unlike the Red Air Force or VVS, it was a separate service co-equal with the army (*Heer*, although the term Wehrmacht is normally used) and navy (Kriegsmarine).

MAP: *Ministerstvo Aviatsionnoy Promishlinnosti*—'Ministry of the Aircraft Industry'. This is what the NKAP was renamed to in 1946. In 1946, all the 'People's Commissariats' were renamed to 'Ministries'.

Manchurian Strategic Offensive Operation: The Soviet name for the August 1945 campaign against the Japanese Kwantung Army in Manchuria. Although not part of the Great Patriotic War, this offensive was the last major campaign of the Second World War.

NATO: North Atlantic Treaty Organisation. This organisation was founded in 1949 to counter the military might of the Soviet Union and included, among other countries, the United Kingdom and the United States of America. It developed a system of reporting names or nicknames by which many Soviet aircraft were known post-war. The Tu-2 was given the nickname of the Bat (the 'B' signifying that it was a bomber, and the single-syllable name signifying that it was propeller-driven, jets having two-syllable names, such as the Il-28 Beagle). NATO's communist equivalent was the Soviet-led Warsaw Pact (which was formed in 1955), which included most of the countries of Eastern Europe.

NII VVS: *Nauchno-Issledovatel'skiy Institut Voyenno-Vozdushnykh Seel*—'Scientific Research Institute of the Red Air Force'. The testing facility for the VVS (Red Air Force).

NKAP: *Narkomaviaprom* (from *Narodniy Kommissariat Aviatsionnoy Promishlinnosti*) —Soviet Air Ministry (literally 'People's Commissariat of the Aircraft Industry'). This was the ministry responsible for aircraft development. During the Great Patriotic War, it was headed by Aleksei Ivanovich Shakhurin (1904–75).

NKVD: *Narodniy Komissariat Vnutrennik Del*—People's Commissariat of Internal Affairs, the ministry that included the security or secret police, in addition to normal police and border guards. It was this ministry that arrested Andrey Nikolayevich Tupolev (1888–1972) and other aviation specialists and imprisoned him in a special prison, or *sharashka* (see entry further on). It later became the MVD in 1946, when the 'People's Commissariats' became 'Ministries'. This was the precursor to the KGB of Cold War fame.

OKB: *Opitnoye Konstruktorskoye Byuro*—'Experimental Design Bureau', OKB being the acronym. A state-run research institute that was something like an engineering company tasked with the design of prototypes. These organisations were not intended for mass producing the aircraft they designed. However, they usually had the facilities and resources to construct prototypes. Designs accepted by the state were then assigned to factories for mass production. A bureau was officially identified by a number or an acronym (such as TsKB) and later by initials from its head engineer's last name (such as 'Il' for Ilyushin).

Also known as a Design Bureau, they were a collection of Soviet designers grouped around a single head designer, with the bureau being under the name of the head designer (from mid-December 1940 onwards). In the case of the Tu-2 bomber, the head designer was Andrey Tupolev. Design bureaux would respond to (or be directed to respond to) government specifications for aircraft. In contrast to Western aircraft companies, Soviet design bureaux did not own their own production facilities, but factories were assigned to produce their designs as described previously.

Operation Barbarossa: This operation, named after a twelfth-century German king, was the name the Germans gave for their initial campaign against the Soviet Union. Opened on 22 June 1941, this operation was designed to defeat the Soviet Union by the end of 1941, but ultimately failed with huge losses to both sides.

Orlov, Mikhail: A modern Russian expert on Soviet VVS Great Patriotic War colours. When he is referred to in the text, he may be simply referred to as 'Orlov'. Along with the late Vasiliy Vakhlamov, he produced a series of very important articles on VVS colours in 1999, and produced a small, but very important work of his own on VVS Great Patriotic War colours (see Bibliography for further descriptions of these works). His research has been largely followed in this book regarding Soviet colours used during the Great Patriotic War.

Para: A pair of aeroplanes, two of which composed a *zveno* (flight).

PARM: *Polevaya Aviaremontnaya Masterskaya*—'Field Aircraft Repair Work Shop'. These repair shops, in addition to repairing damaged Tu-2s, rebuilt the sometimes poorly constructed aircraft that came directly from the factories, before releasing them to the front-line units. Ironically, one of the reasons that so many Soviet aircraft were often of poor manufacture is that the experienced machinists and mechanics were in the Red Army and not on the production lines, where their place was often taken by semi-skilled and unskilled labourers.

Pe-2: The main Soviet dive bomber during the Great Patriotic War, designed by Vladimir Mikhailovich Petlyakov (1891–1942). It was sometimes known as the Peshka, or Pawn. It was a superior dive bomber to the Tu-2 and they sometimes flew together during the war. Following the war, the Pe-2 was known as the 'Buck' by NATO.

Polk: Regiment. As used in this book, it refers to an air regiment.

RKKA: *Rabochye-Krestiyanskoy Krasnoy Armiy* (PKKA in Cyrillic)—'Red Army (taken from the Cyrillic acronym for the Workers and Peasants Red Army). The Air Force during the Great Patriotic War was the VVS RKKA (BBC PKKA in Cyrillic).

Red Air Force: Also known as the 'VVS'. See entry further on for a definition of VVS. This term will be used interchangeably with VVS in this book. Note that after the war it was often called the 'Soviet Air Force', but the term Red Air Force continued to be used, as did the term VVS.

Red Army: The main fighting force of the Soviet Union, consisting of rifle (infantry), tanks, cavalry, and the air force (although the long-range bomber force, the ADD, was until 1944 under the direct command of the Soviet High Command, the *Stavka*, and not part of the Red Air Force). The name was officially changed to the Soviet Army in late 1944, although it was still commonly referred to as the Red Army until the end of the war and for a long time thereafter. The Soviet Navy was a separate military arm from the Red Army.

SMF: Northern Fleet. Based at Murmansk, it was responsible, among other things, for providing protection to Allied convoys bringing lend-lease equipment to the Soviet Union.

Second World War: The most important event of the twentieth century, this worldwide conflict lasted from 1 September 1939, when Germany invaded Poland, until 2 September 1945, when the Japanese formally signed the documents of surrender on board the American battleship, the USS *Missouri*. Estimates vary, but as many as 55 million people may have perished in this conflict. Of that number, as many as 30 million were Soviet citizens.

Serial Number: Applied at the factory, this number could consist of from six to ten digits and incorporated the *zavod* number, such as '1660920', where *Zavod* 166 was the producing factory. Sometimes, this number is referred to as the construction number (c/n).

Sharashka: Special prisons organised by the NKVD for special prisoners, such as scientists and engineers. These prisons had better conditions than the run-of-the mill Gulag prisons and the prisoners were allowed (or coerced) to continue their work under NKVD supervision. Andrey Tupolev designed the Tu-2 in a *sharashka*, known as *Zavod* 156 or Z.156. Vladimir Petlyakov also designed his dive bomber, the Pe-2, in the same *sharashka* as Tupolev.

Shturmovik: Russian for 'ground attack aeroplane' (Штурмовик) became synonymous with the Il-2 ground attack aircraft designed by Sergey Vladimirovich Ilyushin (1894–1977). Note that the accepted standard transliteration for this word into

English is *Shturmovik*, not Sturmovik, Stormovik, or other variations you will see. This was the standard Soviet ground attack for the Red Air Force throughout the Great Patriotic War. Normally, it will be referred to as the 'Il-2' in this book.

Soviet Air Force: Another name for the Red Air Force. Both these terms (and VVS) will be used interchangeably in this work.

Soviet Navy: A separate military arm from the Red Army, unlike the Red Air Force, which was part of the Red Army. The Soviet Navy included the AVMF (naval air forces).

Soviet Union: This term, the shortened version of the Union of the Soviet Socialist Republics, will be used throughout this book instead of the commonly used, but inaccurate (especially in the context of the Great Patriotic War) Russia. Likewise, Soviet will be used instead of Russian.

Stavka: The Soviet High Command.

Top Cover: One of the duties of the Red Air Force fighters was to provide 'top cover' for the Tu-2s. This consisted of them flying above the Tu-2s to protect them from Axis fighters.

Tupolev: This refers both to the man, Andrey Nikolayevich Tupolev, and the OKB that he founded. Andrey Tupolev was born in Pustomazovo, near Tver, on 10 November 1888, and died in Moscow on 23 December 1972. He was the most prolific and influential designer in Soviet aviation history, and some of his designs, such as the Tu-95 Bear, continue in use today. He was a pioneer in the use of all-metal aircraft.

USAF: United States Air Force. Founded in 1947 as a fully independent military arm, equal in status with the army and navy, it was formed from the wartime United States Army Air Forces (USAAF).

VVS: *Voyenno-Vozdushnye Sily*—'the Military Air Forces' (Red Air Force), BBC in Cyrillic (Военно-воздушные силы). This acronym will be used interchangeably with the term the Red Air Force in this book. The head of the VVS from 1942 until after the war was Aleksandr Aleksandrovich Novikov (1900–76), who was replaced in 1946 by Konstantin Andreyevich Vershinin (1900–73).

Wehrmacht: The German Armed Forces under the Nazis (including the Kriegsmarine (Navy), and the Luftwaffe, in addition to the *Heer* (Army); see previous entries for descriptions of these services), although now often used to refer to the German Army alone. The actual German term for the army was *Heer*, but this is almost never used in historical books and will not be used in this work. Following convention, the term Wehrmacht will be used to refer to the German Army, and the Kriegsmarine and Luftwaffe will each be referred to as such.

Yakovlev: Refers to both the designer, Aleksandr Sergeyevich Yakovlev (1906–89), and the inline-engined fighter aircraft that he designed. The Yakovlev fighters, often referred to simply as Yak or Yaks, were the main Soviet fighters of the Great Patriotic War, along with the Lavochkin fighters. The Yak-1 through Yak-9 were produced in huge numbers, with more than 36,000 being produced. As with the Lavochkin fighters, one of the main duties of these fighters was providing escort for bombers such as the Tu-2.

Zavod (pl. *Zavodi*): Russian for factory. These factories were owned by the state, and design bureaux would be directed by the NKAP to use a particular *zavod* for a particular aeroplane. *Zavodi* could and did change which aeroplanes they built; for example, *Zavod* 381 at Nizhniy Tagil in 1942 went from producing single-seater Il-2s to producing Lavochkin fighters (this was part of the same effort to produce more fighters that led to cancellation of the first version of the Tu-2). I will use *zavod* and factory interchangeably in the text.

Note on transliteration: I have tried to use generally accepted standards for transliteration from Russian Cyrillic to English language Latin characters throughout this book.

Andrey Nikolayevich Tupolev in front of an early series Tu-2 at Omsk in 1942. (*Viktor Kulikov's Collection*)

Introduction

This book is divided into two mains sections: one dealing with the Second World War service of the Tu-2 and one dealing with its long post-war service, both inside and outside of the Soviet Union. In addition, as mentioned previously, I will cover in some depth the various experimental versions of the Tu-2, many of them built or converted in the post-war period. The development of the two main Great Patriotic War versions will be covered in detail. I will also cover as much as possible the combat operations of the Tu-2, both during and after the Second World War.

The Tu-2 itself is an interesting aircraft, both in its genesis and in its history. Few great aircraft were designed in a prison, but that is exactly where the Tu-2 was designed, in an NKVD prison under the ever-watchful eyes of the feared head of the NKVD, Lavrentiy Pavlovich Beria (1899–1953). Despite the circumstances (or perhaps because of them—his life depended on success), Andrey Tupolev was able to design an outstanding aeroplane, one that, except for a strategic blunder by Josef Stalin (his decision to cancel production), would have been able to contribute much more to the victory of the Soviet Union over the Germans. That brings us to the second interesting part of the Tu-2 story, its apparent 'death' and then phoenix-like rebirth, which carried it far into the post-war period.

In 1942, the Soviet Union was undergoing huge losses in fighter aircraft. In an effort to redress this deficit, Josef Stalin turned the industrial might of the Soviet Union towards producing more fighters, somewhat reminiscent of the Germans' Emergency Fighter Programme of 1944–45, when all efforts were bent towards producing fighters. The result of this was that the Tu-2's production was stopped after a mere eighty had been produced. As (bad) luck would have it, this cancellation occurred just as the combat reports started coming in from the front, extolling the combat virtues of this new tactical bomber. Realising his mistake, Stalin reversed his original decision to stop the production and production resumed on the Tu-2. The last of the early Tu-2s had been delivered from Tupolev to the VVS in January 1943, and the first of the new Tu-2s (the Tu-2S) would not enter service in significant numbers until the middle of 1944—a year and a half had been lost. Nevertheless, from the middle of

1944 onwards, the Tu-2 played an important role in the remaining Soviet offensives, starting with Operation Bagration, which began in June 1944 and resulted in the destruction of the German Army Group Centre. The Tu-2 was in the middle of the successful Soviet effort to take the German capital, Berlin, in April 1945. Even after the end of the Great Patriotic War in May 1945, it continued to see heavy action until the end of the Second World War, taking part in the Soviet invasion of Manchuria in August 1945. Its Second World War career was over, but that was not the end for the Tu-2 by any means, as a long post-war career lay ahead of it.

Still, one has to wonder how much more the Tu-2 would have contributed to the Soviet war effort if production had not been mistakenly terminated in 1942. As it was, the 'new' Tu-2 continued to be produced into the 1950s and was used by the Soviet Union and satellite and allied states until perhaps as late as 1982 in the case of mainland China.

1

Tactical and Medium Bombers: A Definition

Tactical and medium bombers are not a new phenomenon; from the moment an Italian biplane dropped a few bombs at a Turkish position in Tripolitania (Libya) in 1911, the tactical bomber was born. The first large, four-engined bomber, the Russian Ilya Muromets (designed by Igor Sikorsky of helicopter fame), dates from the First World War. Twin-engined bombers, like the Gotha G.IV, between the size of the four-engined heavy bombers, like the Ilya Muromets and the German Zeppelin-Staaken R.VI, and light bombers, like the single-engined Airco DH.4, were also initially used in the First World War. These could be considered medium bombers for their time.

The Tu-2 was certainly not the first aircraft to be described as either a tactical or a medium bomber. Before I get into the subject of this book, perhaps this might be a good time to review what exactly a tactical bomber or a medium bomber is. The short (and obvious) answer is that a tactical bomber is not a strategic bomber—that is, it does not (usually) bomb strategic targets, it bombs tactical targets. Then the question shifts to, what is a strategic target or a tactical target? Although there are (and probably always will be) arguments over where tactical targets stop and strategic targets begin, there are some targets that are clearly one or the other. A case in point, if you bomb a single locomotive, it is a tactical target. If you bomb the factory where the locomotive is made, that is a strategic target. Today we have bombers that can destroy whole cities with a single bomb or cruise missile—these are clearly strategic bombers. The A-10 Thunderbolt II, with its excellent ground attack capability, is clearly a tactical bomber.

A medium bomber is somewhat easier to define. It is a medium-sized (for its time) bomber. During the Second World War, this would include aircraft of around 50 feet (15.24 metres) in length, with a wingspan of around 60 feet (18.29 metres) or more. There are a number of aircraft that fit it into this category, some of which are discussed further on. They are also multi-engined, usually with two engines, with defensive gunners, and they usually have an internal bomb bay, although they also often having the capability to carry bombs externally. The Tu-2 certainly fits into this category, being twin-engined with a length of more than 45 feet (13.72 metres) and a wingspan of around 61 feet (18.59 metres), with a capacious internal bomb bay, and three crew members who manned defensive guns. American bombers such as the twin-engined B-25 Mitchell and B-26 Marauder fit well into this category, and were also much like smaller versions of the American heavy (strategic) bombers, such as the four-engined Boeing B-17 Flying Fortress and Consolidated B-24 Liberator. Like their four-engined counterparts, the Mitchell and Marauder were multi-engined, with a heavy defensive armament, including manned turrets, and had internal bomb bays. However, their smaller size also gave them more versatility than the four-engined 'heavies', especially in the case of the B-25. Not only was the B-25 used as a level bomber, much like its heavier brethren, but it could also be used for ground attack duties as a low-level strafer. The B-26 could even be used as a torpedo bomber. The German Ju 88 was similarly versatile to the American medium bombers, if not more so. It served as a level bomber, dive bomber, reconnaissance aircraft, torpedo bomber, fighter-bomber, long-range fighter, and a night fighter. It was the medium bomber's smaller size that gave it the manoeuvrability (and in some cases the speed) to perform duties that were not practical or even possible for the larger bombers. That is what made medium bombers so useful and popular during the Second World War, their versatility. It should also be remembered that twin-engined medium bombers are cheaper and quicker to produce than larger, four-engined bombers, resulting in larger numbers of the medium bombers.

The Tu-2 shared this versatility with its American and German counterparts—it was used during the Second World War as a level bomber, a dive bomber, a ground-attack aircraft, and as a reconnaissance aircraft. After the war, it likewise served as a torpedo bomber, a bomber trainer, and was even tested experimentally as a fighter. It was the 'medium' size of the Tu-2 that enabled it to excel as a warplane. It had a manoeuvrability and speed approaching that of a fighter, yet it was also capable of carrying a large bombload and it had a greater range than most fighters. Its twin engines and larger size also made it more survivable in combat than a fighter, as it could easily fly on one engine and it is simply harder to shoot down a larger target, as the chances of hitting a vital part of the aeroplane are less than with a small, single-engined fighter.

One final point should be made. Just because an aeroplane is labelled as a tactical bomber, medium or otherwise, does not mean that it is always used that way. The American medium bombers were used on strategic missions, attacking factories in German-occupied Europe, for example. In the same way, it could be argued that the Tu-2's missions against the fortress city of Königsberg in East Prussia and against the German capital of Berlin were strategic in nature. It was this flexibility that made medium bombers useful. Nonetheless, the Tu-2 was mainly used against tactical targets, such as troop concentrations, convoys, and fortified areas of the front lines.

2
Soviet Bombers Before the Tu-2

By the opening of Operation Barbarossa (22 June 1941) and the beginning of the Great Patriotic War, the Red Air Force was still mostly equipped with obsolete and obsolescent bombers such as the TB-3 (although by 1941 it was in second-line duties) and the SB. Newer, more modern bombers such as the DB-3 (Il-4), Pe-2, and TB-7 (Pe-8) were also in service, but only in relatively small numbers. The following chapter focusses on some of the Soviet multi-engined bombers that preceded the Tu-2 into service with the Red Air Force.

TB-1 (ANT-4)

Designed by Andrey Tupolev, this cantilever all-metal twin-engined monoplane bomber was a trendsetter when it first flew on 26 November 1925; it first entered service in 1929, at a time when other air forces were still using fabric-covered biplanes as bombers. It was the world's first all-metal heavy bomber. This aircraft led directly to the larger, four-engined TB-3. The designation 'TB' was derived from the Russian for 'Heavy Bomber', *Tyazhyoliy Bombardirovshchik*. The other designation of ANT-4 was derived from the first initials of Andrey Nikolayevich Tupolev's name, the '4' signifying that this was his fourth design. The '1' in TB-1 signified that this was the Soviet Union's first heavy bomber (later, usually only fighters would have odd numbers in the Soviet naming system, although there were a few exceptions, such as the Tu-95 Bear bomber).

The TB-1 flew as a front-line bomber until 1936. It also flew in second-line roles during the Lake Khasan incident in 1938, the Khalkhin Gol (Nomonhan) incident in 1939, the Winter War with Finland in 1939–40, and it was still flying as a transport during the Great Patriotic War, beginning in 1941. Indeed, this tough and sturdy aeroplane continued to fly in the Arctic until 1948, and one of these aircraft is still preserved in Russia at the Ulyanovsk Aircraft Museum.

TB-3 (ANT-6)

This very large four-engined aircraft, designed by Andrey Tupolev, was one of the first large multi-engined all-metal cantilever monoplane bombers to go into service anywhere in the world when it entered Soviet service in 1932. It was essentially a four-engined development of the earlier twin-engined TB-1. Constructed of an all-metal structure with a corrugated metal covering typical of the German Junkers aircraft (which influenced Tupolev), it featured a fixed landing gear and was thoroughly obsolete by the beginning of the Great Patriotic War. As with the TB-1, it saw service at Lake Khasan, Khalkhin Gol, and the Winter War. It was also used by the Chinese against the Japanese in the Sino-Japanese War. In these conflicts, it was used in its primary role as a bomber.

By the time of Operation Barbarossa (June 1941), as obsolete aircraft, the TB-3s were no longer front-line aircraft so they were based to the rear, where they fortuitously survived the initial aerial attacks of Operation Barbarossa. This luck was not to last long, however.

Since it had escaped destruction (for the moment), the TB-3 saw action in the opening days of the war as an unescorted day bomber out of necessity, in what were little more than suicide missions in the Soviets' vain attempt to halt or even slow down the seemingly unstoppable German advance. Nonetheless, it was still being used as a night bomber as late as the Battle of Kursk in the summer of 1943 and continued in service until the end of the war; it was even being used as late as 1949 in the Arctic. It was utilised during the war mostly as a transport, especially for transporting paratroopers. It was superseded as a long-range bomber by the much more modern TB-7 (Pe-8—see further on).

MI-3 (ANT-21)

This aircraft was significant in that it was the first of Andrey Tupolev's multi-engined aircraft to employ some smooth stressed-skin construction (on the fuselage), instead of the corrugated skin that had characterised previous Tupolev aircraft (although this construction was retained for the wings). Designed as a multi-role 'cruiser'—aircraft that were in some vogue during the 1930s (especially with the French)—it was intended to use it as a multi-role fighter (the 'MI' designation deriving from *Mnogomestniy Istrebitel*, Russian for 'Multi-Seat Fighter'), although it is likely it would have eventually been fitted with bombs. It addition to the smooth stressed-skin monocoque fuselage, it was also the first aeroplane Tupolev built that had a retractable undercarriage (along with the I-14 fighter, or 'ANT-31', flown at about the same time).

It first flew on 23 May 1933. Interestingly, the main landing gear was similar to the much later Tu-2, with a single oleo strut that forked around a single main wheel and retracted aft hydraulically. In its developed version, the MI-3D (ANT-21bis), the engines were made more powerful and the previously open cockpit position was enclosed. Although it was the first of Tupolev's multi-engined modern designs, it did not enter production.

Tupolev SB (ANT-40)

By far the most numerous bomber in the VVS inventory at the start of the Great Patriotic War was the Tupolev SB. First flown in 1934, the twin-engined Tupolev SB (and not 'SB-2' as you will often see) was one of the first modern all-metal cantilever monoplane bombers to fly and to enter production and service anywhere. It first entered service with the VVS in 1936. It was used extensively by the Spanish Republicans in the Spanish Civil War, where its speed made it difficult for the Nationalist (Falangist) fighters to intercept (the designation 'SB' standing for *Skorostnoiy Bombardirovshchik* or 'Fast (Speedy) Bomber'). Like the TB-1 and TB-3, it also saw service in the Lake Khasan Incident in the Soviet Far East and the Battle of the Khalkhin Gol in Mongolia, against the Japanese in the Sino-Japanese War (flying with the Chinese against the Japanese), and in the Winter War against the Finnish in 1939–40.

The SB was a very advanced aeroplane when it first appeared in the mid-1930s. However, such was the pace of aircraft design and development during the mid- to late 1930s that, by the start of the Great Patriotic War in 1941, although as noted previously it was numerically the most important VVS bomber, it was obsolescent, if not actually obsolete (at least in its earlier versions). As such, more modern types, such as the slightly later and larger Il-4 and the much faster Pe-2, soon replaced it as a front-line bomber, although it continued in use in the Far East and in second-line roles until the end of the war. The Tu-2 itself had originally been designed as a fast bomber replacement for the SB.

Il-4

First flying in 1935, the DB-3 (the designation was changed to Il-4 in 1940), designed by Sergey Ilyushin, was slightly larger, faster (than the earlier SBs), and had a longer range than the SB. Most importantly, it had nearly twice the bombload. In many ways, the Il-4 was the Soviet equivalent to the German Heinkel He 111, both being twin-engined medium bombers designed in the mid-1930s that continued to serve until the end of the Second World War (both being produced until 1944). The Il-4 was the Soviet Union's standard long-range bomber, despite its obsolescence. Indeed, it continued in service after the war as a torpedo bomber, a role that it had fulfilled with some success during the Great Patriotic War, and it was replaced by the Tu-2T in this role post-war. Post-war, the Il-4 was given the NATO (ASCC—Allied Self-Coordinating Committee) reporting name or nickname of 'Bob'.

Pe-8 (TB-7, ANT-42)

Excepting the obsolete TB-3, which by 1941 was no longer even a marginally modern warplane, the only four-engined strategic bomber that the Soviet Union possessed by the start of the Great Patriotic War was this massive aircraft, designed by Vladimir

Petlyakov. Although it remained in use throughout the war and saw some heavy usage (for example, during the Battle of Kursk in 1943 and in the bombing of Königsberg in 1943, where it dropped enormous 11,023-lb (5,000 kg) bombs on that city's massive fortifications), it was not produced in large numbers and was not a major factor in the war. For most of the war, it was not a part of the Red Air Force, but was a part of the independent ADD (*Aviatsionnaya Dalnaya Diviziya* or long-range aviation), which was an independent military arm under the direct control of the *Stavka*, the Soviet High Command. The ADD was dissolved in late 1944 and its aircraft were incorporated into the Red Air Force. After the war, the Pe-8 saw service as a transport in the Soviet Arctic, the Arctic seeming to be the last stop for several large Soviet bombers.

Ar-2

A dive bomber development of the Tupolev SB, it was designed by Aleksandr Aleksandrovich Archangelskiy (1892–1978), a close associate of Andrey Tupolev and one of the original designers of the SB. The Ar-2 was designed with much smaller wings and included dive brakes and was quite a bit faster than the SB, having a top speed of nearly 300 mph (298 mph (480 kph)). Although a reasonably good aeroplane, its career was cut short by the Great Patriotic War, in which many were destroyed in the first few months, and by the appearance of the superior Pe-2, which led to the cancellation of its production. The Ar-2 disappeared from front-line units in 1942.

As an interesting side note, even though the Ar-2 was a development of a Tupolev design, and Archangelskiy had been a member of the Tupolev OKB, the aircraft was named after Archangelskiy ('Ar'-2) instead of Tupolev because Tupolev was technically an enemy of the state while the Ar-2 was being designed and flown. Otherwise, it might have been designated as the Tu-2.

Pe-2

This twin-engined aircraft, designed by Vladimir Petlyakov, was originally a high-altitude fighter project, designated as the '100' and designed, like the Tu-2 (103) as with Andrey Tupolev, while Petlyakov was still under NKVD detention. As the VI-100, it first flew on 22 December 1939. However, what the VVS desired (and needed) at the time was a modern dive bomber (the VVS had seen the success of the German Ju 87 dive bomber in Western Europe), not a high-altitude fighter. Therefore, the Pe-2, as it was designated from 1942, was redesigned. First entering service in 1940, the Pe-2 was used throughout the Great Patriotic War as a dive bomber, level bomber, reconnaissance aircraft, and ground-attack aircraft, and eventually over 11,000 were produced, four times the number of Tu-2s that were produced. Indeed, even after the entry into service of the Tu-2, it continued in use as a dive bomber as it was found to be more suitable for that role than the Tu-2, which had originally been designed and built with that capability. A fighter version, the Pe-3, was even built in small numbers. The Pe-2 continued to be used post-war, when it was given the NATO nickname of 'Buck'. Like the Tu-2, it was provided by the Soviet Union post-war to other Soviet Bloc countries, such as Poland, Bulgaria, and Hungary.

Yer-2 (Er-2)

A twin-engined long-range bomber, this aircraft had a history somewhat reminiscent of the Tu-2's. It was developed by Vladimir Grigoryevich Yermolaev (1909–44) from the civilian transport Stal-7 designed by the Italian-Soviet designer Robert Ludvigovich Bartini (1897–1974). It first flew on 14 May 1940. Around fifty aircraft were in service by the time that the Germans invaded in 1941. Like the Tu-2, production was halted, this time in 1941 so Il-2 ground attack aircraft could be produced at its factory, and was not resumed until late 1943. By the time production restarted, the Yer-2 had been changed significantly. As with the Tu-2, the Yer-2 was re-engined, although in this case with Charomskiy ACh-30B diesel engines (replacing the original Klimov M-105 engines) and it had a completely redesigned cockpit, among other changes. It participated in operations late in the Great Patriotic War and was not retired until the late 1940s. Occasionally, this aircraft is referred to as the Er-2 in western publications, but this is the result of an incorrect transliteration from the Cyrillic.

Soviet Bombers Before the Tu-2: Specification Table (data from various sources)

Specifications	Tu-2S	TB-1 (ANT-4bis)	TB-3/M-17F	MI-3 (initial configuration)
Year	1944	1931	1933	1933
Maximum Speed (mph (kph))	340 (547)	128 (206)	109.9 (177)	218 (351)
Range (miles (km))	1,305 (2,100)	858 (1,380)	838 (1,350)	N/A
Service Ceiling (feet (metres))	31,168 (9,500)	16,142 (4,920)	12,500 (3,800)	25,870 (7,885)
Offensive Armament	2 × ShVAK 20-mm cannon	N/A	N/A	4 × PV 7.62-mm machine guns
Defensive Armament	3 × Berezin UBT 12.7-mm machine guns	6 × DA 7.62-mm machine guns	6 × DA 7.62-mm machine guns	1 × PV 7.62-mm machine gun, 1 × DA 7.62-mm machine gun
Rocket Armament	N/A	N/A	N/A	N/A
Maximum Bomb Load (lb (kg))	6,614 (3,000)	2,892 (1,312)	4,409 (2,000)	N/A
Empty Weight (lb (kg))	16,477 (7,474)	9,965 (4,520)	24,177 (10,967)	7,522 (3,412)
All-up Weight (lb (kg))	22,839 (10,360)	N/A	37,918 (17,200)	11,217 (5,088)
Maximum Weight (lb (kg))	25,044 (11,360)	14,925 (6,770)	N/A	N/A
Engines and take-off hp	2 × Shvetsov ASh-82FN (M-82FN) 1,850	2 × Mikulin M-17F 680	2 × Mikulin M-17F 715	2 × Mikulin M-17F 715
Crew	4	6	6	4
Length (feet (metres))	45.28 feet (13.8)	59 feet 3 inches (18.06)	80 feet (24.4)	35.6 feet (10.85)
Wingspan (feet (metres))	61.88 feet (18.86)	94 feet 1⅞ inches (28.7)	129.6 feet (39.5)	62 feet 8⅛ inches (19.11)

SB-2M-103	Il-4 (DB-3F)	Pe-8	Ar-2	Pe-2	Yer-2 (M-105)
1939	1940	1941	1939	1944	1941
279.6 (450)	255 (410)	275.2 (443)	298.2 (480)	360 (580)	271.5 (437)
1,180 (1,900)	2,361 (3,800)	2,299 (3,700)	932 (1,500)	721 (1,160)	2,485 (4,000)
30,500 (9,300)	28,543 (8,700)	30,500 (9,300)	33,100 (10,100)	28,870 (8,800)	25,250 (7,700)
N/A	N/A	N/A	N/A	1 × Berezin UBT 12.7-mm machine gun, 1 × ShKAS 7.62-mm machine gun	N/A
4 × ShKAS 7.62-mm machine guns	1 × Berezin UBT 12.7-mm machine gun, 2 × ShKAS 7.62-mm machine guns	1 × ShVAK 20-mm cannon, 6 × ShKAS 7.62-mm machine guns	4 × ShKAS 7.62-mm machine guns	2 × Berezin UBT 12.7-mm machine guns, 1 × ShKAS 7.62-mm machine gun	1 Berezin UBT 12.7-mm machine gun, 2 ShKAS 7.62-mm machine guns
N/A	2 BETAB-750DS 305-mm	N/A	N/A	N/A	N/A
3,306 (1,500)	6,000 (2,700)	8,818 (4,000)	3,306 (1,500)	3,520 (1,600)	8,818 (4,000)
10,511 (4,768)	12,787 (5,800)	40,941 (18,571)	9,766 (4,430)	12,952 (5,875)	N/A
14,065 (6,380)	N/A	73,853 (33,500)	14,660 (6,650)	16,639 (7,563)	24,911 (11,300)
N/A	20,878 (9,470)	N/A	N/A	18,728 (8,495)	N/A
2 × Klimov M-103 960	2 × Tumanskiy M-88B 1,100	4 × Mikulin AM-35A 1,340	2 × Klimov M-105R 1,100	2 × Klimov M-105PF 1,210	2 x Klimov M-105 1,050
3	4	10	3	3	4
40 feet 4 inches (12.27)	48 feet 5 inches (14.76)	76 feet 1¼ inches (23.2)	41 feet (12.5)	41 feet 6 inches (12.66)	53 feet 9 ½ inches (16.4)
66 feet 8¼ inches (20.33)	70 feet 4 inches (21.44)	128 feet 4 inches (39.13)	60 feet 8¼ inches (18.5)	56 feet 3 inches (17.16)	75 feet 6 inches (23)

3
Genesis of the Tu-2

The leaders of the Red Army (of which the Red Air Force was an integral part and not an independent military arm, like the Luftwaffe was) were not unaware of the relative obsolescence of their bombers and had begun development even before the Great Patriotic War for modern replacements of some of the bombers listed previously.

PB Bomber

The Soviets felt that, in the European war that most sensed was coming, the United Kingdom and Nazi Germany would combine forces to try to defeat the Soviet Union. In order to counteract this threat by defeating what was considered the United Kingdom's greatest asset, its naval fleet, the Soviet Union felt that a long-range dive bomber was needed to attack the fleet in its UK bases. A dive bomber was called for, in order to hit potentially moving targets in the form of the British ships. Moreover, in order to stay out of the range of British flak, the aircraft needed to be able to fly at altitudes of 29,528 to 32,808 feet (9,000 to 10,000 metres). This dive bomber was to have four engines to give it the range it needed and was designated as the PB (ANT-57) (presumably the 'PB' was from *Pikiruyushchiy Bombardirovshchik*, or 'Dive Bomber'). Although having four engines, it was much smaller than the long-range four-engined Pe-8 (TB-7) heavy bomber. In April 1939, Andrey Tupolev was given the task of designing this aircraft.

In addition to the previous features, the PB was to have the following characteristics: a range of 3,107 to 3,728 miles (5,000 to 6,000 km), pressurised cabins for the crew because of the high altitudes at which it was to fly (29,528 to 32,808 feet (9,000 to 10,000 metres)), and it also needed to be able to dive at high speeds, up to 559 mph (900 kph). As finalised, the specifications called for an aircraft 49.38 feet long (15.05 metres), with a wingspan of 85.3 feet (26 metres), a maximum bombload of 8,818 lb (4,000 kg), and a maximum level speed of 354 to 373 mph (570 to 600 kph). The maximum range was to be 2,175 to 2,485 miles (3,500 to 4,000 km), with six

ShKAS 7.62-mm (30-calibre) machine guns and a crew of three. The engines were to consist of four of the supercharged Klimov M-105TKs. These were quite ambitious specifications for 1939.

FB Bomber

With the actual outbreak of war, however, when the United Kingdom (and France) declared war on Germany, another prospect opened up for the Soviet Union—that of allowing these capitalist countries to weaken themselves in the war, then the Soviet Union would take advantage of the situation and seize as much of Europe as it could. What was needed in this case was an aeroplane that would operate over the battlefields of Europe; a smaller, twin-engined dive bomber, which would be simpler, cheaper, and easier to produce than the original four-engined design.

The decision to switch to a twin-engined design ('FB' from *Frontovoiy Bombardirovshchik*, or 'Frontal Bomber') from the four-engined design (PB) was made after the technical design had been examined in September 1939. P. A. Alexeyev of the People's Commissariat of Defence ended the work on the PB; from then on, work was to be concentrated on the design of the FB. There is some dispute regarding how Andrey Tupolev came to design the twin-engined FB. According to one account, Tupolev had already come up with the idea of a twin-engined dive bomber, designated the ANT-58, in 1938. He was then told in a meeting with Lavrentiy Beria, the head of the NKVD, to design a four-engined aeroplane, the PB. Tupolev was upset by the decision and, while he was supposed to be working on the four-engined PB, which he considered an unrealistically ambitious design, he was surreptitiously continuing to work on the twin-engined design, the FB.

Another source has him willingly working on the PB, indeed, this source indicates that Tupolev came up with the idea and the specifications for a long-range dive bomber, able to attack the British from long range. With the outbreak of the Second World War and the success of the Ju 87 and Ju 88 as dive bombers, Tupolev decided to go with a smaller, more easily produced twin-engined design. Whichever account is correct (perhaps both are, in part), the four-engined PB design remained a paper project only, while the twin-engined FB became first the 103, then the Tu-2.

What is known is that there was a meeting on 1 February 1940 between Tupolev and representatives of the OTB NKVD (A. Balashov and G. Ya. Kutepov) and the UVVS (Air Force Institute—A. I. Filin and I. F. Petrov) in which the FB was discussed. In this meeting, Tupolev described the project. Evidently the meeting went well as work on the FB or ANT-58 continued.

4

First of the Breed: The 103

The decision to build a twin-engined dive bomber led to the design of the ANT-58, as the design was initially called. A committee that included A. I. Filin of the UVVS and test pilots M. A. Nyukhtikov and F. F. Opadchiy approved the mock-up on 21 April 1940 (Andrey Tupolev, who was a carpenter in addition to being an aircraft designer, helped in building the mock-up). After approval, the aircraft was then given the designation of '103'. Three 103s were to be built, with one featuring Mikulin AM-37 liquid-cooled inline engines and two with Klimov M-120 'Y'-type air-cooled inline engines with TK-2 turbo-superchargers.

A Very Special Workplace

It might be a good idea here to give some background on the very interesting circumstances under which what would become the Tu-2 was designed. Before the Great Patriotic War, Andrey Tupolev had been head of the TsAGI, the Central Aerodynamic and Hydrodynamic Institute, the Soviet equivalent of the American NACA (the predecessor of NASA). While still head of the TsAGI, Andrey Tupolev was arrested by the NKVD, the State Security Police, on 21 October 1937 on trumped-up and frankly absurd charges of being part of a Russian-Fascist party, during Josef Stalin's purges of the mid- to late 1930s. This arrest came despite the fact that he was the most renowned and best aircraft designer in the Soviet Union at the time, and indeed was known worldwide.

Tupolev was taken by an infamous Black Maria (an NKVD automobile) to the NKVD camp at Bolshevo, Moscow, in the fall of 1938. This camp consisted of three huts built near the Bolshevo station. Tupolev's imminent arrival was known in advance and he was given a bed near the stove. Kutepov, the deputy chief of the OTB NKVD (Technical Office of the NKVD), which was responsible for 'special' prisoners like aviation designers, informed Andrey Tupolev about his new project, which would eventually become the Tu-2. The special NKVD prison was called a *sharashka*.

The 103, the first prototype of the Tu-2 during tests in June to July 1941. (*Viktor Kulikov's Collection*)

Other aviation specialists who had been arrested, such as Vladimir Petlyakov (the designer of the Pe-8 heavy bomber and later the Pe-2 dive bomber, see above), were housed in this *sharashka* under the supervision of the OTB NKVD. The head of the OTB NKVD was General V. A. Kravchenko.

The OTB NKVD was also apparently referred to as the TsKB-29, or Central Design Bureau 29. The designers were moved from the Bolshevo camp to this installation on 23 February 1940. The OTB NKVD was housed in a building that had been built for Tupolev for his OKB at the beginning of the 1930s, when he was still in the good graces of Stalin, and overlooked the Yauza River in Moscow. This installation was officially called *Zavod* (factory) 156 or Z.156 (also known as the TsKB-29) and was even surrounded by barbed wire, leaving no doubt that however relatively comfortable the working conditions may have been the NKVD still considered this to be a prison and its workers, prisoners.

Tupolev was not the only aviation designer housed here. As mentioned previously, Z.156 also housed Vladimir Petlyakov. Z.156 was divided into four specialised technical departments or stations. The abbreviation for these departments was STO, which then became '100' (*sto* being Russian for 100). Since Petlyakov's group was the first, his department was assigned the number 100, which then became the number of his project. Vladimir Myasischev's group was second and was assigned the number 102 (one wonders what happened to number 101). This became the number of his project, the DVB-102, an advanced high-altitude long-range bomber that first flew in 1942, but did not enter production.

Andrey Tupolev's department was the third, so, not surprisingly, it was assigned the number 103, which became the number for his project. For some reason, the designer Dmitriy Lyudvigovich Tomashevich's (1899–1974) group, which was formed last, was given the number 110, although it was not the tenth group. This number became the number of his project, a single-engined high-altitude fighter, which first flew in late 1942, although it was not produced. The stations each functioned as a separate design bureau to work on their separate projects. Generally, the NKVD was responsible for providing the stations with what they needed for their work, but did not intervene in the design process itself. The NKVD did sign off on the technical documents prepared by the stations, however. The designers were still their prisoners, after all.

Design Work on the 103

The design work started in the fall of 1939 at the Bolshevo camp, even before the move to Z.156. However, most of the design work for the FB, as the 103 was initially called, took place at Z.156. Beria had promised Andrey Tupolev that, if his aircraft flew, he would be released from prison. If it did not fly, one can well imagine Tupolev's fate. For Andrey Tupolev, therefore, the success of the 103 was not just a matter of professional pride, but of life (and freedom) or death. There can be little doubt that Tupolev threw himself into the new project with all of his considerable energy and designing ability. No doubt, the designers helping him, such as Dmitriy Tomashevich, were in much the same situation. That the eventual design was an outstanding one could be ascribed to being one part inspiration and one part desperation.

Two innovations were necessary to make the 103 a viable design. The first concerned the internal bomb bay, which needed to be able not just to drop bombs in horizontal flight, but from a dive. This design was accomplished by the engineer A. I. Nekrasoviy, another NKVD prisoner. The second involved the development of a bomb sight that would enable the aircraft to accurately dive bomb. This sight, called the OTB, was designed by the mathematician, navigator, and engineer G. S. Frenkel, also an NKVD prisoner.

By March 1940, the VVS had given the project the green light and the aircraft was renamed from the FB to the 103 (or ANT-58 under what was effectively the Tupolev Bureau, or OKB) after the mock-up was approved on 21 April 1940. Work on the PB project had apparently already ended by this time (perhaps in September 1939). In order to assist in the design of the 103, Andrey Tupolev was asked to present a list of engineers he wanted; the NKVD obligingly scoured its prisons and camps to secure these engineers for Tupolev.

It appears that initially two prototypes were to be built—one with M-120TKs and one with Mikulin AM-35As (the AM-35 also powered the high-altitude MiG-3 fighter and was developed into the low-altitude AM-38, which powered the Il-2 Shturmovik). Before testing, this engine was replaced with the AM-37. By May 1940, it had been decided to build three prototypes—one with the M-120TK (which aircraft became the 103V) and two with the AM-37s (the 103 and 103U). One source states that it was a GKO resolution dated 1 August 1940 that directed Z.156 to build the three prototypes, one with the AM-37s fitted and two with the M-120s, with TK-2 turbo-superchargers. The engines were to be equipped with two VISh-42 propellers, with a diameter of 9.19 feet (2.8 metres). This resolution may have superseded a GKO order No. 239 of 1 June 1940, which required that three prototypes be built—one with AM-35A engines and two with the M-120 engines.

As finalised in February 1940, the specifications called for an aircraft 42.42 feet long (12.93 metres), with a wingspan of 59.06 feet (18 metres), a maximum bombload of 4,409 lb (2,000 kg), and a maximum level speed of 435 to 460 mph (700 to 740 kph—which were unrealistically high figures). The service ceiling was to be 42,651 to 45,932 feet (13,000 to 14,000 metres—also very ambitious numbers), and the maximum range was to be 1,243 to 1,553 miles (2,000 to 2,500 km), with six ShKAS 7.62-mm (30-calibre) machine guns and a crew of three. The dive speed was to be the same as that stipulated for the PB—559 mph (900 kph).

The 103 (ANT-58)

The first of the Tu-2 series to fly was equipped with two Mikulin AM-37 V-configured twelve-cylinder liquid-cooled inline engines of 1,380 hp at take-off. The propellers fitted were VISh-61T three-bladed units with a diameter of 11 feet 1⅞ inches (3.4 metres). Construction of the first prototype of the 103 began in May 1940 and was completed on 8 January 1941. After completion of the prototype, it was transported to Shchelkovo Airfield. The first flight took place on 29 January 1941, being flown by test pilot Mikhail A. Nyukhtikov. Andrey Tupolev actually watched the first flight of his creation from the roof of Z.156, which was still effectively his prison. The OKB tests ran from January to May 1941 and the state tests went from June to July 1941. The state tests were not completed because of the outbreak of war. During the tests, the maximum speed recorded at sea level was 300 mph (482 kph) and the overall top speed was 395 mph (635 kph) at 25,591 feet (7,800 metres)—impressive figures indeed. The normal bombload was to be 2,205 lb (1,000 kg), with a maximum bombload of 4,409 lb (2,000 kg).

The main landing gear were of a single oleo type, with a forked attachment to trap the main wheels (a similar arrangement was used for the retractable tail wheel, which had its own doors). The main landing gear, like the tail wheel, retracted to the rear and was completely enclosed by doors. The main wheels were 1,142 mm by 432 mm in size, while the tail wheel had a 470 mm by 210 mm tyre. The main landing gear doors were slightly bulged to accommodate the main wheels.

The aircraft, as befitted its high top speed (faster than that of operational fighters at the time), was very streamlined, with a low cockpit canopy flush with the top of the fuselage and a dorsal gunner's canopy that was raised only slightly. Although not affording good vision to the crew, the canopy arrangement did contribute to the overall excellent streamlining and speed of the aircraft. A single pilot sat in the cockpit, with the navigator housed in the nose. The ventral gun position was flush with the underside of the fuselage, the radio operator/gunner operating this gun in addition to the dorsal (or mid-upper) gun. The total number of the crew was three, comprising a pilot, navigator, and radio operator/gunner. The two inline engines were housed in well-streamlined cowlings. Even after the conclusion of regular flight testing, the 103 continued to be used for other tests. In 1943, it was returned to Moscow and a year later it was converted into the SDB-1 fast day bomber (see Chapter 7 for information about this version).

The 103U (59)

During the brief period of the Soviet-German 'thaw', after the signing of the Molotov-Ribbentrop Non-Aggression Pact on 23 August 1939, a Soviet delegation of aviation specialists visited Germany in 1940 to examine some of the latest Luftwaffe aircraft, including the Ju 88 bomber, which, like the 103, could be used as a dive bomber. This aircraft impressed these aviation experts, who were particularly interested in the way that the crew were concentrated in the front fuselage. The Germans believed that this crew configuration improved communication and morale during combat and the Soviets were impressed enough to install these changes into the 103 design. The number of the crew was now increased from three to four on the 103.

This redesigned 103 was christened the 103U (OKB designation ANT-59, the 'U' apparently standing for *Uluchshenniy*, Russian for 'Improved'). Instead of having the navigator in the nose as in the original 103 design, the navigator was now seated behind the pilot, from which position he could move around to also operate a defensive gun directed aft. Both the pilot and the navigator sat under a raised canopy, quite different from the low, streamlined canopy of the first 103. The navigator was also equipped with a fold-away control column, from which, in his new position behind the pilot, he could control the aircraft in an emergency.

The 103U from the front during official tests at the NII VVS in June 1941. Note the characteristic hexagonal paving slabs of the NII VVS airfield. Note also the holes in the spinners, which allowed air into the cowlings for cooling purposes. (*Viktor Kulikov's Collection*)

The 103U from the side towards the back during official tests at the NII VVS in June 1941. (*Viktor Kulikov's Collection*)

The 103U from the back during official tests at the NII VVS in June 1941. (*Viktor Kulikov's Collection*)

Rear fuselage and tail unit of the 103U. The rear dorsal and ventral gun positions can be clearly seen. (*Viktor Kulikov's Collection*)

Work on the 103U began in July 1940. The nose was lengthened by around 300 mm or 1 foot. The dorsal gunner's position was now flush with the fuselage between the cockpit canopy and the dorsal gunner's canopy, with the fuselage aft of the gunner's canopy being slimmer than on the original 103 design to give the ventral gunner better vision (overall, the fuselage was slimmer in side profile). The ventral gunner was still equipped with a small circular window above his position to give him some light. Eventually, a slightly larger vertical tail was also installed to improve stability and compensate for the greater length of the 103U as compared to the original 103 design.

As an interesting side-note, one might well ask why Germany would be showing some of their latest (and best) front-line aeroplanes to a country that they fully intended to invade and soon. The answer is rooted in the Nazi's contempt for what they saw as the Jewish-controlled Slavic/Asiatic 'sub-humans' that they supposed the Soviets to be. They did not believe that the Soviets would be able to understand the advanced features of these Luftwaffe aircraft, or, if they did, the Germans believed that they would not have time to make the changes to their aircraft before the Soviet Union were overrun and defeated by German forces. Unfortunately for the Germans, they were wrong on both counts. This would not be the last time that the Germans underestimated Soviet capabilities.

This aircraft still featured the inline AM-37 engines (now of 1,400 hp at take-off), but the new cockpit configuration was the one that was to be featured on all production Tu-2s until the end of production in 1951 (or 1952). The redesigned aircraft was completed on 9 April 1941. The propellers used were VISh-61P three-bladed units, with a diameter of 12 feet 5⅝ inches (3.8 metres). An interesting feature of the propellers was that the spinners featured a hole of 5.9 inches (150 mm), which allowed air into the cowling for cooling. The first flight of the 103U was made on 18 May 1941 by pilot M. A. Nyukhtikov and engineer V. A. Miruts. On 27 May 1941, the results of the testing were reported to Beria, Zhigarev, and Shakhurin (the heads of the NKVD, VVS, and the aircraft industry, or NKAP, respectively). The 103 design was obviously considered an important aeroplane. State testing of the 103U was done at basically the same time as the 103, from May to July 1941.

Due to its greater weight and wider cockpit, the 103U was somewhat slower than the 103. The drag of the wider front fuselage was actually lower than it might have been because Tupolev had inadvertently created an 'area rule effect', whereby the widening of the fuselage in front of the wing roots actually lessened what the drag would normally be expected to be. It had a maximum speed at sea level of 291 mph (469 kph) and 379 mph (610 kph) at 25,600 feet (4,800 metres). Its service ceiling was 34,500 feet (10,500 metres) and the 103U had a range of 1,180 miles (1,900 km). Although slower than the 103, the performance was considered sufficient enough for the GKO to issue an order on 27 June (or July according to one source) 1941 to begin production (Operation Barbarossa had started on 22 June 1941). The 103U crashed on 6 July 1941, but this did not affect the decision to produce the aircraft. Also, despite this eventual crash, Beria kept his word and duly freed Andrey Tupolev, who was finally released from NKVD detention on 21 July 1941. However, Tupolev had been convicted in 1940 and given a ten-year sentence—he was not finally exonerated and officially rehabilitated until 1955, some two years after Josef Stalin's death.

The tests revealed that there were problems with the propellers and instability. The instability was dealt with by increasing the area of the vertical stabilisers. A much more serious problem showed itself on 6 July 1941 when the right engine caught fire and the fire could not be extinguished. The pilot Mikhail A. Nyukhtikov survived, but the navigator and an engineer named A. Akopyan were killed. This happened during weapons testing. An investigation revealed no defects in the design and, as noted previously, the order to begin production was proceeded with. However, first, one more major change to the basic design had to be made—the choice of engines.

The 103V (60)

Both the GKO and NKAP orders had specified that the third 103 prototype be equipped with the experimental air-cooled M-120TKs. However, the unavailability of these engines led to the decision to re-engine the third 103 prototype aircraft with Shvetsov M-82 radial engines, which were, for reasons explained further on, available in abundance. The lack of development on the experimental AM-37 engines and the need for the plant manufacturing the AM-37 to build AM-38 engines for the desperately needed Il-2 Shturmovik ground-attack aircraft, also led to the decision to use the M-82 engines instead. The M-82s, on the other hand, were available in abundance as the aircraft that they were designed for, the Su-2 light bomber, was slated to have its production cancelled in 1942, leaving the Shvetsov OKB, which produced the engines at Z.19 in Molotovo (now Perm), with hundreds of surplus M-82s stored in warehouses. This re-engining led to the 103V, the true prototype of the first production Tu-2s.

While these design changes were being proposed, the first air raid on Moscow occurred on 22 July 1941, during which the prisoners of Z.156 had to use their freshly constructed bomb shelters, which they had built themselves, beginning on 23 June 1941, the second day of the Great Patriotic War. As a consequence of the now exposed position of Z.156, the decision was made to transfer the OKB to Omsk in Siberia. This new factory was to be called *Zavod* 166 and included personnel evacuated from the Moscow aviation factory, *Zavod* 81. They were also joined by personnel from Z.288 in the Kalinin area. Z.166 itself was built partly out of an unfinished automobile factory. Two areas for the plant had been secured by the Regional Committee of the Communist Party by 23 August 1941. There were actually two plants built, 164 feet (50 metres) from each other—one had an area of 290,626 square feet (27,000 square metres), the other had an area of 149,618 square feet (13,900 square metres), for a total of 440,244 square feet (40,900 square metres). The Tu-2 was not a small aeroplane and its factory buildings were correspondingly large. In addition to the factory buildings, a runway had to be built and barracks to accommodate the workers. Even a hospital had to be built.

Interestingly, the initial conditions at Omsk were not that different from what they had been in Moscow. The prisoners, for such they still were, lived at first in a brick two-storey building, not far from what would become Z.166, surrounded by a fence,

The 103V during joint tests at the NII VVS in 1942. (*Viktor Kulikov's Collection*)

The 103V during official tests at the NII VVS on 5 July 1942. (*Viktor Kulikov's Collection*)

with bars on the second storey windows, where the prisoners were accommodated. This prison was not closed until an NKVD order of 1 September 1943 directed it to be closed.

The 103V aircraft was completed at Z.166 in Omsk in mid-November 1941. Known as the 103V 2M-82A (OKB designation 60), it first flew on 15 December 1941 with test pilot M. P. Vasyakin at the controls (Vasyakin would later fly the Tu-2 in combat). Due to the 'V' in the designation, the aircraft acquired the nickname of 'Vera'.

Joint OKB and state tests ran from 15 December 1941 to 22 August 1942 (one source states 1 August 1942), by which time the aircraft was nearly ready for combat trials, such was the length of these tests. Part of the problem with the tests was that the aircraft originally tested was so unsatisfactory due to the poor reliability of its engines that it was replaced by a production 103V (actually Tu-2 No. 308) so that the tests could be completed. During the tests on the original 103V, the engines had to be changed no less than eight times.

The tests showed the maximum speed to be 323 mph (521 kph) at a height of 10,500 feet (3,200 metres). This top speed was well below that of the 103 and 103U and was at least partially due to the greater drag of the radial M-82 engines. The service ceiling was also less at 29,500 feet (9,000 metres) and the range was 1,255 miles (2,020 km). The armament consisted of two ShVAK 20-mm cannon in the wing roots, two ShKAS 7.62-mm (30-calibre) machine guns for operation by the pilot, and one ShKAS machine gun and two UBT 12.7-mm (.50-calibre) machine guns for defence to be operated by the navigator, the radio operator, and the ventral gunner. Ten RS-132 132-mm rockets could also be mounted under the wings. It is not clear from the record how much the rockets were used in combat (or even if they were used at all, even by the early versions of the Tu-2). The normal bombload was 2,205 lb (1,000 kg), with a maximum overload of 6,614 lb (3,000 kg) for short-range missions.

Other than the reliability of the engines, other problems were noted, such as the equipment layout not being optimal and the hydraulic system needing to be simplified.

The first production 103V at Omsk, Siberia, at Z.166 in spring 1942. (*Viktor Kulikov's Collection*)

The first production 103V, view from the front, at Omsk, Siberia, at Z.166 in spring 1942. It appears that construction work was still being undertaken on the factory. (*Viktor Kulikov's Collection*)

The first 103V at Omsk in December 1941. (*G. F. Petrov Photo Archive*)

However, the one-engine-only performance was noted to be good, and with one engine the aircraft could even climb at the normal weight of 23,149 lb (10,500 kg). The diving characteristics were also found to be good. The aircraft was cleared for production at Z.18 by NKAP order No. 533 dated 17 June 1941, which was just five days before the opening of Operation Barbarossa and the start of the Great Patriotic War.

The Early Tu-2 Series (Tu-2VS)

At first, the Tu-2, sometimes known as the Tu-2VS (although it is unclear if this name was ever used during the Great Patriotic War), was to be produced at Z.18 at Voronezh on the Don. Then the Germans invaded and Z.18 was evacuated to Kuibyshev (now Samara), on the Volga River. Here it became the main factory for the production of the Il-2. As it was, it never produced a single Tu-2.

With the evacuation of Z.18, the initial series of Tu-2s were now to be produced at Z.166 in Omsk, by NKAP Order No. 163, dated 29 July 1941. This was a bit of a problem, as no such plant existed at this time. Hastily, a production plant was built (as described previously in the section on the 103V). The first factory equipment from Z.156 in Moscow arrived at Omsk on 12 July 1941 and the last arrived by the end of August. By September 1941, Tupolev had completed the transfer of drawings to Z.166 from Z.156. The plant manager was Director L. P. Sokolov.

The plan was for forty-five aircraft to be produced by the end of 1941 and 600 during 1942, but the plan was much too optimistic and only ten had actually been produced by early 1942. Tupolev had been appointed the head of Z.166 by the NKAP on 7 October 1941 and by the end of 1941 his entire Tu-2 design staff were in place. The head of the design team was Dmitriy S. Markov and the head engineer in charge of flight testing was E. K. Stoman, who had been with Tupolev in NKVD detention at Z.156. As it was, the testing of the 103V was not completed until 22 August 1942 for the reasons given previously, by which time the aircraft was already in production. By NKAP Order No. 234, issued on 28 March 1942, the aircraft's name was changed from the 103 to the Tu-2, the 'Tu' reflecting Andrey Tupolev's family name.

All the production documentation had been completed by January 1942. The first production Tu-2 was produced by February 1942 (one source says March 1942) and five were produced by April 1942, with an additional series produced by 5 April 1942. Most of the initial series of Tu-2s, eighty in all, were produced as dive bombers, although a few were produced as reconnaissance aircraft.

From 17 May 1942 until 29 July 1942, three serial production Tu-2s were used for tests at the NII VVS to determine their suitability for military trials. They did not have an auspicious start. On 23 May, aircraft c/n 100102 crashed during landing. A second aircraft crashed on May 26. The remaining Tu-2 continued with the NII VVS tests. Despite the crashes, an NII VVS report issued on 22 August 1942 stated that the Tu-2 was suitable for use in the horizontal bombing role, limited to a 16,404 feet (5,000 metres) altitude. It was noted that the wheel braking system needed to be improved because of problems while landing (the aircraft would veer unexpectedly on landing, sometimes causing it to crash) and that the defensive armament needed to be strengthened. In addition, there were problems with the rudders' sensitivity. The radio operator, in the dorsal position, had his ShKAS 7.62-mm (30-calibre) machine gun replaced by a Berezin UBT 12.7-mm (.50-calibre) heavy machine gun in the spring of 1942, and the navigator had his ShKAS replaced by the heavier UBT in the fall of 1942. The ventral gun may have continued to be a ShKAS machine gun on these early Tu-2s, but the record is unclear on this.

Another problem that was noted for the Tu-2 was the relative complexity of the systems, especially the hydraulic system, and there were also problems with the constant-speed propellers. A special commission set up by the NKAP, with the famous fighter designer Nikolai Nikolaevich Polikarpov (1892–1944) as its chairman, specifically noted the complexity of the Tu-2 and that it cost more to produce than other aircraft. On the other hand, the commission did note some positive aspects of the Tu-2, such as it was stable around all three axes, was easy to pilot, and could fly easily on one engine. The hydraulic system was picked out for special note as being complex to produce and operate and lowered the combat survivability of the Tu-2. The report also noted that, with its forward-firing two ShVAK cannon, two ShKAS machine guns, and ten RS-132 rockets, the Tu-2 could be used as a ground-attack aircraft if frontal armour were provided for the pilot and the navigator.

One of the recommendations of the commission was that the wheel brakes for the Tu-2 be replaced with 'Douglas' brakes, presumably those used on the Li-2, the Soviet license-built version of the Douglas DC-3 (C-47). It was hoped that this would ameliorate some of the landing problems with the Tu-2, where it could turn unexpectedly upon landing, due in part to the inadequate brakes, with their lack of synchronisation and difficulty in use. Evidently, the lack of an ability to lock the tail wheel also contributed to these landing difficulties, although it is unclear when the tail wheel was made lockable.

From 13 September 1942 to 28 October 1942, when the aircraft crashed, a production Tu-2 (c/n 100308, the eighteenth production Tu-2) was tested at the NII VVS, flying forty-four flights to determine the flight characteristics of the production Tu-2. This aircraft did not have the dive brakes fitted, perhaps so rockets could be fitted under the wings. The maximum speed at sea level was 276 mph (444 kph), the top speed at 10,499 feet (3,200 metres) was 324 mph (521 kph), the service ceiling was 29,528 feet (9,000 metres), and the range was 1,255 miles (2,020 km). For this particular aeroplane, the armament was three ShKAS (with two mounted in the nose and with one of the three being for defensive purposes), two UBT machine guns for defence, and two ShVAK cannon in the wings. Ten RS-132 rockets could be carried under the wings (these do not appear to have been carried very often by the Tu-2—although this is certainly not conclusive by any means, there seems to be no evidence where the rockets were installed). The production Tu-2 was fitted with three-bladed AV-5V-167A propellers, with a diameter of 12.47 feet (3.8 metres). Although both the speed and ceiling were less than what had originally been contracted for, the top speed by a considerable 41 mph (66 kph) and the ceiling being less by over 2,625 feet (800 metres), the climbing and landing data were in line with the contract.

One of the test pilots, Vladimir Ivanovich Zhdanov, made some observations about the aeroplane, such as the aircraft handled well, was able to climb up to 9,843 feet (3,000 metres) at a weight of 23,149 lb (10,500 kg) on one engine, and that the aircraft dove normally even without the dive brakes. He also noted that the cabin lighting was poor for night flying, and that it was difficult to make a coordinated turn. Overall, however, he seems to have been impressed by the aircraft. Test pilot Mikhail A. Nyukhtikov also had some opinions about the machine. For example, the view compared to the 103 with its inline AM-37 engines (because of the larger diameter of the M-82A radial engines) had deteriorated, but that the control of the aircraft was easier and that it was dynamically stable around all three axes. However, he felt that it was impossible to make a coordinated turn. He recommended that the navigator's seat be moved forward and that the armour be made thicker and larger.

Although it appeared almost identical to the 103U, except for the replacement of the AM-37 inline engines with the radial M-82 engines, there were quite a few detail differences between the production Tu-2 and the 103U: there was more armour protection for the crew; the second wing spar in the centre section was strengthened; and the control of the flying surfaces was made easier. Since no water radiators were needed for water-cooled engines, this space in the centre section was now occupied by two additional fuel tanks with a capacity of 137.37 gallons (520 litres). The radio compass was changed from the RPK-22M to the RPK-7. The wing leading edges were now free of air intakes, as the radiators had been removed from the wings.

It was proposed, due to the shortage of aluminium during the earlier part of the Great Patriotic War, that much of the covering be changed from dural (aluminium alloy) to plywood. This was developed by the OKB at the end of July 1942, where such elements as the bomb-bay doors, the wing flaps, the wingtips, much of the fuselage, the engine nacelles, and the fins would be covered in plywood. The Red Air Force agreed to the changes, but only if the plywood was strong enough and did not weigh more than the metal it was replacing. The plywood panelling was to be attached to the metal structure using countersunk rivets. If all the changes were made, it was estimated that some 1,764 lb (800 kg) of aluminium would be saved per aircraft and that the weight would be increased by 331 to 441 lb (150 to 200 kg), which was considered acceptable. Although some of the changes were not made, the wingtips, forward fuselage, and the tail cone were made of wood on the production Tu-2s to conserve aluminium.

The Early Tu-2 Series in Combat

The Tu-2 in its initial production incarnation saw combat for the first time on 14 September 1942, near Kalinin, north of Moscow, flying with the 3rd VA (commanded by Colonel General Mikhail Mikhailovich Gromov (1899–1985), a famous record-setting test pilot before the war), based at Migalovo Airfield. A team from the Tupolev OKB, led by Dmitry S. Markov, supported the aircraft. Twenty-five missions were flown by three Tu-2s and were manned by pilots and crew from the NII

VVS. The missions took a total of sixty-five hours. There were no losses to aircraft or flak, although one Tu-2 sustained some damage to an engine from flak, but was still able to land safely. The aircraft averaged one sortie a day and the missions averaged 311 miles (500 km) in distance. The bombloads varied with the mission, being 2,205 lb, 3,307 lb, or 4,409 lb (1,000 kg, 1,500 kg, or 2,000 kg). The Tu-2s were always accompanied by a heavy fighter escort.

These missions revealed that the Tu-2 compared more than favourably with the Pe-2 as it could carry more bombs, was faster at low and medium altitudes (perhaps not surprisingly since the VI-100, from which the Pe-2 was developed, was a high-altitude fighter), and had a stronger armament. In terms of speed, it was 62 mph (100 kph) faster at a height of 2,625 to 3,281 feet (800 to 1,000 metres), flying at a speed of 292 to 298 mph (470 to 480 kph). It also had a better single-engine performance than the Pe-2 because of its more powerful engines and was overall considered a superior aircraft, at least for level bombing. There were problems with the hydraulic and lubrication systems, and the Tu-2 needed a long runway with a bombload of 4,409 lb (2,000 kg), up to 3,609 feet in length (1,100 metres). The Pe-2 was still considered a better dive bomber, due at least partially to a much better view for the pilot and navigator while in a dive. At this time, both aircraft featured dive brakes under the wings.

The breakdown of the missions or sorties flown by each pilot were as follows: Senior Lieutenant Sviridov flew seven sorties; Lieutenant Musinsky flew seven sorties;

An early series Tu-2 of the 12th BAP in winter 1943. (*Viktor Kulikov's Collection*)

Captain Chernyshenko flew six sorties; Senior Lieutenant Parshin flew three sorties; and Major Laukhin flew two sorties, for a total of twenty-five sorties flown.

A mission that showed the ability of the Tu-2 even during its early combat trials was a raid conducted against a German installation near the town of Trostin. This installation had already been assaulted by Pe-2s, unsuccessfully, and it was now time for the Tu-2s to try their luck against this target. On 27 September 1942, equipped with FAB-100 bombs (220 lb (100 kg), although one source states that it was FAB-1000s), as the Pe-2s had been equipped, and escorted by ten LaGG-3 fighters, the three Tu-2s were able to attack the depot, which was underground, and destroy it. Despite the aerial opposition of nine Bf 109s, the Tu-2s suffered no losses, no doubt due partly to their heavy fighter escort.

As part of the combat trials in September 1942, the 132nd OBAP (Independent Bomber Air Regiment), commanded by Lieutenant Colonel A. Khlebnikov, was equipped with twenty-nine Tu-2s on the Kalinin Front. This regiment had been working up on the Tu-2 from May 1942 (or April 1942) and had been equipped before with the SB and Pe-2. It now received twenty-nine Tu-2s, and this regiment, or *polk*, fought on the Kalinin Front from 29 October 1942 to 4 January 1943 (one source states from 5 November 1942 to 1 January 1943). While on the Kalinin Front, it was used in raids against Smolensk, Velikiye Luki, and Vitebsk. It fought on the Southwestern Front from 5 February 1943 to 13 April 1943.

Although the combat trials had shown the Tu-2 to be a durable and modern bomber with good handling, easy maintenance, and a large bombload there were still problems, however, as the Shvetsov M-82A engines suffered from an unacceptably high failure rate. There were sixteen full or partial engine failures in the air and twelve on the ground during the combat trials and the NKAP asked that urgent measures be taken to correct the engine issues (it was these failures that eventually led to the M-82A engines being replaced by the M-82FN in the Tu-2S).

In an indication of the almost semi-experimental nature of these early Tu-2s, crews were told that if their aircraft landed behind enemy lines, they were to completely destroy their aircraft.

In October 1942, four Tu-2s were sent from Z.166 to the front, three of these being used for reconnaissance by the 2nd DRAP (Long-Range Reconnaissance Regiment). Evidently, this regiment was also flying Pe-3s for long-range reconnaissance. The 2nd DRAP was renamed the 47th GvDRAP (Guards Long-Range Reconnaissance Regiment) in February 1943. One of its Tu-2s was lost in a dogfight with German fighters. In this mission, while returning from a mission photographing enemy positions near Staraya Russa, a Tu-2, flown by V. F. Stolyarov, was attacked by six Fw 190s. In the ensuing dogfight, the Tu-2 was set afire and lost, with only the navigator surviving. The Germans were not always so lucky, however. The Tu-2 was well-armed and fast for a large plane, and, in one encounter near Minsk in May 1943, a Tu-2, flown by V. N. Tereschenko, was able to fend off four Bf 109s, shooting down one in the process.

The remaining three Tu-2s of the 47th GvDRAP continued in their reconnaissance duties, now based at an airfield near Andreapol, close to the Byelorussian border.

From here they photographed enemy movement in such places as the town of Parnu, a port on the Gulf of Livonia in the Baltic Sea. In addition to its reconnaissance duties, the Tu-2s of the 47th GvDRAP participated in bombing missions; for example, against enemy concentrations in Minsk, Borisov, and Vitebsk. These aircraft were used heavily and, by May 1943, the three Tu-2s of the 47th GvDRAP had actually flown more sorties than the twenty-nine Tu-2s of the 132nd OBAP.

By November 1942, seventeen Tu-2s were operational with the 3rd VA, with fifteen of these being combat ready. However, by this time, the decision to halt production of the Tu-2 had already been made. The Omsk plant was to switch production from the Tu-2 to the Yak-9. The last of the eighty production Tu-2s was delivered to the Red Air Force in January 1943 (or was produced in January; sources differ on this—one source states that Z.166 was allowed to produce Tu-2s only until 15 November 1942, other sources indicate that the last Tu-2s were produced in October 1942). Apparently, only sixty-three of the early version of the Tu-2 were delivered to the VVS and made it to the front. This was, however, far from the end of the story for the Tu-2, even for those relative few from this initial production. They continued to be used in combat throughout 1943, such was their utility, even as the improved Tu-2 was being developed and put into production.

In December 1942, Tu-2s from the 132nd OBAP on the Kalinin Front attacked the German-held town of Velikiye Luki (as mentioned above). In this action, the Tu-2s attacked their target with FAB-1000 bombs (2,205 lb (1,000 kg)) from a height of only 3,281 feet (1,000 metres), which no doubt increased their accuracy and made the mission a successful one. The large bombs dropped created suitably large craters, 59 feet (18 metres) in diameter.

By 16 March 1943, fourteen Tu-2s were being used by the 132nd OBAP on the Southwestern Front (this regiment had been based on the Kalinin Front when it had received its first Tu-2s in September 1942). One regiment that flew throughout 1943 with the original series Tu-2s was the 47th GvDRAP, which then received the new Tu-2S when they became available. By this time, the Battle of Stalingrad, in which the Tu-2s did not take part, had ended (on 2 February 1943), but the combat career of the early Tu-2s was not over.

Before Kursk (von Manstein's Counteroffensive)

The German retreat after the defeat at Stalingrad was stopped only by Field Marshal Erich von Manstein's brilliant counterstroke against the Soviets, when the Germans recaptured the city of Kharkov, which had just been retaken by the Soviets. It was this counterattack that established the huge Soviet-held salient in the German lines, centred around the city of Kursk, with the northern German lines anchored around Oryol (often spelled 'Orel', a poor transliteration of the Russian), and the southern lines anchored around Belgorod. This salient was the most distinguishing feature of the Eastern Front at this time, and was an obvious target for the Germans if they wished to stop the Soviet advance and regain the fighting initiative.

Kursk

Both the German strategy for attacking the salient and the Soviet plan for defending it were simple: the Germans would attempt to pinch it off at its neck by simultaneous attacks from the north, under General Walther Model, and from the south, under Field Marshal Erich von Manstein. General Model was under the overall command of Field Marshal Gunther von Kluge (1882–1944), the commander of Army Group Centre, while the reorganised Army Group South was under Field Marshal von Manstein. If successful, this operation would capture large numbers of Soviet troops and would shorten the German lines considerably, enabling the Wehrmacht to better defend the lines and possibly use them as a launching point for further attacks against the Red Army, including future offensives against Moscow. The Soviet plan was to use three concentric main lines of defence that would soak up the German attacks and then, when the German forces were exhausted, launch their own counterattacks in the north and the south against the weakened German forces. In addition to its defences, the Soviets had also amassed thousands of aircraft, of which only a handful were Tu-2s, such as the eighteen aircraft of the 285th BAD (Bomber Aviation Division—it was mainly equipped with Pe-2s), which despite being few in number saw heavy action. For the Kursk Offensive, the Germans had gathered some 2,000 aircraft out of a total of 2,980 aircraft for the entire Eastern Front.

Despite the disruptions caused by Soviet attacks on roads and railroads, the attack on the Kursk salient went ahead, opening on 5 July 1943. In the north, General Model was forced to attack the forces of Soviet General Konstantin Konstantinovich Rokossovkiy (1896–1968) on a narrow front through forest; the Germans soon became bogged down and were unable to penetrate the third Soviet defensive line, foundering on the Soviet defences around Olkhovatka and Ponyri. Field Marshal von Manstein, however, had much more success in the south, where the open steppe offered many possible lines of attack, thereby complicating the Red Army's defence considerably. It was here in the south where the most serious threat to the Soviets occurred.

In the south, against Soviet General Nikolai Fyodorovich Vatutin (1901–44), the main Soviet defensive lines were actually penetrated and the Germans advanced as far as Prokhorovka, where a huge tank battle developed, generally considered to be the largest tank battle of all time. The Soviets had some 600 tanks, while the Germans had 300. Even though the Soviets suffered much heavier losses, the German advance was stopped on July 12, just as the Soviet attack in the north towards Oryol was beginning. The Germans had lost the Battle of Kursk, and with that they had permanently lost the initiative on the Eastern Front. From here on, the Germans would be in almost continuous retreat, all the way to Berlin. That the fighting would last for nearly two more deadly years was due to the tactical ability of the German Army and the individual bravery of the German soldier, but, after Kursk, there was no doubt about the Germans' ability to retrieve the situation on the Eastern Front. Nazi Germany would be defeated—it was only a matter of time.

The Tu-2s, small in numbers though they may have been in 1943, were considered very valuable combat assets and as long as they could fly they were used.

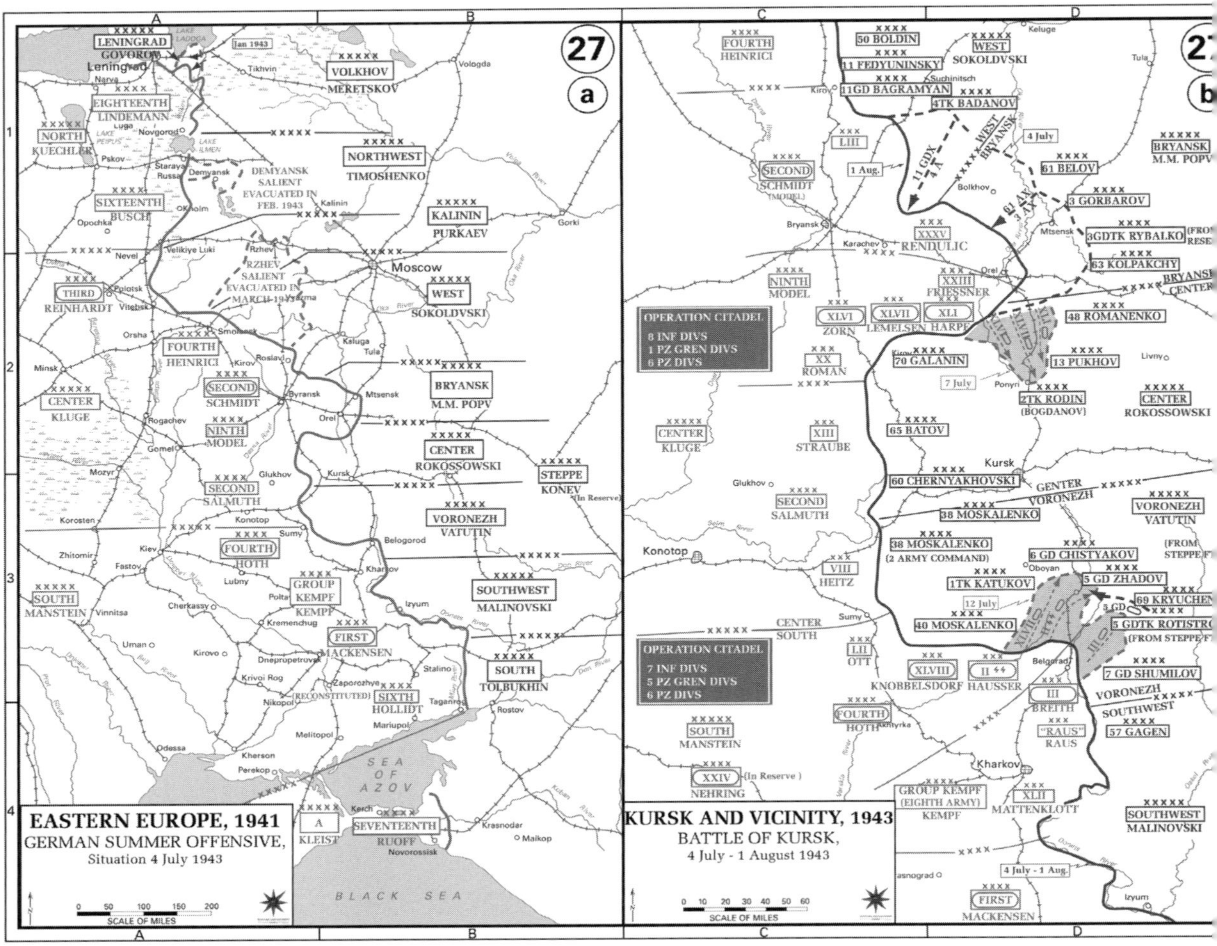

The Battle of Kursk. (*History Department of the United States Military Academy*)

They normally carried FAB-500 (1,102 lb (500 kg)) and FAB-1000 (2,205 lb (1,000 kg)) high-explosive bombs. The Tu-2s were apparently only used as level day bombers, as they were found lacking as dive bombers (apparently because of the relatively inadequate view for the pilot and navigator during dive bombing), and dive bombing was a role that the Pe-2 filled well, with a good view for the pilot while diving.

The Tu-2s were used to attack German airfields, such as those at Smolensk and Zaporozhye. In the bombing of the Zaporozhye airfield, the attack was carried out at low altitude with FAB-100 220 lb (100 kg) bombs, dropped from a height of 1,312 feet (400 metres) with reportedly excellent results, eighteen enemy aircraft being claimed as destroyed. The attack against the Germans in Pskov in December 1942 was considered very successful. The Tu-2s were also utilised in bombing raids against large railroad junctions, such as those at Dnepropetrovsk, Pavlograd, Sinelnikovo, and Zaporozhye.

Assessment of the Early Tu-2 Series in Combat

In April 1943, a report was issued that looked at some of the combat missions that the Tu-2 had flown to date as part of the continuing combat evaluation of this new warplane. On the Kalinin Front, from 4 December 1942 to 4 January 1943, the Tu-2s had flown forty-six combat sorties, attacking fortified German positions and airfields. From 12 February 1943 to 16 March 1943, Tu-2s on the Southwestern Front flew thirty-nine combat sorties and eight solo reconnaissance sorties. Of the total of ninety-three sorties flown on these two fronts during these periods, some twenty-three sorties were unsuccessful. The reasons for the unsuccessful sorties were varied—engine problems, bad weather, bomb failures, aircrew errors, etc. Evidently, during these sorties, nine Tu-2s in total were lost or damaged. Of these, five crash-landed, two were lost over Soviet territory, and two did not return from their missions. Of these aircraft, five were repaired at a PARM, factory, or a repair workshop, so only four of the Tu-2s were irrecoverable losses, which speaks well of the Tu-2's sturdiness.

During this period, the 132nd OBAP had dropped 386 bombs on their targets for a total tonnage of 7.45 tons (6,755 kg). This included nine FAB-500s, twenty-five FAB-1000s, twenty-eight FAB-250s, and 297 FAB-100s.

Although not without its problems, the Tu-2 was generally well-liked by the pilots and crew, who found it to be a fast, robust, and powerful aeroplane. The main problem seemed to be with the reliability (or lack thereof) of the M-82A engines, although some directional instability was also noted. Overall, however, the Tu-2 was considered a more than capable modern warplane and the decision to cancel its production was a controversial one.

Naval Service

None of the first version of the Tu-2 were used by the AVMF, as the relatively few examples of this first variant that were built were all issued to VVS units.

Cancellation of Production

During 1942, when production and combat testing of the Tu-2 were taking place, the Soviet Union was suffering from a shortage of fighter aircraft because of the huge losses that the Red Air Force had suffered in 1941 and were continuing to sustain in 1942. Due to these losses, Josef Stalin made the decision to halt production of the Tu-2, and even assigned one of the factories making the invaluable Il-2, *Zavod* 381 in Nizhniy Tagil in the Urals, over to producing La-5 fighters. The last of eighty Tu-2s rolled out from Z.166 in Omsk in October 1942 (or January 1943; sources differ, it may have been produced in October 1942 and not finally delivered to the front until January 1943). The order, NKAP Order No. 763, issued on 7 October 1942 (one source has 10 October 1942), stopped production of the Tu-2 at Z.166, the factory that was now to start producing Yakovlev fighters (the Yak-9). This decision was made despite the strong opposition of the head of the People's Commissariat of the Aircraft Industry (the NKAP), A. I. Shakhurin, who saw the Tu-2's potential. It was a decision that Stalin himself would soon regret.

Understandably, Andrey Tupolev was none too happy about the order. In an effort to keep production of the Tu-2 going, he proposed to have Z.166 produce the fighters on another production line from the Tu-2, thus preserving the production of the Tu-2. This proposal was rejected and production of the Tu-2 was stopped at Z.166 with the 7th series (see production table in Appendix III). As an interesting side note, the NKAP issued an order No. N-8/4229, dated 16 October 1942 to 'interested parties', including the director of Z.166 L. P. Sokolov, and Andrey Tupolev himself directing that the production jigs, tools, and documentation for the Tu-2 be kept in good order and safely stored. It would seem that the NKAP were looking to the possibility of the resumption of the Tu-2's production. This is perhaps not surprising because, as noted previously, the head of the NKAP, A. I. Shakhurin, had strongly opposed the decision to stop the production of the Tu-2.

Camouflage and Markings

The standard early Great Patriotic War camouflage, introduced in June 1941, was black (A26m) and green (A24m) over blue (A28m Blue). These were enamels for use on all-metal (or mainly metal) aircraft. These colours were applied to all Soviet combat aircraft, although mixed-construction aircraft, such as the Il-2 Shturmovik, and all-wooden aircraft, such as the U-2/Po-2 utility biplane, used analogous AMT nitrocellulose lacquers. The topside was painted with alternating bands of black and green, although there does not seem to have been any single standard application of these bands for the first variant of the Tu-2. This is a bit odd, since the Pe-2 (which was similarly configured with twin tails) did have a standard scheme specified for it. It is not clear why the Tu-2 did not use the Pe-2's standard scheme. Perhaps the semi-experimental nature of the first Tu-2 variant also extended to its paint scheme. Since this first Tu-2 version had disappeared from the front-lines by the end of 1943, it does not appear to have ever been used or repainted in the later three-colour scheme, seen beginning in September 1943. This scheme used A32m Dark Grey, which was similar to the British Extra Dark Sea Grey, A24m Green, A21m Light Brown (actually more of a greyish-tan), and A28m Blue underside, and was the scheme used on the Tu-2S.

The brown and green schemes, seen in some colour profiles, were actually black and green (A26m Black and A24m Green), and the brown colour that appears in these colour profiles (and in kit instructions, drawings, and other artwork) is a misinterpretation of wartime photographs and should be disregarded.

5

A New Beginning for the Tu-2: The Tu-2S

At about the same time that the decision was being made to stop production on the Tu-2, glowing reports started coming in from the front extolling the combat capabilities of the Tu-2. Stalin soon realised his mistake and the GKO instructed in Order No. 3754, dated 17 July 1943, for Andrey Tupolev to restart production. In a somewhat amusing exchange in Moscow, Stalin asked the head of the NKAP, A. I. Shakhurin, why he had not complained to the Central Committee of the Communist Party about Stalin's decision to terminate the Tu-2's production. Shakhurin was too polite (or perhaps more precisely, wise) to give the obvious answer; he had not complained about Stalin to the Central Committee because he had wanted to continue living.

The Tu-2 Redesigned: The Tu-2S (61)

Convinced that the Tu-2 was a good design, Tupolev sought to improve it, even after production of the first version had ended. Tupolev believed that a 'standard' bomber could be created from the Tu-2 that could be used, with modifications, for a variety of tasks: a dive bomber, a reconnaissance aircraft, a long-range bomber, and a trainer. The bomber needed to be simple and easy to produce. Three of the early Tu-2s, produced in October 1942, were used to test structural improvements, including simplification of its various systems. These improvements included removal of the dive brakes and their attendant dive recovery system, the control system was simplified, the two ShKAS machine guns in the nose were removed per VVS recommendation, and the fuel system was simplified. The hydraulic system was simplified by going to a high-pressure system. The most fully modified of these three machines was Tu-2 serial no. 100716, also known simply as '716'. With these modifications, 716 became the *Etalon*, or Standard for what became the Tu-2S.

When production resumed on the Tu-2, the exact same bomber was not produced, as some improvements had been made to the design, some of these changes being detailed previously. These improvements took into consideration suggestions and complaints regarding the original version. These changes also reflected Andrey Tupolev's desire to simplify the design and make it easier and cheaper to produce.

One of the main complaints regarded the engines, as there had been considerable problems with the M-82As fitted to the original version, such as with the magnetos and carburettors. These engines were replaced by the boosted and fuel-injected ASh-82FNs (M-82FNs, originally M-82FNV) on the Tu-2S. At 1,850 hp at take-off, these engines were more powerful than the earlier engines, which only produced 1,700 hp at take-off. The installation of these fuel-injected engines removed the problems that had been occurring with the carburettors on the earlier M-82s, as the ASh-82FNs did not have carburettors, instead featuring direct fuel-injection. High-altitude performance was also improved. These engines were first tested on the 103V, now designated the 103V 2M-82FNV. The tests were conducted at the beginning of July 1943 and were successful enough that the NKAP Order No. 430, dated 20 July 1943, prescribed these engines for the production Tu-2s. These new ASh-82FN engines were identical to those fitted to the La-5FN and were fitted to all subsequent mass-produced Tu-2s.

There were changes made to simplify this 'new' Tu-2, with an eye towards streamlining production, reducing weight, and improving survivability. One change involved fixing in place the previously moveable stabiliser at an angle of 1 degree, 10 minutes. Some of the other changes made were reducing the number of hydraulic instruments and controls from ninety-three to thirty-eight, reducing by half the weight of the wiring, and making the hydraulic system simpler in part by reducing to a fourth the original length of the hydraulic piping (from 1,467 feet (447 metres) to 367 feet (112 metres)). The hydraulic tank was moved to the front of the aircraft. These simplification measures decreased the weight of the structure of the production Tu-2S by 882 lb (400 kg). Some of the weight reduction was from the following systems: 331 lb (150 kg) from the hydraulic system, 243 lb (110 kg) from the fuel system, 187 lb (85 kg) from the electrical system, and 55 lb (25 kg) from the navigation system.

In addition to the previous changes, other changes were made to simplify the design and construction of the Tu-2. The electrical system was considerably simplified, for example, with fewer fuses and less wiring. Similar efforts were made to simplify the fuel system; the number of valves was reduced from 100 to 38 valves and the flexible connections were reduced from 258 to 126 connections. Fuel tanks eight, nine, and ten were removed and the wing tankage was able to be increased due to the removal of the dive brakes and their related equipment (one source states that the number of fuel tanks was reduced from twenty to fourteen tanks). There were other changes, such as adding armour plate to the starboard side of the navigator's position, the electrical system was now powered by one generator instead of two, the dive brakes were no longer fitted (as noted previously), the AFA-B camera was replaced by the AFA-BI camera, the hydro-magnetic compass GMK-2 was fitted, etc. The previous is only a very partial list of all the myriad design changes made to the structure and systems of the early version of the Tu-2 to transform it into the Tu-2S. Despite the very close external similarity of the two versions and similar performance, and having the same basic structure, internally they were quite different aircraft, with the Tu-2S being much simplified.

An early series Tu-2 (number 717) re-engined with M-82FNs (ASh-82FNs), seen here during tests with the new engines. The aircraft is still in the black and green scheme. Note the plain stars. (*Viktor Kulikov's Collection*)

A photograph of 717 from the sides towards the back. (*Viktor Kulikov's Collection*)

A photograph of 717 from the back. (*Viktor Kulikov's Collection*)

As noted previously, all these changes made the Tu-2S lighter by 882 lb (400 kg) and easier to produce and maintain than the initial Tu-2 series. These changes also made the Tu-2S tougher and more survivable as there were fewer lines, pipes, and equipment to be knocked out of action. Supposedly, these changes made to the Tu-2 reduced the manufacturing complexity by 15 to 20 per cent, which made the Tu-2S easier, cheaper, and faster to produce. With these changes, the Tu-2S now took at least 3,000 fewer hours to produce than the early version of the Tu-2.

This improved version of the Tu-2 was given the service designation of 'Tu-2S' ('S' for *Standart*, Russian for 'Standard'), while the Tupolev OKB designation was '61'. In addition to the improved engines, the defensive armament was standardised on three aft-firing 12.7-mm (.50-calibre) UBT machine guns, with one being fired by the navigator in a gun position at the back of the cockpit canopy and one being fired by the radio operator in the rear dorsal position. The ventral gunner fired the third gun through the ventral canopy. The two ShKAS guns in the nose were deleted as the VVS felt that these were unnecessary, while the 20-mm ShVAK cannon in the wing roots were retained for use by the pilot. In addition to bombs in the bomb bay, the Tu-2 could now carry torpedoes on under-wing racks, in addition to bombs of up to 2,205 lb (1,000 kg) on these same wing racks.

Aircraft 716 had these modifications applied to it at Z.156 in July through August 1943. Aircraft 716 was also fitted with the new M-82FNV (ASh-82FN) engines. With these modifications, it first flew on 26 August 1943 with the OKB, before being handed over to the NII VVS in September 1943 for state tests; the state tests ended on 16 December 1943. The GKO Order No. 3754, dated 17 July 1943, had required that the aircraft have a maximum speed of 342 mph (550 kph), a ceiling of 29,528 feet (9,000 metres), and a range of 1,243 miles (2,000 km). It was this order that also reinstated the Tu-2 into production, to be built now at Z.23 in Moscow.

During the tests, 716 showed an improvement over the earlier Tu-2, with a top speed of 315 mph (509 kph) at sea level compared to 276 mph (444 kph) for the earlier version of the Tu-2. The top speed overall increased to 340 mph (547 kph) at 17,717 feet (5,400 metres) as compared to 324 mph (521 kph) at 10,449 feet (3,200 metres) for the earlier machine. The service ceiling was 31,168 feet (9,500 metres) compared to the early Tu-2's 29,528 feet (9,000 metres) and the range was also increased by 75 miles (120 km) compared to the earlier Tu-2. These numbers were close to or exceeded the numbers specified by the GKO order. Nonetheless, some problems still remained, such as directional instability, which had been apparent in the earlier version of the Tu-2, and the view of the navigator was still considered lacking. However, despite these shortcomings, it was decided to put this improved version of the Tu-2 into full-scale production as it was felt that the Tu-2 had better performance than both Soviet and foreign bombers in the same class.

By the time of these tests, Tupolev and his OKB staff had already moved from Omsk (Z.166) back to Moscow, to Z.23 (at Fili, a former suburb of Moscow that had been annexed by Moscow in 1935). In accordance with GKO Order No. 3754, this factory was now tasked with the production of the Tu-2S; this aircraft incorporated the changes made to 716 as fitted with the ASh-82FN engines. This factory would

An early series Tu-2 (number 716) re-engined with ASh-82FNs during tests. This aircraft served as the prototype for the Tu-2S aircraft. (*Viktor Kulikov's Collection*)

A photograph of 716 from the side. (*Viktor Kulikov's Collection*)

A Tu-2S being tested in the T-101 wind tunnel at the TsAGI. (*Viktor Kulikov's Collection*)

produce all the Tu-2S used during the Second World War. It appears that Z.22 in Kazan was also considered for producing the Tu-2S, but it does not seem to have manufactured any.

During the state tests, the Tu-2S was tested against a captured Fw 190A-4 fighter. The results were interesting. At low levels, for example at an altitude of only 3,281 feet (1,000 metres), the Fw 190 had difficulty catching up to the Tu-2S because of the small difference in speed between the two aircraft at this altitude. At higher altitudes, it was easier for the German fighter to overtake the Tu-2S as the difference in speed increased. Nonetheless, it was difficult for the Fw 190A-4 to attack the Tu-2S from the front, due to the relatively high speed of the Tu-2S, and it was normally relegated to attacking the tail. While attacking from above, the Fw 190 was always within the zone of fire from the defensive guns of the Tu-2S.

The Tu-2S in Combat

Sixteen of the new Tu-2S were ready for combat by the end of January 1944. The first VVS unit to receive the new Tu-2s was the 47th GvDRAP, located in the Smolensk area. As the 2nd DRAP (before its redesignation to the 47th GvDRAP), this regiment had flown the early series Tu-2s. These new aircraft were used in photographing the Berlin area.

The missions were accomplished by 24 April 1944 (flights resumed in spring 1945, in preparation for the Berlin offensive). Due to the range involved, at least some of the aircraft were equipped with drop tanks for the mission, the drop tanks probably being attached to the under-wing bomb racks. Among the targets they photographed were airfields, anti-aircraft units, and defensive lines in and around Berlin, the aircraft sometimes flying directly over Berlin, despite the heavy flak they encountered. They apparently encountered little aerial opposition, even over Berlin, perhaps because these were single aircraft flying at high altitude and not thought worth the waste of fuel by the Luftwaffe in trying to intercept them.

The 'new' Tu-2 first saw combat action in June 1944, with the beginning of service trials with the 334th Red Banner BAD (Bomber Air Division), commanded by Colonel I. P. Skok (later the commander of the 6th BAK of the 16th VA or Air Army). The division had three regiments with eighty-seven Tu-2s in total, with seventy-four being operational (a combat readiness rate of 85 per cent, which was quite respectable bearing in mind that this was essentially a new aeroplane).

These aircraft were under the personal control of Josef Stalin, who perhaps mindful of his earlier mistake in cancelling the Tu-2's production constantly questioned Marshal Aleksandr Novikov, the commander of the VVS, regarding the status and combat performance of these Tu-2s.

Two Tu-2s in flight in 1944. (*Viktor Kulikov's Collection*)

One of the first regiments to work up on the new Tu-2S was the 12th BAP, which began training on their new mounts at Kubinka, near Moscow, in late 1943. By late April 1944, the regiment was ready for service and joined the 334th BAD. In May 1944, the 12th BAP was sent to the Leningrad Front.

The 132nd OBAP, which had first used the early version of the Tu-2 in September 1942, was withdrawn from the Southwestern Front for reformation (ten of their early Tu-2s were sent to the 47th GvDRAP, eight were sent to the factory to be repaired, and seven were sent to front-line airfields). After reequipping with the Tu-2S, the 132nd OBAP, now as part of the 334th BAD, was transferred in June 1944 to the Leningrad Front, along with the rest of the 334th BAD. As noted previously, by this time, the 334th BAD had three regiments of Tu-2s, the regiments being the 12th BAP, 132nd BAP, and the 454th BAP, for a total of eighty-seven Tu-2s, of which seventy-four were operational. The 334th BAD was part of the *Stavka* reserve.

Stalin was evidently not enamoured by the idea of sending his precious Tu-2s to the Leningrad Front, as he did not want the Germans to know about the existence of this 'new' bomber, before Operation Bagration. In the end, he was persuaded in the efficacy of using the Tu-2s against the Finnish positions in the Karelian Isthmus. He did make it clear to the commander of the Red Air Force, Aleksander Novikov, to keep a close eye on the Tu-2s.

Operations Against Finland

One very successful Tu-2 operation was against the Vyborg railway terminal on 17 June 1944, with fifty-nine Tu-2s of the 334th BAD participating in the action. The action was so successful that the 334th BAD was awarded the honorific title of '*Leningradskaya*', signifying 'of Leningrad' in Russian. During the same time, Tu-2s were also operating against the Finnish defensive 'Mannerheim Line', as the Soviets were determined at this time to knock Finland out of the war one way or the other, in order to clear their northern flank in preparation for their coming offensives against the German forces. The 12th BAP alone flew 700 sorties against the Mannerheim Line, losing a squadron commander named A. A. Shumeyko to flak in the process. In addition to attacking the Vyborg terminal, Tu-2s attacked Finnish positions at Kivennapa, Kiviniemi, and Valkyari. There was evidently little aerial opposition and the Tu-2s were ordered to carry out daylight missions without fighter escort. The only losses were claimed to be from anti-aircraft fire. On 19 September 1944, Finland signed an armistice with the Soviet Union, ending the Continuation War (Finland's contribution to the Axis war effort against the Soviet Union).

Operation Bagration

The first large operation that the Tu-2S participated in was Operation Bagration, the reconquest of Byelorussia from the Germans, which resulted in the destruction

A Tu-2S on the ground. Note the three windows in the rear fuselage for the ventral gunner's position. (*Viktor Kulikov's Collection*)

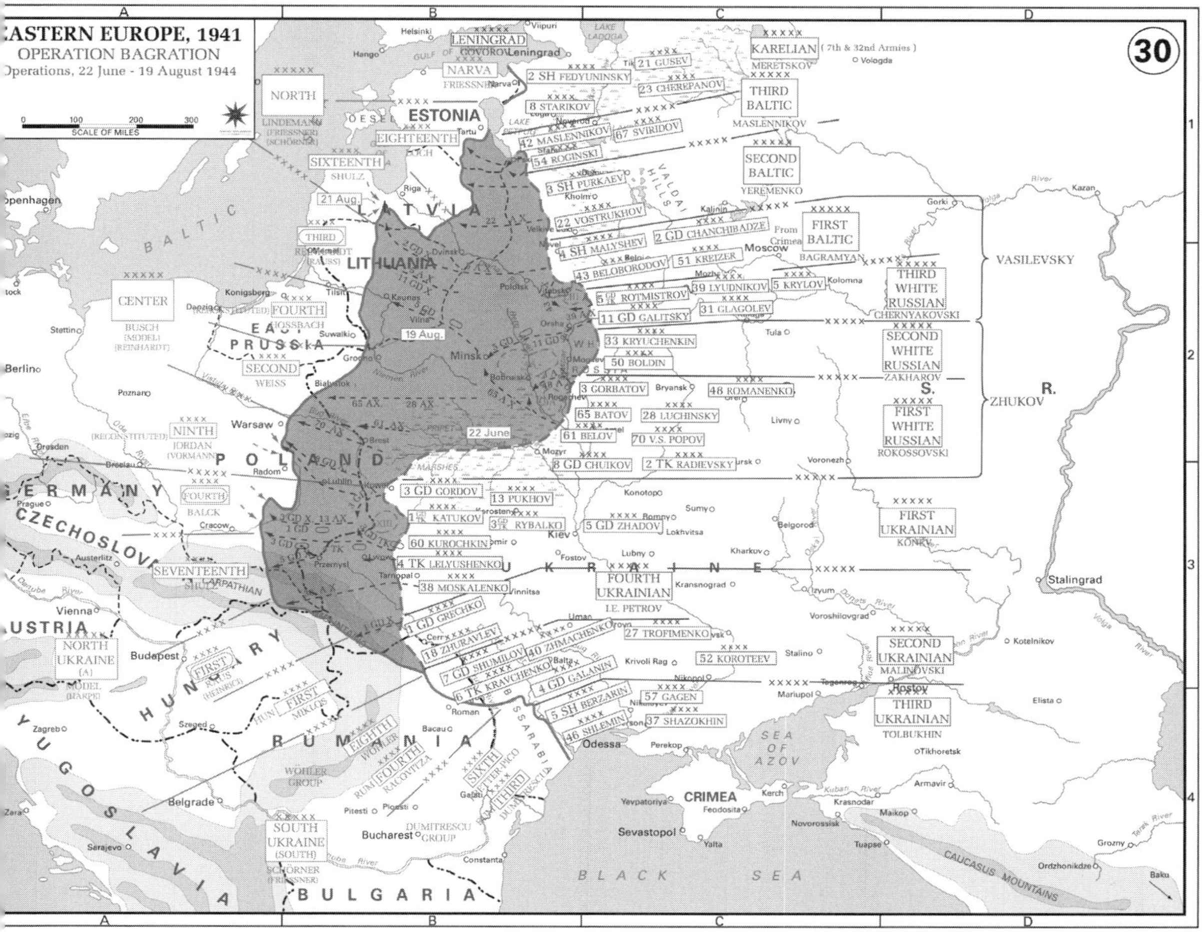

Operation Bagration. (*History Department of the United States Military Academy*)

of the once-mighty Army Group Centre. Once the Germans had been cleared from most of the western Ukraine and the area around Leningrad, the only substantial part of the Soviet Union still occupied by German forces was in the Soviet Republic of Byelorussia in a huge salient, with its southern end resting on the Pripyet Marshes (a large area of forests and swamps with few good roads). After the clearing of the Ukraine, this so-called 'Byelorussian Balcony' was to be the next site of a large-scale Soviet offensive. Although the Germans were well aware of the exposed nature of this sector of the front, they believed that the next big Soviet attack would be in the Ukraine, and disposed their forces, both land (including most of their panzer forces) and aerial (including most of their remaining fighters), accordingly.

In a brilliant feat of deception, or *maskirovka* (camouflage) as the Soviets called it, the Red Army were able to hide their intentions from the Wehrmacht. So effective was this deception that, when the invasion commenced in full on 23 June 1944 (preliminary battalion-sized probing attacks had already started on 22 June 1944, the third anniversary of the opening of Operation Barbarossa), the Germans still thought that it was a diversionary attack, with the main attack yet to come in the Ukraine. By the time they had realised their mistake, it was far too late to do anything about it and their outnumbered forces were routed, with even the Soviets being surprised by the rapidity of their advance.

The main Red Air Force units that were involved in the operation were the 1st, 3rd, 4th, and 16th Air Armies in the opening phases, while the 6th Air Army took part in the second phase of the operation. The Tu-2-equipped 334th BAD was attached to the 3rd Byelorussian Front at the end of June, with which the division participated in this operation until mid-July. In this operation, called Operation Bagration (named for the Georgian General Pyotr Ivanovich Bagration (1765–1812), who had been killed at the Battle of Borodino in the war against Napoleon—the Patriotic War)—one of the biggest and best-planned operations of the war—thousands of aircraft, including the Tu-2s, took part. By now, the Luftwaffe had largely disappeared from the Eastern Front, so the Tu-2s operated with little fear of aerial attack, although they still had to contend with heavy ground fire. The general of the 4th Army, Kurt von Tippelskirch (1891–1957), stated that the 6th Air Fleet of the Luftwaffe had only forty fighters operational because of a lack of fuel and spare parts. In addition, other operational German fighters had been shifted to what were considered higher risk fronts, such as the Ukraine (where the Germans expected the main Soviet assault) and the Western Front (Operation Overlord, the Anglo-American invasion of Normandy, having commenced on 6 June 1944).

During Operation Bagration, the Tu-2s saw heavy usage, flying two to three sorties a day. Even regimental commanders flew missions, with the commander of one of the regiments, the 12th BAP, M. P. Vasyakin (a former test pilot who had flown the 103V), flying two sorties a day. He had been appointed the commander of the 12th BAP in August 1943. The Tu-2s flew with up to 6,614 lb (3,000 kg) of bombs for short-range missions and were used to strike railroad yards deep behind the enemy's front lines.

After its participation in Operation Bagration, the 334th BAD (including the 12th BAP) was transferred to the 1st Baltic Front in July. There it flew missions against German positions in the Baltic ports of Libava (Libau) in Latvia and Klaipeda (Memel) in Lithuania, until January 1945.

Right: Two Tu-2s in flight. (*Viktor Kulikov's Collection*)

Below: A Tu-2 in flight. Note the large area of light paint on the top of the fuselage and wings (A21m Light Brown), typical of many Tu-2s. (*Viktor Kulikov's Collection*)

Vistula to Oder Operation

The Vistula to Oder operation was the follow-on to Operation Bagration and took the Soviets from Warsaw and the eastern border of East Prussia to the Oder River, only 30 miles (48 km) from Berlin. This operation was not as straightforward as Operation Bagration had been as the closer the Soviets got to Berlin, the fiercer the German resistance was, and the operation started in the dead of winter, beginning on 12 January 1945. Indeed, the start date of the operation had been moved forward due to a personal request from British Prime Minister Winston Churchill (Winston Leonard Spencer-Churchill, 1874–1965) to Josef Stalin. Churchill was concerned about Germany's initial success in the Ardennes Offensive (the Battle of the Bulge) and wanted pressure on the Germans from the Soviets to relieve the pressure on the Western Front. Stalin, perhaps surprisingly, obliged and moved the start date forwards to accommodate Churchill.

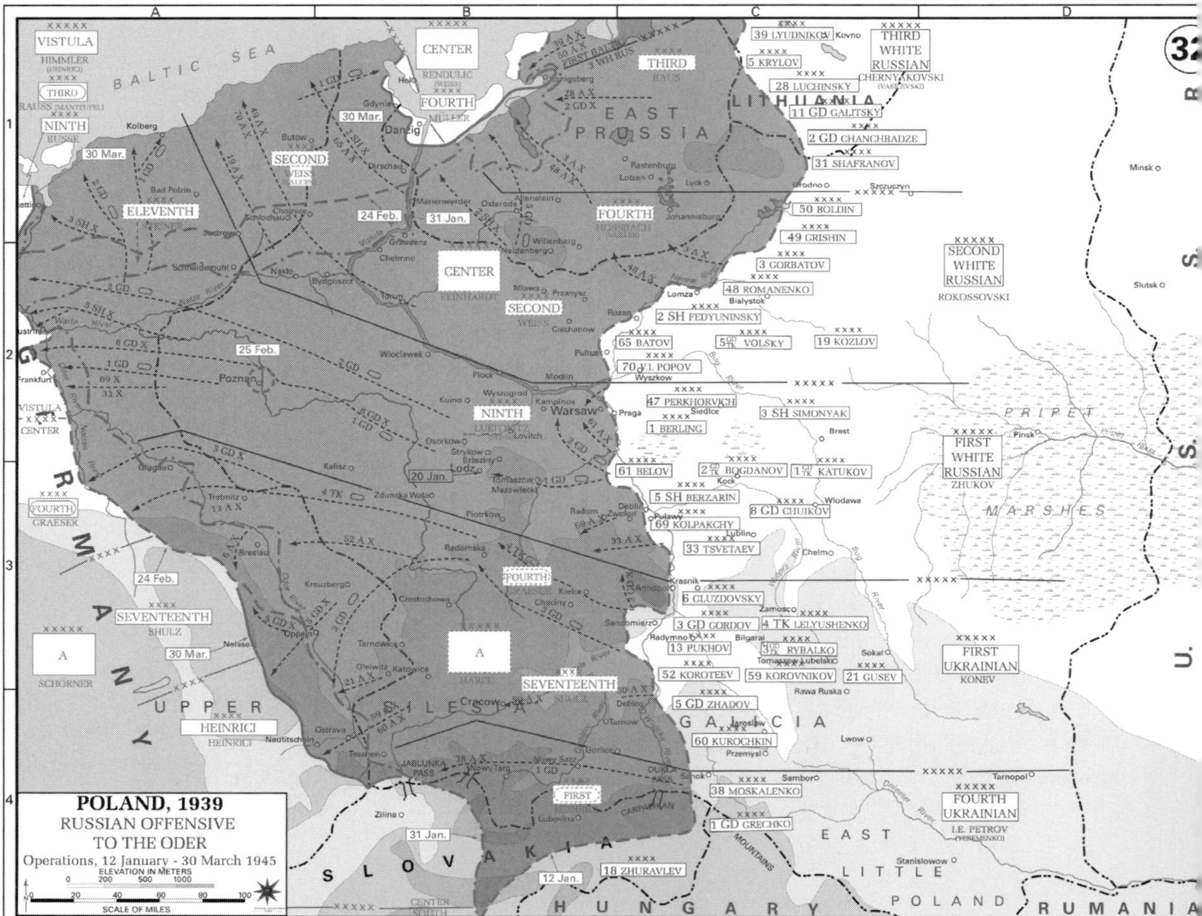

The Vistula to Oder operation. (*History Department of the United States Military Academy*)

From January 1945 until April 1945, the 334th BAD as part of the 18th Air Army supported the 3rd Byelorussian Front. The 326th BAD was now under the command of General I. P. Skok. The Tu-2s were used in the assault against Warsaw and against German cities and towns on the Baltic coast, such as Königsberg, Allenstein, Heilegenbeil, and Danzig. In particular, the Tu-2s saw heavy use against the fortress city of Königsberg, which as the capital of East Prussia was heavily fortified and fiercely defended. On 7 April 1945, in concert with Pe-2s, Tu-2s were used to suppress flak positions and bombed aircraft on the ground, as well as attacking other German positions in Königsberg. On 10 April 1945, Königsberg surrendered to the Soviet forces.

Battle of Berlin (Berlin Strategic Offensive Operation)

From their positions on the Oder, the Soviets launched their last great operation of the Great Patriotic War, the Battle of Berlin or the Berlin Strategic Offensive Operation as they called it. At the start of the Berlin Operation, the Soviets had some 7,500 aircraft arrayed against the Germans, mainly from the 16th and 18th Air Armies, the Tu-2s being a part of the 18th Air Army. The commander of the VVS, Marshal Aleksandr A. Novikov, took direct command over these forces, such was the importance of this last huge operation of the Great Patriotic War. For the Soviets, the ground forces were composed of around 2.5 million men and women (of which up to 200,000 were Polish troops), some 6,000 tanks and self-propelled guns, 75,000 guns and mortars, and 400 rocket launchers (Katyushas). Against them, the Germans were able to field between 750,000 and 1 million men (with the actual number probably being closer to the low end), around 500 tanks and 1,000 assault guns, over 9,000 artillery pieces, and 2,200 or so aircraft.

After the fall of Königsberg, the 334th BAD was used to assist the 1st Byelorussian Front in its assault on Berlin. Under the command of Marshal Georgiy Konstantinovich Zhukov (1896–1974), it was the 1st Byelorussian Front that was given by Stalin the order (and distinction) to take Berlin itself. The Tu-2s were to assist in this vital operation. That the Tu-2s were chosen to participate in this most important part of the Berlin Operation is a good indicator of the high esteem in which the Tu-2 was held by the Red Army. It was planned for the first day of the operation to employ 406 Tu-2s and Pe-2s in attacking the Germans, with 133 fighter-bombers in support.

The battle itself opened in full on 16 April 1945, a day after the initiation of battalion-sized probing attacks (as was normal with large Soviet operations). The Soviets moved out from their Oder bridgehead at Kustrin and their bridgeheads on either side of Frankfurt-an-der-Oder. By the end of the first day of the operation, the VVS had flown 6,548 combat sorties according to Soviet accounts. Although the Germans were able to slow the Soviet advance in the centre at the Seelow Heights for three days, with considerable Soviet casualties inflicted, against which defences the Tu-2s were heavily engaged in bombing operations, there was little the Germans could do to stop the huge Soviet army facing them. By 25 April, the encirclement of Berlin

Several Tu-2s in flight. This aircraft, No. 6, is the subject of a profile in the colour plates section. (*Viktor Kulikov's Collection*)

A Tu-2 in flight. (*Viktor Kulikov's Collection*)

had been consolidated. It was also on this day that advance elements of the Red Army met up with their American counterparts at Torgau, on the Elbe River. The Eastern Front had met the Western Front and Germany had now been cut in two.

Operating against the city itself, on 22 April 1945, fifty-four Tu-2s in two regiments dropped 97 tons of bombs on areas of resistance in the central part of the city. During the Battle of Berlin, they also attacked German areas of resistance in the heavily defended Tiergarten District. It is doubtful if they faced much aerial opposition, such was the parlous condition of the Luftwaffe by this time, but flak would have still been a problem and indeed a huge and nearly indestructible flak tower dominated the Tiergarten District. Nonetheless, by 2 May 1945, the fighting had ended in Berlin (Hitler had killed himself on 30 April) and, by 11 May 1945, the last major German forces in the field, in Bohemia and Moravia, had surrendered to the Red Army, with the formal surrender date being 9 May 1945 according to Soviet/Russian tradition. Victory Day in Russia is still celebrated on 9 May 1945. However, the Tu-2's combat use during the Second World War had not ended—Japan had still not surrendered.

A Tu-2 in flight over Moscow in 1945. (*Viktor Kulikov's Collection*)

Manchurian Campaign (Manchurian Strategic Offensive Operation)

As indicated previously, the Battle of Berlin was not the last operation of the war for either the Soviet Union or the Tu-2. Stalin had promised US President Franklin Delano Roosevelt (1882–1945) at the Yalta Conference in February 1945 that, with the conclusion of the war in Europe, the Soviet Union would join the fight against the Empire of Japan within three months. Thus the campaign against the Japanese forces in Manchuria (or the Kwantung Army as this army is often known) was born. The Soviet name for this campaign was the Manchurian Strategic Offensive Operation.

The 113th Red Banner Leningrad OBAD had worked up on the Tu-2s by March 1945, after having flown the Il-4 until December 1944. It participated in the Berlin operation for only three days, after which it was moved to the Far East to take part in the upcoming Manchurian offensive under the command of the 7th BAK of the 12th Air Army of the Trans-Baikal Front. The 326th and 334th BADs became part of the 6th BAK under General I. P. Skok, also under the 12th Air Army.

Although not a part of the Great Patriotic War, this campaign was not only the last campaign for Soviet forces in the Second World War, it was the last major land campaign for any side during the war, occurring during August 1945. It was also the last time that the Tu-2 would be used in combat by the Soviets. Although the fighting was short, lasting only a couple of weeks, it was intense and saw heavy usage of the Tu-2s of the 113th OBAD, and the 326th and the 334th BADs. Flying under the command of the 6th and 7th BAKs of the 12th Air Army of the Trans-Baikal Front, these Tu-2s were used against ground targets, such as troop concentrations, railway

The Manchurian Campaign (Manchurian Strategic Offensive Operation). In Russian. (*Wikimedia*)

stations, bridges, and enemy airfields. The Tu-2s took part in attacks against the Manchurian cities of Mukden, Hailar, and Harbin and were used for both bombing and reconnaissance work. The Tu-2s saw action from 8 August 1945, the opening day of the operation, until 3 September 1945, a day after the official end of the Second World War. In all, the Tu-2s of the 113th OBAD of the 7th BAK alone flew some 1,600 sorties. The end of the war found the Tu-2s of the 6th BAK based on Sakhalin Island.

Naval Service

Unlike the earlier version of the Tu-2, the Tu-2S was issued to AVMF units, such as the Red Banner Fleet (KBF or Baltic Fleet) and the Black Sea Fleet, with which they continued to serve post-war, sometimes as torpedo bombers.

Tu-2S Combat Tactics

Much of the success of any aeroplane is dependent on using the proper tactics. For the Tu-2S, this consisted of carrying the correct bombs for the mission involved and flying in proper formations. The bombs that were used could be high-explosive FAB-100, FAB-500, or FAB-1000, depending on the size and strength of the target. For example, the large FAB-1000 (2,205 lb (1,000 kg)) bombs were useful against enemy fortifications. Armour-piercing PTAB and BRAB bombs could also be carried, the PTABs being especially useful against tanks. Even with the maximum bombload of 6,614 lb (3,000 kg), the aircraft was still found to be easy to handle. Earlier in its usage, there was a shortage of the large calibre bombs and the Tu-2s were forced to carry smaller bombs, and therefore a smaller bombload.

For the most part, the defensive armament provided a good area of protection for the aircraft, especially in the case of attacks from the rear. The pilot's two 20-mm cannon would have proved to be a deterrent to frontal attacks. It was also found that flying in formations of three aircraft or nine aircraft provided a density of fire that helped repel attacks by German fighters.

The optimum altitude for bombing depended on the target. For larger targets, the bombing altitudes were mostly from 3,281 to 9,843 feet (1,000 to 3,000 metres), but bombing from an altitude of up to 13,123 feet (4,000 metres) did occur. For smaller targets, such as bridges and fortified strong points, the altitudes used were 984 to 1,640 feet (300 to 500 metres) or 1,640 to 3,281 feet (500 to 1,000 metres).

In terms of their use, the Tu-2s were used mainly for level day bombing against large targets. At first, the Tu-2s were limited to only a 2,646-lb (1,200-kg) bombload. By September 1944, this was increased to 2,976 lb (1,350 kg). Eventually, the full load of 6,614 lb (3,000 kg) was allowed and was used for short-range missions.

Assessment of the Tu-2S in Combat

By early 1945, the 326th BAD was equipped with 94 Tu-2s, while the 334th BAD had 111 Tu-2s. Overall, there were a total of 278 Tu-2s in service, of which 264 were airworthy, for an airworthiness rate of 95 per cent—a very impressive percentage for a heavily used warplane and a testament to the ruggedness and maintainability of the Tu-2S. The Tu-2s comprised around 9 per cent of the total bomber force of the Red Air Force. Even though widely considered a better aircraft than the Pe-2, the Pe-2 continued to be used in far great numbers than the Tu-2, partly due to the fact that it had been in continuous production since 1940, and it continued to be used as a dive bomber, a role for which it was better suited than the Tu-2. The Pe-2 was also better known to the crews, who were used to its strengths and weaknesses.

Despite the general toughness and survivability of the Tu-2, operations were not flown without loss. While operating with the 334th BAD, despite fighter escort flown by Bell P-39 Kobras (Airacobras) and Yak-9s, in three months, the Germans were able to destroy ten Tu-2s and damage another fourteen aircraft. In September 1944, the very experienced pilot M. P. Vasyakin (a former Tupolev OKB test pilot) was killed in air combat near Tukums in Latvia. Seven more Tu-2s were brought down during this period by German flak. By the end of 1944, seventy-seven Tu-2s were reported to have been lost to various causes, including forty-five lost in combat operations, eighteen in accidents, and fourteen to wear and tear (they did see very heavy usage).

As with the first version of the Tu-2, the Tu-2S was well-regarded by its pilots and crew, who found it to be a fast and rugged aircraft, easy to handle, with good defensive capabilities, and an excellent bombload. Colonel Bugay, who commanded the 132nd BAP as a part of the 334th BAD, praised the Tu-2 for its high speed, ability to be operated safely on only one engine, its capability to carry large-sized bombs, and for its good handling. As reported in *Soviet Combat Aircraft of the Second World War: Volume Two: Twin-Engined Fighters, Attack Aircraft, and Bombers*, by Yefim Gordon and Dmitry Khazanov (p. 156), Colonel Bugay stated that 'the pilots of the regiment appreciated the Tu-2 and successfully flew combat missions'. A terse, but accurate combat assessment of the Tu-2S.

Tu-2R Reconnaissance Variant: Great Patriotic War Version

From the beginning of the design of the 103, it was felt that it could be adapted to a reconnaissance aircraft due to its good load-carrying capabilities and overall good performance. The VVS had a need for a high-performance reconnaissance aircraft, so, in 1942, Tupolev investigated the possibility of turning the production early Tu-2 version into a reconnaissance aircraft. Working in cooperation with the VVS, the Tupolev OKB had the design of the aircraft ready by June; on 2 June 1942, the design was presented to a VVS commission. The VVS signed off on the proposed design and presented Tupolev with its basic requirements. Once this was done, work started on converting a production Tu-2 into a Tu-2R ('R' for *Razvedchik*

Russian for 'Reconnaissance'), while the VVS completed its technical specifications for the aircraft.

The specifications required that the Tu-2R must have a range of 1,553 miles (2,500 km) at a speed of 233 to 249 mph (375–400 kph) for day reconnaissance missions, and a range of 1,243 miles (2,000 km) for night reconnaissance missions. The reason that the range for the day missions could be longer was that an extra fuel tank could be carried in the bomb bay (for the night missions it is possible that the bomb bay would be occupied by flash bombs). The aircraft had to have the special equipment for these missions (i.e., cameras). The cameras were to be aimed using an OPB-1m sight. In addition, apparently more armour was to be provided to protect the crew.

The cameras to be installed were the AFA-1 or two AFA-3s, with these installations being interchangeable. Two AFA-33s were also to be installed. The cameras were to be protected by lids to prevent dirt on the ground from obscuring the lenses. The lids were to be opened on take-off, which then allowed the cameras to take their photographs in flight. The lenses protruded from the bomb bay and were protected (and streamlined) by using fairings. The bomb bay could accommodate flash bombs such as eight or nine of the FOTAB-35s. The FOTAB flash bombs were used for illumination purposes on night missions. The cameras were to be arranged so that the photographs could be taken from the port and starboard sides. An NAFA-19 night camera was also installed, as it was on the standard Tu-2.

The VVS's need for a reconnaissance aircraft was such that, by 5 June 1942, only three days after the proposal had been approved, the VVS made a request to Tupolev that he equip four Tu-2s with two of the AFA-3s cameras and the extra fuel tank. The installation of the extra fuel tank was to be tested on the 103V. By 18 June 1942, a meeting was held at Z.166 with Tupolev in attendance, along with the deputy chief engineer of the *zavod* Polonsky and a military representative named Brovko. The result of the meeting was that the construction of five Tu-2Rs was approved. The aircraft were to be ready by 15 July 1942, that is, in less than a month, which was clearly unrealistic. In fact, only three of the five aircraft were ready by December 1942, such was the pressing need for the Tupolev OKB to concentrate on producing the standard tactical bomber version of the Tu-2.

Aircraft Nos 508 and 601 were equipped with only one fixed camera, but aircraft No. 603 had two twin AFA-33/50 cameras on moveable mounts that enabled one to swing to the right up to 7 degrees and one to swing to the left up to 7 degrees. This enabled this aircraft to photograph a wider area than the aircraft with the fixed camera. It was found that the large bomb bay allowed larger cameras to be fitted. The tests with these aircraft were deemed successful and led the Tupolev OKB to perform further work on the development of the Tu-2R. The fuel tank installation was tested on aircraft No. 406. Two AFA-33/50s were mounted on moveable supports, as with aircraft No. 603. These mounts could now move the cameras up to 9.5 degrees to the left or right, depending on whether the port or starboard camera was being used. State tests of this aircraft were carried out from 18 December 1943 to 20 March 1944.

In 1944, it was decided to convert aircraft No. 304, produced at Z.166. The conversion work was to be carried out by Z.23, which by 1944 was now producing the production version of the Tu-2. After modernisation (probably to bring it up to Tu-2S standards) and factory tests of the aircraft in May 1944, the aircraft was sent to the 47th GvDRAP for combat tests. The combat tests showed that the extra fuel tank in the bomb bay increased the range to 1,324 miles (2,130 km).

As a result of the combat tests, additional modifications and additions were specified, such as moveable installations of the AFA-33/50, AFA-33/75 cameras, and a fixed AFA-33/20 installation. In addition, the navigator had the ability to open the protective camera lids in flight (this would protect the lenses on take-off). The underside of the nose was also to gain a new clear panel, as the nose glazing was extended to the rear on the starboard side. These changes led to continued development of the reconnaissance Tu-2 version after the war, which led to the development of the post-war version of the Tu-2R, the Tu-6 (see Chapter 7 for information on this version).

The Tu-2S Refined

Development of the Tu-2 did not stop with the initial development of the Tu-2S, as Tupolev strove to refine the design even well into the post-war period, as production continued. To improve the aerodynamics and decrease the drag of the Tu-2S, smaller diameter cowlings were fitted from the series 20 onward, which necessitated that small fairings or 'bumps' be fitted to cover the rocker heads on the ASh-82FN engines. These smaller cowlings appeared during the war. From the series 20 onward, the original wooden nose was replaced with a metal one, the acute aluminium shortage of the early part of the war having now been overcome, at least partly because of the shipment of aluminium from the United States. At some point in the development of the Tu-2S, the three small windows on either side of the fuselage above the ventral gunner's position was replaced by one large window, possibly from the series 49 aircraft onward.

After the Second World War, four-bladed propellers, with square ends, replaced the three-bladed propellers with rounded ends found on the wartime Tu-2s. The rear dorsal gunner's (radio operator's) canopy was modified, with a fixed portion replacing the portion that moved to the front to enable the gun to be used. The advantage of this change is not completely clear; most probably, it simplified operation of the gun and may have simplified production (Tupolev always worked hard to simplify the design and the ease of production of the Tu-2). De-icing boots were fitted to the leading edge of the wings and horizontal tail planes as well as the twin vertical tails. (Some of these changes will be dealt with in a more comprehensive manner in Chapter 10.)

The 1947 Standard Tu-2S

Including the changes noted previously, the post-war versions of the Tu-2S were progressively improved and featured modernised electronics. These changes were

A Tu-2S with four-bladed propellers being tested at the NII VVS in 1946. (*Viktor Kulikov's Collection*)

A late post-war Tu-2S being tested at the NII VVS (note the hexagonal pavement) in 1949. (*Viktor Kulikov's Collection*)

brought about partly because of the poor performance of two production aircraft, Nos 1/44 and 2/44, which when tested in March 1945 failed their tests. The USSR Council of Ministers reacted to this by issuing a Resolution No. 12-82-524 on 20 June 1946, which directed the MAP to produce ten Tu-2s with modifications to eliminate the defects found in the tested aircraft and defects that had been found in combat. These aircraft were to be the standard for 1946 and 1947 production aircraft.

The aircraft had the same length and wingspan as unmodified Tu-2s. They also had the same propellers, the three-bladed AV-5V-167A with a diameter of 12.47 feet (3.8 metres) (this would change in 1947 to a four-bladed propeller as described further on). The flight weight was 24,163 lb (10,960 kg) and the top speed was now 342 mph (550 kph), a slight improvement. The range was 1,398 miles (2,250 km), which was also an improvement.

One of the most noticeable external changes between the 1947 standard Tu-2S and the wartime version was the replacement of the three-bladed propellers with four-bladed units (as mentioned previously), the propellers being the AV-9VF-21K four-bladed propeller with blunt tips. The four-bladed units had a diameter of 11.81 feet (3.6 metres) as compared to the 12.47-foot (3.8-metre) diameter of the three-bladed AV-5V-167A propellers. De-icing units were applied to the leading edges of the flying surfaces. There were also upgrades to the avionics and a VEU-1 B-20 20-mm cannon installation may have replaced the rear dorsal gunner's VUB-68 UBT 12.7-mm machine gun installation in the last production examples.

The upgraded avionics included an RSB-5 radio instead of the RSB-3bis, a GPK-47A artificial horizon instead of the AGP-2, and a GPK-46 gyrocompass instead of the GMK-2 gyromagnetic compass. Other changes included a RARK-5 instead of the RPKO-26 radio compass and a RV-2 altimeter.

Apparently, Z.39 in Irkutsk built 218 of these updated versions from 1947–50. Note that probably only the latest of the Tu-2s built there would have included all of the changes described above, as some of the changes were progressively applied during production.

Camouflage and Markings

The Tu-2S was finished in the three-colour scheme introduced in 1943. The three-colour scheme (1943–45) came from Order No. 389S/0133 NKAP and VVS RKKA, '3 July 1943, for the beginning of painting new aircraft at the aircraft factory, scheduled from 15 July 1943, and attack aircraft and bombers from 1 August [1943]'. The three-colour scheme started appearing on Soviet aircraft from autumn 1943 until the end of the war (and even after, at least in the case of the Tu-2).

This scheme used A32m Dark Grey, which was similar to the British Extra Dark Sea Grey, A24m Green, A21m Light Brown (actually more of a greyish-tan), and A28m Blue underside. The interior colour was A-14 Steel Grey, a very neutral medium grey, similar to the American Neutral Gray. Some late war Tu-2s may have received the 'fighter-type' two-grey scheme consisting of A32m Dark Grey and AMT-11 Grey Blue (there apparently was not an Axxm oil enamel equivalent to this colour) over A28m

A late post-war Tu-2S being tested at Z.39 in Irkutsk in 1949. The rear dorsal gun appears to be a 20-mm cannon and not the UBT 12.7-mm machine gun normally fitted to Tu-2s. (*Viktor Kulikov's Collection*)

A front view of a late post-war Tu-2S at Z.39. (*Viktor Kulikov's Collection*)

Blue. This use is controversial, however, and it is problematic whether or not the available photographic evidence supports the use of this scheme, although you will sometimes see profiles with this scheme for GPW Tu-2s. This scheme was evidently not used following the war in any case, and the three-colour scheme appears to have been used for several years after the war, before being replaced by an overall topside green over blue scheme, typical of early post-war Soviet bombers.

Although the NKAP issued a drawing, indicating how the Tu-2 was supposed to be painted in the three-colour scheme, with few exceptions this does not appear to have been followed in service. For example, wide areas of the top of the fuselage and central parts of the wing were often painted in the A-21m Light Brown on service Tu-2s. Although service aircraft often did not follow the NKAP schemes exactly, they were usually close to the recommended scheme (this was at least the case with the Il-2). There appears to be no explanation for why the Tu-2 deviated so much from its recommended pattern. It may be that it was determined in actual service that the wide area of A-21m on top served to better camouflage the aircraft than the recommended scheme.

6

The Tu-2 *vs* other Medium Bombers of the Second World War

The Tu-2 was of course not the only medium bomber to take part in the Second World War. This chapter will focus on the comparison between the Tu-2 and other medium bombers used by some of the other participants in the war. This list is by no means completely comprehensive, but it does cover some of the main types used by the main combatants. The countries are listed alphabetically, with the aircraft listed alphabetically under their country, where appropriate. A table showing the specifications of the aircraft will follow the comparisons.

Germany

Dornier Do 217

This twin-engined bomber was a development of the Do 215, which was itself a development of the Do 17 (a mid-1930s design); both the Do 17 and Do 215 served on the Eastern Front, with the Do 17 primarily operating as a reconnaissance aircraft. Evidently, before the Great Patriotic War, the Soviet Union purchased two Do 215s from Germany, although their ultimate fate is unknown. The Do 217 was basically a larger and more powerful version of the Do 215, and it saw use as a bomber, night fighter, and a reconnaissance aircraft. It was as a reconnaissance aircraft that it saw service on the Eastern Front. With some versions matching and even exceeding the Tu-2 in speed, the considerably larger Do 217's career was cut short by the destruction of Nazi Germany, whereas the Tu-2 enjoyed a very long post-war career. As with most German bombers (except for jet bombers such as the Ar 234), production had stopped in 1944 with the initiation of the Emergency Fighter Programme, which made the production of fighters the main priority of the German aviation industry.

Heinkel He 111

As the Luftwaffe had no true four-engined strategic bombers, except for the problem-plagued He 177 Greif (Griffin in German), with its troublesome coupled Daimler-Benz DB 610 engines (and excluding the four-engined BV 222 and the Ju 290, which were maritime reconnaissance aircraft), the twin-engined He 111 of necessity continued as the main strategic bomber of the Germans throughout the war. A reliable and well-built design, the He 111 suffered from a weak defensive armament and a relatively slow speed, much slower than that of the Tu-2. In many ways, it was analogous to the Soviet Il-4, not the later Tu-2; like the Il-4, it had been designed in the mid-1930s and continued to serve out of necessity until the end of the war, despite its obsolescence. In Spanish service, it continued in post-war use until as late as 1973 with the Spanish Air Force.

Junkers Ju 88

This was perhaps the most analogous aircraft to the Tu-2 during the Second World War, and even directly influenced its development. Designed before the war as a fast day bomber that also had dive bombing capabilities, it was also a very versatile design, serving not just as a horizontal and dive bomber, but also as a torpedo bomber, reconnaissance aircraft, long-range fighter, and as a night fighter. In its later bomber versions, such as the Ju 88S, it was faster than the Tu-2, having a top speed of 378 mph (608 kph) to the Tu-2's 340 mph (547 kph). In its long-range fighter versions, such as the Ju 88C (which saw considerable service on the Eastern Front), it possessed a heavy forward-firing armament that enabled it to undertake ground-attack missions with some success. It also proved to be a successful night fighter, developed from the long-range fighter versions, forming with the Bf 110 twin-engined fighter the core of the German night fighter force in the latter half of the Second World War. Indeed, the Ju 88 may have been the most outstanding medium bomber of the Second World War, with the possible exceptions of the American Douglas A-26 Invader and the Tu-2.

Italy

Savoia-Marchetti SM.79 Sparviero

Featuring the three motors so typical of Italian aircraft of the 1930s, this bomber excelled as a torpedo bomber during the Second World War. Designed during the mid-1930s, it was of mixed construction, with a metal and fabric-covered metal-structured fuselage and tail planes, wooden wings, and retractable main landing gear. Like the Tupolev SB, it saw much action during the Spanish Civil War, where its high speed made it difficult for the Spanish Republican fighters to intercept. By the Second World War, its speed was no longer fast enough to avoid interception, though it still proved to be a reliable and tough aeroplane and a good torpedo bomber, although compared to the Tu-2 it was much slower, not as well armed, and had a smaller bombload.

Japan

Mitsubishi G4M Betty

Although a large plane, with a long range and a length of 65 feet 6¼ inches (19.97 metres), in terms of weight and payload, the G4M Betty (its American nickname) was in truth a medium bomber. The standard Japanese Navy long-range bomber, the twin-engined Betty did have an excellent maximum range of more than 3,000 miles (4,828 km). It was also equipped with a 20-mm cannon in the tail, which proved to be a useful and powerful defensive weapon. On the other hand, it was much slower than the Tu-2, could not carry nearly the same bombload, and was not nearly as tough, lacking armour protection for the crew and lacking self-sealing tanks. It would have been near-suicidal to have used it for daytime bombing on the Eastern Front, even with heavy fighter escort.

Mitsubishi Ki-67 Hiryu (Peggy)

The Hiryu or Peggy (its American nickname) was considered a heavy bomber by the Japanese, but, in comparison with other bombers of the Second World War in terms of bombload and capability, it should be considered a medium bomber and is so considered here.

The Peggy was a very good aeroplane and was tougher than most Japanese aircraft as it incorporated armour and self-sealing tanks into the design. The armament was also fairly heavy, consisting of four 12.7-mm (.50-calibre) machine guns and one 20-mm cannon for self-defence. It compared favourably with the Tu-2 in terms of speed (334 mph (538 kph) compared to 340 mph (547 kph) for the Tu-2S) and was also quite manoeuvrable. It did have a smaller bomb bay, only able to accommodate 2,359 lb (1,070 kg) compared to the Tu-2's 4,409 lb (2,000 kg). On the other hand, the Peggy had a better range as Soviet aircraft were built to operate near the front, while Japanese aircraft were built to operate over the vast expanses of the Pacific.

The Peggy was one of the best medium bombers of the war, but only 750 or so were produced due to the dire situation with Japanese industry late in the war. As with the German Ju 88, its career essentially ended with the Second World War, although Indonesia operated a few ex-Japanese examples in the immediate post-war period.

Soviet Union

Ilyushin Il-4

Designed in the mid-1930s by Sergey Ilyushin, the Il-4 was designed well before the Tu-2 and was not as advanced. Although a reliable design, it had neither the speed, nor the armament—both defensive (two ShKAS 7.62-mm machine guns and one UBT 12.7-mm machine gun in a dorsal (mid-upper) turret) and offensive (none)—that the Tu-2 had. Indeed, the Tu-2 was essentially a replacement for the obsolescent Il-4 (and the SB). It was too slow and poorly armed to act as a day bomber during the Great Patriotic War, so it was used mainly at night. Nonetheless, the Il-4 continued to serve throughout the war as a bomber, primarily as a night bomber, and as a torpedo bomber. Indeed, as a torpedo bomber it was not completely replaced until some time after the war (by the Tu-2).

Petlyakov Pe-2

Although really more of a light bomber (and dive bomber), the Pe-2 is included here as there was some overlap with the Tu-2 in terms of roles. In fact, the Tu-2 had originally been intended to function as a dive bomber, among other roles, and if it had succeeded in this role it might very well have replaced the Pe-2. As it was, the Pe-2, although smaller and with a lighter bombload than the Tu-2, continued to be used by the Soviet Union until the end of the war (and beyond) because it was a superior dive bomber when compared to the Tu-2. Over 11,000 Pe-2s were constructed (there was never a pause in production), which was some four times more than the Tu-2s built, and it saw service from the first day of the Great Patriotic War to the last. Like the Tu-2, it also saw service in the Manchurian Strategic Offensive Operation in August 1945. It continued in service after the war and was given the NATO nickname of 'Buck'. After the war, it was used by several Communist countries such as Bulgaria, Poland, and Yugoslavia.

United Kingdom

De Havilland Mosquito

This very famous British aircraft, unusual for the time in being a warplane made almost entirely out of wood, was used as a night fighter, fighter-bomber, bomber, and reconnaissance aircraft. As a bomber, it could carry up to 4,000 lb (1,814 kg) of bombs, which gave it a bombload comparable to that of some medium bombers. It was considerably faster than the Tu-2, with a top speed of over 400 mph (644 kph) in some versions, but in its bomber version it lacked any gun armament of any kind, neither offensive nor defensive. As such, its only defence was speed and, once its bombs had been dropped, it was useless for ground attack. The fighter-bomber version on the other hand, with four Browning .303-inch (7.7-mm, 30.3-calibre) machine guns and four Hispano 20-mm cannons mounted in the nose, in addition to bombs under the wings and in the aft bomb bay, proved to be a very useful ground-attack aircraft indeed. It is interesting to note that the Mosquito directly influenced the Soviets in their development of a fast day bomber variant of the Tu-2, the SDB.

Vickers Wellington

The Wellington was among the first series of modern bombers used by the RAF, along with the Armstrong Whitworth Whitley and the Handley Page Hampden, all being twin-engined designs. The Wellington was notable for its unusual construction; instead of using a stressed-skin metal construction, it utilised a fabric covering over an all-metal geodesic construction (the geodesic structure being designed by the British inventor Barnes Wallis). This structure was light, but very strong and the Wellington could withstand a great deal of structural damage, although its initial lack of self-sealing fuel tanks made it quite flammable. It was much slower than the Tu-2 and only had .303-inch (30.3-calibre) machine guns for defence. Due to its vulnerability during daylight missions (a vulnerability shared with all British bombers of the time), it was moved to nocturnal missions, as was the case with the Soviet Il-4. It served in the RAF until after the end of the Second World War in various duties, including as a maritime patrol aircraft.

United States

Douglas A-20 Boston (Havoc)

Although a light bomber by designation (A-20, with the 'A' for 'Attack' in USAAF usage), the Tu-2 was destined to replace this American-designed aircraft in Soviet service, which it did after the war. A lend-lease aircraft, it was a well-liked machine, with a good top speed (especially in its earlier versions, with the A-20B topping out at 350 mph (563 kph)), good power, and was tough and durable. It is an interesting fact that the single largest user of the A-20 was the Soviet Union, which used even more of this very useful aeroplane than the United States. It found use in the Soviet Union as a level bomber, ground-attack bomber, and a torpedo bomber, in which guise the Tu-2 replaced it after the war. The Tu-2, being a larger aircraft, had a much larger bombload and had better defensive armament. The Tu-2 could also carry two torpedoes with ease, while the A-20 was normally restricted to one torpedo when being used as a torpedo bomber. However, crews actually preferred the DB-7S (the torpedo-carrying variant of the Soviet Boston) over the Tu-2T because they found it to be a more comfortable aircraft in which to fly.

Douglas A-26 (B-26) Invader

The 'big brother' of the A-20, in some ways the Invader was the aircraft that was most analogous overall to the Tu-2. It was conceived and first fought in the Second World War, and it had a long and varied post-war history with a number of different air forces. It was designed to replace both light bombers such as the A-20 Havoc (Boston) and medium bombers such as the B-25 Mitchell and the B-26 Marauder. Although carrying the 'A' for attack (light bomber) designation during the Second World War, the Invader was really a medium bomber as can be appreciated from the fact that it was also intended to replace medium bombers in American service. Compared to the Tu-2, it was faster and had a longer range, but it could not quite carry the same amount of bombs that the Tu-2 could carry. On the other hand, the Invader often carried a very heavy nose armament of up to eight .50-calibre machine guns and could carry rockets, which made it very useful for ground attack. The Invader's two remotely controlled defensive turrets, with two .50-calibre guns each, were probably more effective than the three hand-held .50-calibre (12.7-mm) UBT machine guns of the Tu-2.

The Invader was used by over a dozen different countries after the war and it fought in both the Korean War (1950–53) and the Vietnam War (1965–73) with the USAF. It also saw combat with the French in Indochina and in Algeria. It was even used on both sides during the unsuccessful Bay of Pigs invasion of Cuba, in 1962, and saw action in the Nigerian Civil War (Biafra). It was not retired in foreign service until the early to mid-1980s (perhaps as late as 1984 by El Salvador). After the Second World War, with the abandonment of the 'A' for attack designation by the USAF, and with the retirement of the B-26 Marauder from USAF service in 1948, the A-26 Invader was re-designated the B-26 Invader.

Martin B-26 Marauder

The Marauder was and is an interesting aeroplane; at one time, it was an underrated aircraft, but now the opposite is true. It is constantly mentioned as being a fast bomber, yet the last version, the B-26G, only had the same top speed as the much larger and heavier four-engined Boeing B-17G Flying Fortress heavy bomber (287 mph (462 kph)), and this was some 53 mph (85 kph) slower than the top speed of the Tu-2S—340 mph (547 kph). In its earlier, faster versions, the B-26 could be a dangerous aircraft to take-off and land in because of the high wing loading and high landing speed caused by its relatively small wings; it suffered multiple landing accidents due to this. Later versions with larger wings were safer to fly, land, and take-off in, but they were also slower, due to the increased drag of the larger wings and the greater weight, while still using the same basic engines as the earlier versions. However, it was a tough and heavily armed aircraft (up to twelve .50-calibre machine guns) and had a good range, with a ferry range of 2,850 miles (4,587 km). Its bombload was normally 4,000 lb (1,814 kg), which was less than the 6,614 lb (3,000 kg) that the Tu-2 was capable of carrying.

Overall, the Marauder was a reasonably good aircraft, but hardly an outstanding one. One piece of evidence would seem to bear this out—the B-26 was out of service with the US by 1948 at the latest, while the B-25 continued in US service until 1960 (as did the B-17; the Invader was not retired from US service until 1972). It is also interesting to note that the B-26 Marauder was test flown by the Soviets, but was rejected for use, while the B-25 was accepted for use, with well over 800 B-25s being used by the VVS and the AVMF.

North American B-25 Mitchell

The B-25 was generally an outstanding aeroplane; better overall than the B-26 Marauder, although not fast, with a top speed of around 275 mph (443 kph) in its later versions. It had a good range, excellent defensive armament, and good reliability. In addition, it was a very versatile aeroplane, being used as a level bomber (against both tactical and strategic targets), ground-attack bomber, reconnaissance, maritime patrol aircraft, a transport, and even for a short time as a night fighter (the B-25G with the nose-mounted 75-mm cannon was used for a short time as a night fighter). Like the B-26 Marauder, it was used to attack both tactical and strategic targets, everything from barges to factories.

The Soviets used over 800 Mitchells that had been provided through lend-lease and found it to be a rugged and dependable aircraft, and it was used to supplement the Il-4 for night bombing missions. In addition, it was used as a night intruder, where its nose-mounted .50-calibre machine guns (up to nine) gave it a very potent firepower. The Soviets appreciated its durability and powerful armament. It continued to serve the Soviets after the war and was given the NATO reporting name of 'Bank'.

Technical Comparison Between Second World War Medium Bombers (data from various sources)

Specifications	Tu-2S	Do 217M-1	He 111H-6	Ju 88A-4	SM.79	Ki-67	G4M1
Maximum Speed (mph (kph))	340 (547)	347 (557)	273 (440)	317 (510)	286 (460)	334 (538)	265 (428)
Range (miles (km))	1,305 (2,100)	1,332 (2,145)	1,429 (2,300)	1,429 (2,430)	1,615 (2,600)	2,361 (3,800)	3,132 (5,040)
Service Ceiling (feet (metres))	31,168 (9,500)	24,180 (7,370)	21,330 (6,500)	29,500 (9,000)	24,600 (7,500)	31,070 (9,470)	27,890 (8,500)
Offensive Armament	2 × ShVAK 20-mm cannon	N/A	N/A	1 × MG FF 20-mm cannon (optional)	1 × Breda-SAFAT 12.7-mm machine gun	N/A	N/A
Defensive Armament	3 × Berezin UBT 12.7-mm machine guns	4 × MG 81 7.92-mm machine guns, 2 MG 131 13-mm machine guns	7 × MG 15 (or MG 81) 7.92-mm machine guns, 1 × MG 131 13-mm machine gun, 1 × MG FF 20-mm cannon	4 × MG 81J 7.92-mm machine guns, 1 × MG 81Z 7.92-mm twin machine guns	3 × 7.7-mm machine guns	1 × Ho-5 20-mm cannon, 4 × Ho-103 12.7-mm machine guns	1 × Type 99 20-mm cannon, 4 × Type 92 7.7-mm machine guns
Rocket Armament	N/A	N/A	N/A	N/A	N/A	N/A	N/A
Maximum Bombload (lb (kg))	6,614 (3,000)	8,800 (4,000)	7,900 (3,600)	6,614 (3,000)	2,645 (1,200)	3,527 (1,600)	1,892 (85
Empty Weight (lb (kg))	16,477 (7,474)	20,062 (9,100)	19,136 (8,680)	N/A	19,675 (7,700)	19,068 (8,649)	14,860 (6,741)
All-up Weight (lb (kg))	22,839 (10,360)	N/A	26,500 (12,030)	18,832 (8,550)	25,132 (10,050)	N/A	20,944 (9,500)
Maximum Weight (lb (kg))	25,044 (11,360)	36,817 (16,700)	30,864 (14,000)	30,865 (14,000)	N/A	30,347 (13,765)	28,350 (12,860)
Engines and take-off hp	2 × Shevtsov ASh-82FN (M-82FN) 1,850	2 × Daimler-Benz DB 603A 1,726	2 × Jumo 211F-2 1,340	2 × Jumo 211J 1,401	3 × Alfa Romeo 128-RC18 860	2 × Mitsubishi Ha-104 Kasei 1,900	2 × Mitsubishi MK4A-11 Kasei 1,5
Crew	4	4	5	4	6	6	7
Length (feet (metres))	45.28 feet (13.8)	55 feet 9 Inches (17)	53 feet 9.5 inches (16.4)	47 feet 2⅞ inches (14.36)	53 feet 2 inches (16.2)	61 feet 4¼ inches (18.7)	65 feet 6¼ inches (19.97)
Wingspan (feet (metres))	61.88 feet (18.86)	62 feet 4 inches (19)	74 feet 2 inches (22.6)	65 feet 10.5 inches (20.08)	66 feet 3 inches (20.2)	73 feet 9⅞ inches (22.5)	81 feet 7¾ inches (24.89)

4 (DB-3F)	Pe-2	Mosquito B.XVI	Wellington Mk 1C	A-20G	A-26B	B-25J	B-26G
410)	360 (580)	415 (668)	235 (378)	339 (546)	355 (570)	275 (443)	287 (462)
(3,800)	721 (1,160)	1,500 (2,414)	2,550 (4,106)	1,051 (921)	1,400 (2,300)	1,350 (2,173)	1,150 (1,851)
3 (8,700)	28,870 (8,800)	37,000 (11,278)	18,000 (5,490)	23,700 (7,225)	22,000 (6,700)	24,000 (7,376)	20,700 (6,309)
	1 Berezin UBT 12.7-mm machine gun, 1 ShKAS 7.62-mm machine gun	N/A	N/A	6 × Browning .50-inch (12.7-mm) machine guns	8 × Browning .50-inch (12.7-mm) machine guns	8 × Browning .50-inch (12.7-mm) machine guns	4 × Browning .50-inch (12.7-mm) machine guns
erezin 12.7-mm ine gun, hKAS mm ine guns	2 × Berezin UBT 12.7-mm machine guns, 1 × ShKAS 7.62-mm machine gun	N/A	6 × Browning .303-inch machine guns	3 × Browning .50-inch (12.7-mm) machine guns	4 × Browning .50-inch (12.7-mm) machine guns	7 × Browning .50-inch (12.7-mm) machine guns	7 × Browning .50-inch (12.7-mm) machine guns
B-750DS mm	N/A	N/A (the fighter-bomber variant could carry rockets)	N/A	N/A	10 × 5-inch (12.7-cm) HVAR	8 × 5-inch (12.7 cm) HVAR	N/A
(2,700)	3,520 (1,600)	4,000 (1,814)	4,500 (2,041)	2,000 (910)	6,000 2,700)	4,000 (1,814)	4,000 (1,814)
7 (5,800)	12,952 (5,875)	14,300 (6,490)	18,556 (8,435)	15,051 (6,827)	22,850 (10,365)	19,480 (8,836)	24,000 (10,886)
	16,639 (7,563)	18,100 (8,210)	N/A	N/A	27,600 (12,519)	33,000 (14,969)	38,200 (17,327)
8 (9,470)	18,728 (8,495)	25,000 (11,340)	28,500 (12,955)	27,200 (12,338)	35,000 (15,900)	41,800 (18,960)	N/A
umanskiy B 1,100	2 × Klimov M-105PF 1,210	2 × Merlin 76/77 1,710	2 × Bristol Pegasus Mk XVIII 1,050	2 × Wright R-2600-A5B Twin Cyclone 1,600	2 × Pratt & Whitney R-2800-27 Double Wasp 2,000	2 × Wright R-2600 Double Cyclone 1,700	2 ×Pratt & Whitney R-2800 2,000
	3	2	6	3	3	6	7
et 5 inches 6)	41 feet 6 inches (12.66)	44 feet 6 inches (13.57)	64 feet 7 inches (19.69)	47 feet 11 inches (14.63)	50 feet (15.24)	52 feet 11 inches (16.13)	58 feet 3 inches (17.8)
et 4 inches 4)	56 feet 3 inches (17.16)	54 feet 2 inches (16.52)	86 feet 2 inches (26.27)	61 feet 4 inches (18.69)	70 feet (21.34)	67 feet 7 inches (20.6)	71 feet (21.65)

Conclusion

Especially in its later Great Patriotic War incarnation (the Tu-2S), the Tu-2 was an excellent aeroplane, with abundant power, good speed, easy handling, a reasonably strong offensive and defensive gun armament, and an excellent load-carrying capability. Overall, it compared very favourably with other medium bombers of the Second World War. The two aircraft that were closest in overall ability to the Tu-2 was firstly the Ju 88 (which had actually influenced the design of the Tu-2). In certain versions, the Ju 88 was faster and was used in larger numbers during the war and for a longer time (from 1940). However, the Ju 88's career was for the most part ended with the defeat of the Third Reich, while the Tu-2 continued to be produced and used long after the end of the war (it does help to be on the winning side).

The second aircraft was the A-26 Invader, which although designated as an attack (light) bomber, was really a medium bomber by the standards of the Second World War. It was also one of the most outstanding Second World War aircraft in that category, exceeding even the Tu-2 in overall ability. (I would give the Tu-2 second place in the medium bomber category for the Second World War.) It is no coincidence that both the Invader and the Tu-2 were still in service long after the Second World War had ended.

I believe an honourable mention should be given to the Ki-67 Hiryu, or Peggy. It was a fast, tough, and manoeuvrable aeroplane, and if Japanese industry had not been in such a parlous state due to American bombing the Peggy might have had a greater impact on the war in the Pacific.

7

Post-war Development and Experimental Variants (Includes Unbuilt Projects)

From the inception of the 103, Tupolev had planned for the aircraft to fulfil different roles, not just that of a dive bomber. Among the other roles considered were that of a reconnaissance aircraft, a long-range bomber, a torpedo bomber, a fighter, and a high-speed daytime bomber. Development of these different aircraft was limited during the Great Patriotic War because of the need to concentrate on producing the standard tactical bomber version. Additionally, since production of the Tu-2 did not cease with the end of the Second World War, development on the production aircraft and on experimental versions continued well into the post-war period. Listed are detailed descriptions of these mainly post-war versions. These Tu-2 variants are listed alphanumerically by their military designation, such as 'Tu-1', or the OKB design number (*Izdeliye* or object number), such as '63' if there is no official Soviet military (service) designation, and not necessarily by when they were built chronologically. Some entries have both designations and in that case they are listed by their service designation (for example, the Tu-10 (68) is listed after the Tu-8 (69)).

Tu-1 (63P) Fighter

The development of an interceptor version of the Tu-2 was spurred on by the development of post-war strategic bombers and the need to develop a long-range and high-speed interceptor to meet this threat. Due to its high speed and load-carrying ability, which enabled it to carry the bulky radar equipment of the day, the Tu-2 was ideally suited for this development. At the same time as the development of the high-speed day bomber, the SDB, the GKO with Order No. 5947, dated 22 May 1944, directed the Tupolev OKB to develop a night-fighter interceptor. Developed from the SDB-2 (which was itself developed from the 103), this version of the Tu-2 was designed to be a three-seat long-range fighter for use in the night-fighter, interceptor, and escort roles.

The Tupolev OKB prepared the initial design by 15 May 1946. The fighter escort version was to have five NS-23 cannon, although it is unclear if this extremely powerful

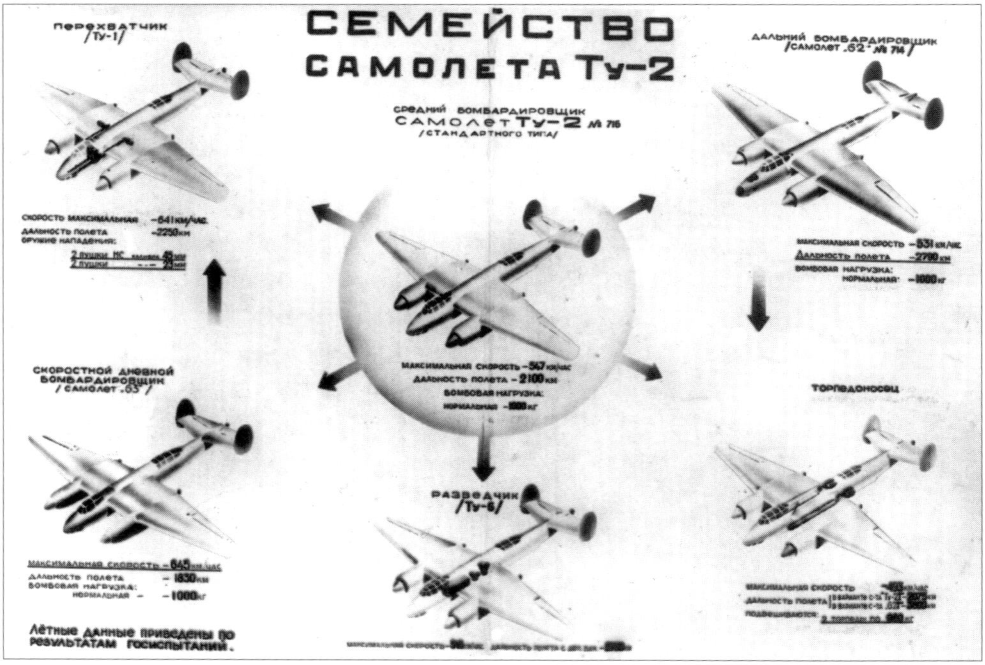

A 'family tree' of the Tu-2S (716 is in the center) showing the different versions of the Tu-2. Clockwise from top right, they are the 62 long-range bomber, torpedo bomber, Tu-6 reconnaissance version, fast day bomber (63), and the Tu-1 interceptor.
(*Viktor Kulikov's Collection*)

armament fit was ever installed. The engines were initially Mikulin AM-39FN-2s, but these were replaced in 1946 by Mikulin AM-43VS powerplants of 1,950 hp, equipped with TK-300 superchargers, and driving four-bladed AV-9K-22A propellers with a diameter of 11.81 feet (3.6 metres). The aircraft was converted at Z.156 by 30 December 1946. It was flown for the first time on 22 March 1947 and testing continued until 3 November 1947 (another source has 3 October 1947), being flown by the test pilot A. D. Perelyot. On 3 August 1947, it had the honour of participating in the annual Tushino flypast, along with other Tupolev designs, including the first three production Tu-4s (the Soviet B-29).

Although based on the SDB-2, the Tu-1 featured many changes. Among those changes were the replacement of the two ShVAK 20-mm cannon in the wings with two NS-23 23-mm cannon, and it reverted to the Tu-2S-type forked landing gear, with a tyre size of 1,100 × 425 mm, instead of the SDB-2's original landing gear. It is not clear from the record, but the 'P' in the designation may have stood for *Pushka*, Russian for 'cannon (-armed)'. The designation 'Tu-1' was chosen as this was the first fighter designed by the Tupolev OKB (Tupolev had designed earlier fighters, but not under his own OKB, and they had used the 'ANT' designation). Fighter aircraft were given odd numbers for their designations (even numbers were used for every other type of aeroplane, for example the Tu-2 and Tu-8 were bombers).

The first version of the Tu-1 featured the extremely powerful armament of two Nudelman-Suranov NS-45 45-mm cannon in the nose, with 50 rounds per gun, two NS-23 23-mm cannon in the wing roots, with 130 rounds per gun, and two UBT 12.7-mm (.50-calibre) machine guns for defence. The two UBTs had 250 rounds for the upper gun and 350 rounds for the lower gun and 2,205 lb (1,000 kg) of bombs could be carried in the bomb bay. The second version of the Tu-1 had two ShVAK 20-mm cannon in the wing roots, along with the NS-45 cannon in the nose, and featured an additional UBT machine gun for defence behind the pilot that was operated by an additional crew member. The aircraft could carry fuel tanks on the external bomb racks to extend its range.

The aircraft were equipped with radar based on the wartime German FuG 220 radar, called the Gneis-5, and had elements located in the nose, rear fuselage, and tail (the aircraft was fitted with tail warning radar). In addition, it initially had an extra fuel tank that extended the range to 1,864 miles (3,000 km). Later, in 1948, the fuel capacity was increased to 1,268 gallons (4,800 litres), which gave the Tu-1 a range of 2,392 miles (3,850 km).

Formally, the reason that production did not proceed with the Tu-1 was because of the unavailability of the experimental AM-43VS engines, which did not go into production, and the Tu-1 was only flown until these engines wore out. However, the unavailability of the engines was clearly not the only reason that the Tu-1 did not enter production. The Tupolev Bureau felt that a better interception radar than the Gneis radar was needed. Perhaps most importantly, it was felt that, in the post-war era, with the increasing use of jet-engined aircraft, including bombers, piston-engined interceptors were obsolete.

Tu-2D Long-Range Bomber (62)

As early as the initial design phase of the 103, a long-range version had been projected, with longer wings housing two additional fuel tanks on each side, the 103D (with the 'D' most likely standing for *Dalniy* or *Dalnaya*, Russian for 'Long-Range', although one source states that the term '103D' was not actually used at the time). This aircraft was never built, due to the need during the war for Tupolev to concentrate on the standard tactical bomber version of the Tu-2. With the Great Patriotic War's successful conclusion no longer really in doubt, in late 1943 or early 1944, Tupolev had time to again begin looking at a long-range version of the Tu-2. In addition, during the later phases of the war, beginning in 1943 there was a need for a longer ranged aircraft to keep up with the fast moving offensive operations of the Red Army.

This long-range development of the Tu-2 featured the longer wings with an additional fuel tank in each wing. This was the first Tu-2 variant to have the Tupolev designation of 62. The first version, modified from the third production Tu-2S (718), still featured the standard production nose configuration, with the navigator seated behind the pilot. It differed by having longer wings, larger vertical tail surfaces, AV-5V-21A propellers with a diameter of 11.81 feet (3.6 metres), a new canopy with

A Tu-1 (63P) during factory tests in 1947. (*Viktor Kulikov's Collection*)

A Tu-1 from the back. Note the tail-warning radar installation. (*Viktor Kulikov's Collection*)

better visibility, and more fuel (from 700 gallons increased to 1,038 gallons (2,650 litres increased to 3,930 litres)). It also still featured the ASh-82FN engines. This aeroplane first flew on 17 June 1944 (or 12 July—sources differ) and underwent OKB tests from 3 July 1944 to 23 September 1944. The state tests went from 20 November 1944 to 23 April 1945. The tests revealed a top speed of 335 mph (539 kph) at 18,865 feet (5,750 metres), a bombload of up to 6,614 lb (3,000 kg), and a range of 1,758 miles (2,830 km). This range was greater than that for the production Tu-2S, but this first version of the Tu-2D was not recommended for production because of the large number of defects encountered. This aircraft was used for experimental work until 1947 when it was retired.

The second version, rebuilt from the Tu-2 714 was considerably different from the first Tu-2D. It had a redesigned forward fuselage, with the navigator now positioned in a lengthened and widened nose section (perhaps the Soviets realised that they had been correct in having the navigator in the nose in the first place). To accommodate the navigator, the nose was extended by 2.03 feet (620 mm) and the horizontal tail planes were increased in width from 17.75 feet to 18.66 feet (5.4 metres to 5.7 metres). The vertical tail surfaces were also enlarged, as with the first Tu-2D. The navigator's former position was now taken up by a co-pilot, sitting behind the pilot, bringing the number of crew members up to five. The co-pilot could turn around to man a UBT defensive gun. The maximum bombload was increased to 8,818 lb (4,000 kg) and the landing gear was strengthened. The fuel load was now 3,860 litres. The top speed was 330 mph (531 kph) at 18,373 feet (5,600 metres) and the range was 1,734 miles (2,790 km).

The factory tests occurred from 20 October 1944 to 1 March 1945. The second version was tested by the state between 18 July 1945 (one source mentions 18 June) and 31 October 1945 at the NII VVS. The main defect noted was the lack of range; tests revealed that the aircraft fell short of the specified range at high speed by 249 miles (400 km), and the maximum range was shorter by 124 miles (200 km). The speed and ceiling were noted as being inferior to the first 62. At one point, a passenger version of the 62 was proposed, with a much modified fuselage accommodating passengers, but there was to be no production ensuing for either version of the 62, although the second 62 would be further modified into other Tu-2 variants.

Izdeliye 62T

The second Tu-2D (62, aircraft no. 714), with the lengthened nose, was modified into a torpedo bomber in July 1946 at Z.156, using the fittings from the original torpedo bomber version, the Tu-2T. This version had four-bladed AV-9VF propellers and larger main wheels, which necessitated bulged doors in the nacelles. The landing gear were strengthened and had a stronger tail wheel. It carried an additional fuel tank in the bomb bay, with a capacity of 269 gallons (1,020 litres).

The first flight was made on 2 August 1946, by the test pilots F. F. Opadchiy and V. P. Marunov and the engineer V. S. Morozov. It underwent OKB tests from 2 August

The first version of the Tu-2D (62) during factory tests in July 1944. Note the broad-chord ailerons and the large vertical tails. (*Viktor Kulikov's Collection*)

The second version of the Tu-2D during factory tests in 1945. Note the different nose from the first version. (*Viktor Kulikov's Collection*)

The 62T at joint tests in 1947. (*Viktor Kulikov's Collection*)

1946 until 28 September 1946. By 10 September 1946, joint tests with the LII were conducted that lasted until 28 September 1946, when the aircraft was damaged by a fire in the port engine. It was repaired and underwent further testing with the Research Institute of the Navy from 2 January 1947 until 3 March 1947. During these tests, it showed a top speed of 311 mph (501 kph) and a good range of 2,360 miles (3,800 km). Production was not proceeded with as the less heavily modified Tu-2T was put into production instead. The 62T's testing days were not over yet, however, as it was then modified in May 1947 into the long-range 69 (Tu-8) bomber.

Izdeliye 63 (SDB)

This was a high-speed bomber development of the Tu-2 (SDB—*Skorostnoiy Dnevnoiy Bombardirovshchik* Russian for 'Speedy Day Bomber'). It was meant to be the Soviet equivalent to the British Mosquito as a day bomber that could escape interception because of its speed, the Mosquito having suitably impressed the Soviets with its abilities. Indeed, the Soviets actually tested a Mosquito B.IV version, provided to them by the British. The GKO issued an order on 22 May 1944 for two SDBs to be built by Z.156. These aircraft were assigned the OKB designation of 63. They were developed from the original 103, with the first prototype SDB being fitted with more powerful AM-39s, which at 1,870 hp were significantly more powerful than the AM-37s originally fitted to the 103 (rated at 1,380 hp). The new engines drove AV-5LV-221 three-bladed propellers with a diameter of 11.81 feet (3.6 metres). The dive brakes were removed and the crew were reduced to two, presumably the pilot and the navigator/bombardier, who also functioned as the defensive gunner. This first version of the SDB retained the low cockpit canopy and unbroken top fuselage line of the original 103. The armament was comprised of two ShVAK 20-mm cannon in the wings and a single UBT 12.7-mm (.50-calibre) machine gun for defensive purposes.

The aircraft first flew on 21 May 1944 and the OKB tests continued until 31 May 1944. The state tests began on 5 June 1944 and ended 6 July 1944. The top speed at sea level was 327 mph (527 kph) and the maximum speed was an impressive 401 mph (645 kph) at 21,800 feet (6,650 metres). The range was 1,137 miles (1,830 km).

The second aircraft was modified compared to the first one and incorporated some of the features of the Tu-2S, with different canopies for the cockpit and the dorsal gunner, although these canopies were still different from those used on the production Tu-2S. The main landing gear was also changed; instead of being forked, there was an axle on the outside of the single oleo leg of the landing gear that the wheel was now attached to. Although the main wheels remained the same, the tail wheel was increased in size. The vertical tails were also increased in size. This second aircraft, the SDB-2, was completed in October 1944.

Compared to the original SDB, it had AM-39Fs instead of the AM-39s, the 'F' (for *Forsirovanniy*, or 'Boosted') indicating that these engines were boosted, but still using the same propellers as the original SDB. An additional UBT machine gun was also

The first version of the SDB (63) during the official tests in 1944. (*Viktor Kulikov's Collection*)

The second version of the SDB (63/2) during tests in the winter of 1945. Note the non-forked main landing gear. (*Viktor Kulikov's Collection*)

Another view of the second version of the SDB (63/2) during tests in the winter of 1945. (*Viktor Kulikov's Collection*)

added, this belonging to the new ventral gun position that had now been included. The maximum bombload was 8,818 lb (4,000 kg). The SDB-2 first flew on 14 October 1944. The NII VVS testing took place from 29 November 1944 to 4 April 1945. The state tests went from 5 April 1945 to 16 May 1945. The maximum speed was slightly lower than that for the first prototype, although it was still an impressive 398 mph (640 kph) at 22,500 feet (6,850 metres). However, the speed at sea level was increased from 327 mph (527 kph) to 339 mph (547 kph). One problem that was noted was the poor view for the navigator.

Despite the excellent overall performance, especially the speed of the SDBs, this version of the Tu-2 did not go into production as Tupolev had decided on using an enhancement of the Tu-2S, the Tu-10 (68) for the fast bomber role.

Izdeliye 65 (Tu-2DB)

This was another attempt by the Tupolev OKB to turn the Tu-2 medium bomber into a long-range bomber (the 'DB' standing for '*Dalniy Bombardirovshchik*', Russian for 'Long-Range Bomber'). In this case, the aircraft was also intended as a high-altitude reconnaissance aircraft flying at altitudes from 26,247 to 31,168 feet (8,000 to 9,500 metres). Production aircraft No. 201 from Z.166 was chosen for modification into the 65. It utilised the long wings of the 62, but had AM-44TK inline engines of 1,950 hp (one source has 2,200 hp), which were equipped with turbo-superchargers—the TK-1B (TK-300B)—and drove AV-5LV-188B (one source has AV-5LV-166B) three-bladed propellers of 12.47 feet (3.8 metres) diameter. The aircraft was modified from Tu-2S c/n 201 in May 1946 according to one source. The armament consisted of two ShVAK cannon in the wing roots, with two UBT 12.7-mm machine guns and a B-20 20-mm cannon for defence. As with the early Tu-2s, the horizontal stabiliser was made so the incidence could be varied. To assist in long-range flights, a PDK-44 compass was fitted. It first flew on 1 July 1946, piloted by F. F. Opadchiy.

The estimated top speed was 360 mph (579 kph) at 30,512 feet (9,300 metres). The range was to be 1,597 miles or 1,659 miles (2,570 km or 2,670 km) and the service ceiling was to be 36,089 feet (11,000 metres). These are all estimates as the aircraft never successfully completed a single flight.

There were constant problems with the engines and the turbo-superchargers, and not a single full flight was ever made in nearly twelve months of testing. Further development was abandoned by the MAP (as the NKAP was renamed after the Great Patriotic War) Order 766, issued on 4 December 1946; as with so many other Tu-2 variants, the experimental engines used were unreliable and never went into production. Work continued on a jet-powered medium-altitude bomber (the 72) based on the piston-engined Tu-8 (69) and a high-altitude reconnaissance aircraft with a pressurised cabin based on the 72 (the 74).

The 65 (Tu-2DB) during factory tests in 1946. It appears to be painted overall light grey, which was common for Soviet prototypes. (*Viktor Kulikov's Collection*)

Another view of the 65 (Tu-2DB) during factory tests in 1946. (*Viktor Kulikov's Collection*)

Izdeliye 67

Still another attempt to create a long-range version of the Tu-2 involved the second 62, which was re-engined in November 1945 with Charomskiy ACh-30BF diesel engines of 1,900 hp. The engines were equipped with AV-7L-22 three-bladed propellers with an R-10 speed regulator. The aircraft was equipped with dual controls. The main tyres were of a 1,260-mm diameter, which necessitated bulged landing gear doors. This aircraft, altered from a production Tu-2S c/n 402, was revised into the 67 in November 1945. Test pilot A. D. Perelyot made the first flight on 12 February 1946. The OKB's testing itself took place from 12 January 1946 until 2 January 1947. Notice that the factory tests apparently started before the first flight—presumably this testing included the pre-flight ground tests. The aircraft's engines were constantly being worked on, as one defect after another was detected. Despite the constant work, the defects could not be eliminated.

Above: The diesel-engined 67. (*Viktor Kulikov's Collection*)

Below: The 67 from the side. (*Viktor Kulikov's Collection*)

As with the 62, the maximum bombload was 8,818 lb (4,000 kg) and it could also carry torpedoes. It had a maximum speed of 316 mph (509 kph) at 20,341 feet (6,200 metres) and had an estimated range of 3,107 miles (5,000 km). The gun armament consisted of a UBT 12.7-mm (.50-calibre) machine gun, two ShVAK 20-mm cannons, and a B-20 20-mm cannon in the rear dorsal position. However, despite the impressive range, due to the unreliability of the engines (a common problem with Soviet aero-diesels), testing was discontinued in 1947. In any event, the success of the reverse-engineered B-29, the Tu-4, made efforts to create a long-range bomber out of the Tu-2 redundant.

Tu-2K

An unofficial designation for two Tu-2s modified to test ejection seats, the 'K' standing for *Katapult*. There were two aircraft used for these tests, the 1944 aircraft having an ejection seat in the space normally occupied by the navigator, and the 1945 aircraft carrying an ejection seat in an open cockpit situated where the radio operator normally was, aft of the cockpit. Interestingly, the Polish had a similarly modified aircraft that has now been preserved in a museum in Krakow.

Tu-2LL Flying Laboratory

Due to its good load-carrying ability and its high ground clearance, the Tu-2 lent itself well as a test bed for jet engines fitted under the fuselage. Accordingly, Z.23 was ordered by the MAP in Order No. 589, dated 30 August 1946, to convert two Tu-2s

One of the Tu-2LLs with an RD-20 jet engine mounted under the fuselage. (*Viktor Kulikov's Collection*)

The preserved Tu-2 at the Central Aircraft Museum at Monino, Russia. Note that the starboard wing-root 20-mm cannon can just be seen to the right of the cowling. This aircraft has the square-tipped four-bladed propellers often found on post-war Tu-2s. It also has the short engine exhausts found on some. Compared to photograph 5, taken when it was still displayed outdoors, it appears to have had a bit of a nose job. (*Taken by Alan Wilson. Wikimedia*)

A Tu-2 at Monino. In this photograph, this Tu-2 almost looks three-finned, but that is just the tail from another aeroplane beside the Tu-2. The single large window for the ventral gunner can be clearly seen just behind the fuselage star. (*Taken by Alan Wilson. Wikimedia*)

A Tu-2 at Monino. Just at the left edge of the photograph, you can see the fixed rear dorsal gunner's canopy. It has been enclosed now to protect the interior of this Tu-2. (*Taken by Alan Wilson. Wikimedia*)

A Tu-2 at Monino. In this photograph, the nose glazing and the short engine exhaust show up well. This aircraft has the extended nose glazing of later Tu-2s. (*Taken by Clemens Vasters. Wikimedia*)

A Tu-2 at Monino. In this photograph, the Tu-2 was still being displayed outside. The wooden structure of the nose can be seen quite clearly here. (*Taken by Pavel Adzhigildaev. Wikimedia*)

A Tu-2 at Monino. A photograph taken from behind that shows how only the starboard rudder has a trim tab, here painted in red. Both elevators have trim tabs, again painted red. The aileron trim tab, present only on the starboard wing, is also painted red. (*Taken by Pavel Adzhigildaev. Wikimedia*)

A Tu-2T at Plovdiv, Bulgaria. From this angle, both top gunners' positions show up, with the cockpit gunner having a blister through which the UBT 12.7-mm machine gun would have originally protruded. The shallow 'vee' of the horizontal tail planes can be seen. (*Wikimedia*)

A Tu-2 at the Chinese Aviation Museum, Datangshan, mainland China. This aircraft has the three-bladed propellers typical of a Second World War Tu-2. The aircraft is finished in North Korean markings. (*Taken by Max Smith. Wikimedia*)

Another Tu-2 at Datangshan. Like the previous example, it has the three-bladed propellers. Note the large spinners, here painted red. (*Wikimedia*)

This Tu-2 at Datangshan has the square-tipped four-bladed propellers typical of post-war Tu-2s. It is painted in PLAAF (People's Liberation Army Air Force—Chinese Air Force) markings.
(*Taken by Ed Groenendijk from airliners.net*)

A Tu-2 at Datangshan. Note that the round-tipped four-bladed propellers on this Chinese Tu-2 are different from the square-tipped four-bladed propellers found on post-war Soviet Tu-2s. This example is also missing the spinners seen on most Tu-2s. (*Taken by Graeme Bay. Wikimedia*)

A Tu-2 at the Polish Aviation Museum, Krakow. This photograph shows off to good advantage the large bomb bay. Note how the nose glazing is extended on the starboard side of the nose, to improve the pilot's view down. (*Taken by Michael Perala. Wikimedia*)

A Tu-2 at the Polish Army Museum, Warsaw. The four-bladed propellers, so common to many post-war Tu-2s, are clearly seen here. (*Taken by Hubert Smietanka. Wikimedia*)

A Harbin H-5 (Chinese-built Il-28 Beagle) in South Korea. (*Taken by Jerry Gunner. Wikimedia*)

An ASh-82FN (M-82FN) engine on display at Monino. (*Photograph by Mike1979Russia. Wikimedia*)

An early version of the Tu-2 in its characteristic black and green camouflage. This aeroplane was produced by Z.166 in 1942.

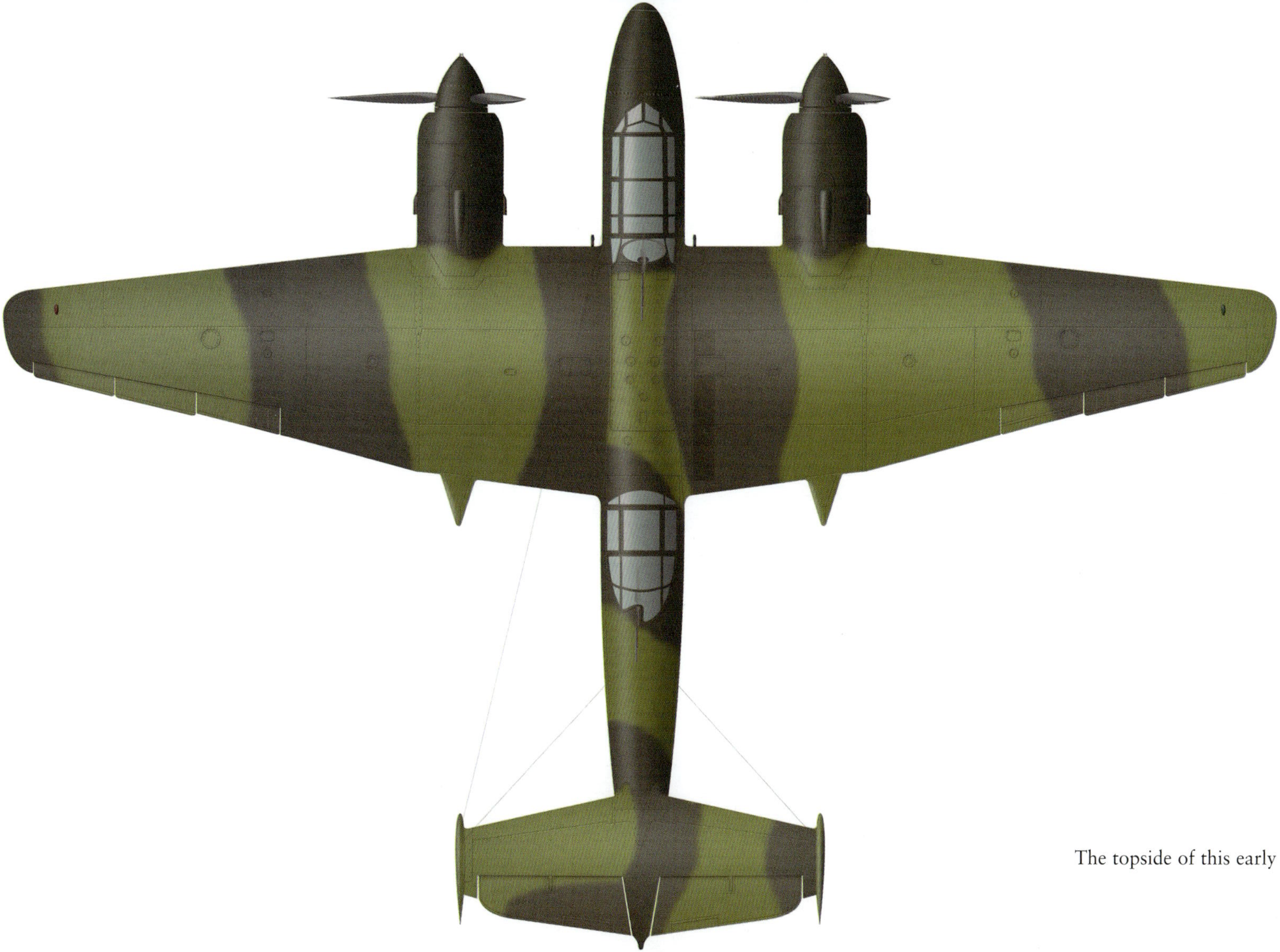

The topside of this early Tu-2.

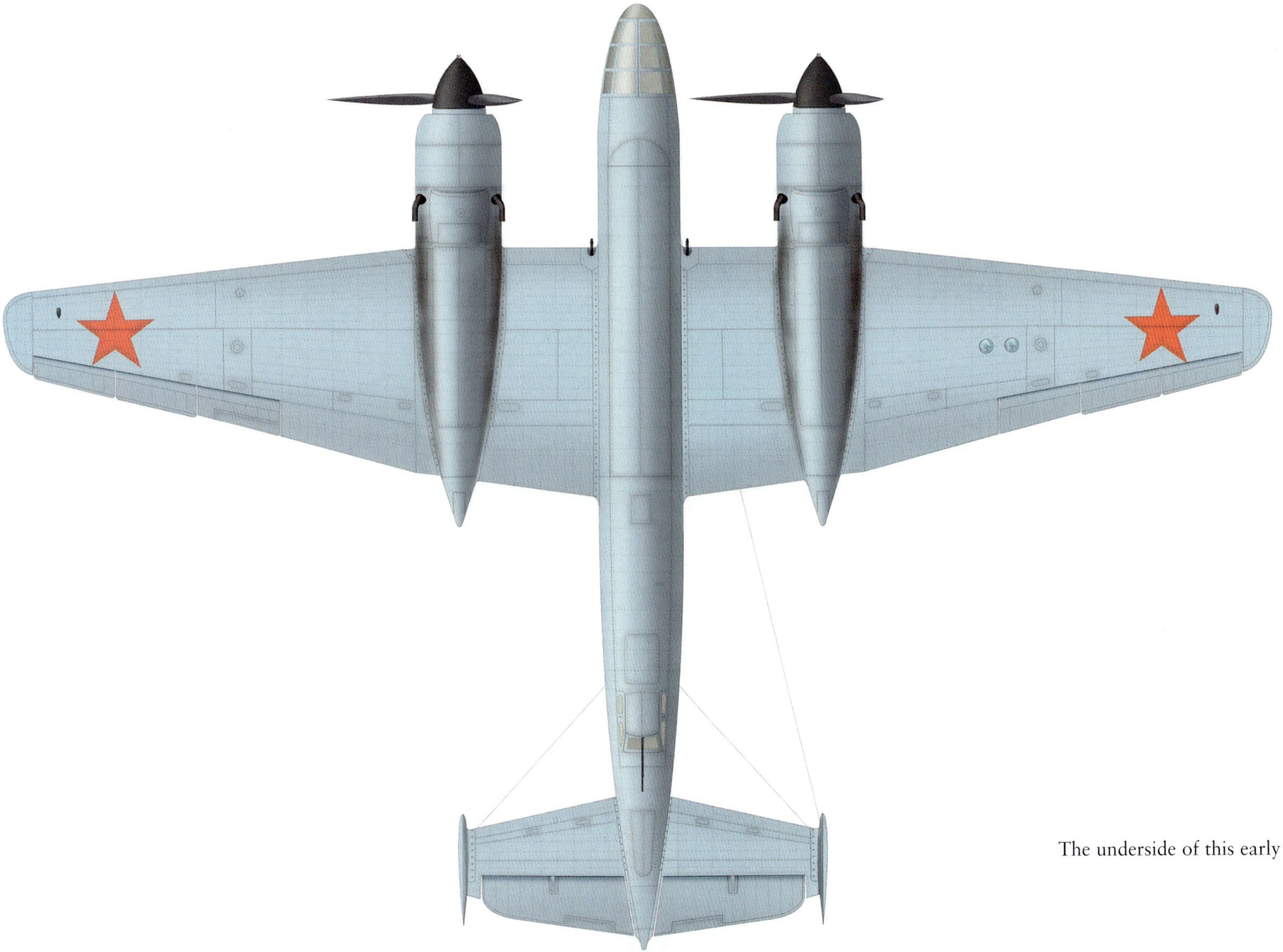

The underside of this early Tu-2.

Top: A Tu-2S in three-colour camouflage. Produced at Z.23 in Moscow in 1944 or 1945.

Bottom: A Tu-2S in three-colour camouflage. Somewhat unusually for a Soviet aircraft, it has no aircraft number (or *bort*).

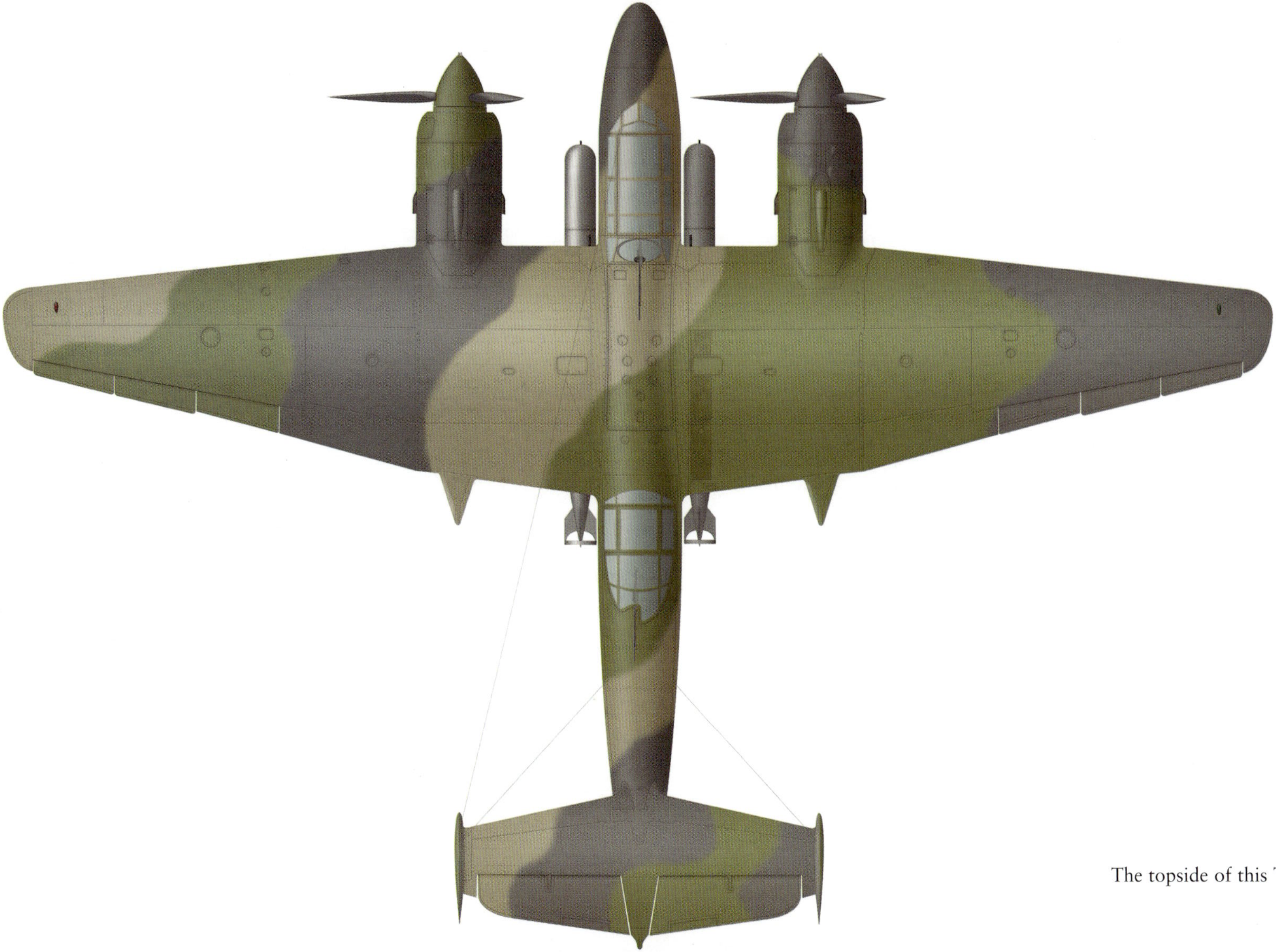

The topside of this Tu-2S.

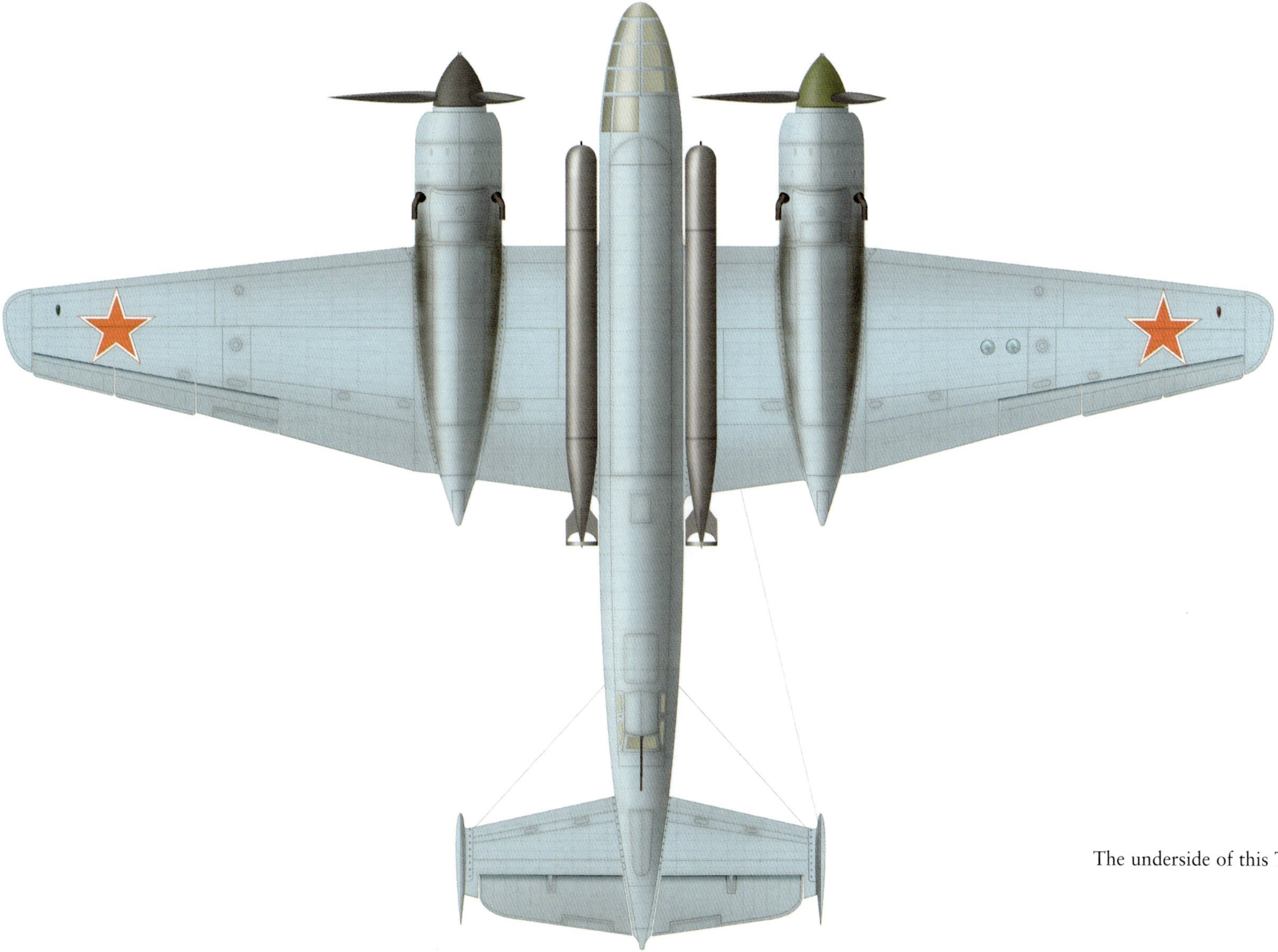

The underside of this Tu-2S.

A post-war Soviet Tu-2S with overall green topside. Note the evidence of repainting on the rear fuselage and the vertical tail. The aircraft number on the fuselage has been painted out.

A post-war Bulgarian Tu-2S. This example has the three-bladed propellers and three small windows for the ventral gunner's position that characterised the Tu-2S in the Second World War.

A post-war Chinese Tu-2S. This version has the four-bladed propellers, fixed rear dorsal gunner's canopy, and single large window for the ventral gunner of a post-war Tu-2S. Like many post-war Tu-2s, it has a shorter engine exhaust to that found on wartime Tu-2s. In this case, the aircraft number is four digits and it is painted on the tail.

Top: A post-war Hungarian Tu-2S. Although this example has the four-bladed propellers and single large window, like the Chinese Tu-2S, it has the early style rear dorsal gunner's canopy.

Bottom: A post-war Indonesian Tu-2S. Like the Chinese example, it has the characteristics of a very late post-war Tu-2S. Note where the Chinese insignia has been painted out on the fuselage and how the number '7' has been painted over the original Chinese aircraft number, '2250'. This aircraft was provided from Chinese stocks.

Top: A post-war North Korean Tu-2S. Also provided from Chinese stocks, it has the large single window for the ventral gunner, but it still retains the early style rear dorsal gunner's canopy and the three-bladed propellers of a Second World War Tu-2S.

Bottom: A post-war Polish Tu-2S. Provided by the Soviet Union, this aircraft has the characteristics of a very late post-war Tu-2S, with the four-bladed propellers, fixed rear dorsal gunner's canopy, and single large window for the ventral gunner. Like so many post-war Tu-2s, it is painted overall green topside; here it is in a rather olive green colour.

as flying test beds. Later, two more were converted. These Tu-2s tested such jet engines as the RD-500 used on the La-15 fighter, the RD-45 (tested in May 1949) used on the Mig-15bis, and the RD-20 jet engine. In addition to testing engines, it was also used to carry and test-fire large missiles. Among the missiles that the Tu-2LL carried was the 16Kh, which was derived from the German V-1 'Buzz Bomb'. The 'LL' in the name stood for *Letayushchaya Laboratoriya* (Russian for 'Flying Laboratory').

Tu-2 2M-93 (Tu-6)

In an effort to improve the performance of the Tu-2, a proposal was made in 1946 to install the M-93 engine. This aircraft was also known as the Tu-6. The engines were never built, so the project was cancelled by MAP Order No. 223, dated 16 April 1947. This projected version should not be confused with the post-war Tu-2 reconnaissance version, which also had the designation Tu-6 and was actually produced.

Tu-2 2M-250

As with the Tu-2 2M-93, this project was proposed in 1946, using the experimental M-250 engine with a take-off power of 2,500 hp. By order of the MAP No. 766, dated 12 April 1946, work on this project was discontinued.

Tu-2N

This was apparently an unofficial designation for a Tu-2 fitted in 1947 to test the Rolls-Royce Nene engine (the 'N' in Tu-2N evidently standing for 'Nene'). It tested the Nene and the Klimov RD-45 with the engines hanging underneath the aircraft. The Klimov engine was the Soviet-built unlicensed copy of the Nene and powered the MiG-15.

Tu-2 Paravan

In order to combat the danger of barrage balloons, this version was developed to enable the Tu-2 to cut the lines that anchored the balloons to the ground. The nose was a 19-foot 8-inch (6-metre) cone made out of aluminium, from which the cutting wires stretched, from the tip of the cone to the wingtips. To maintain the centre of gravity, 331 lb (150 kg) of ballast was added to the tail. Even with the huge nose, the aircraft was capable of 334 mph (537 kph) at 17,880 feet (5,450 metres). State tests were conducted in September and October 1948. Two were converted, but the aircraft did not go into production. The word *Paravan* evidently means something like 'Minesweeper'.

The Tu-2 Paravan in 1948. (*Viktor Kulikov's Collection*)

A side view of the Tu-2 Paravan. (*Viktor Kulikov's Collection*)

Tu-2 RShR-57

One *shturmovik* or ground-attack version of the Tu-2 was the Tu-2RShR-57, fitted with an RShR-57 57-mm auto-cannon in the nose, that extended into the bomb bay, and whose barrel, offset to port, extended some ways from the nose—1.64 feet (0.5 metres) to the end of the substantial muzzle brake. The nose cone was solid, as one can well imagine the result of firing the cannon with a glazed nose. The 'RShR' in the cannon's designation was taken from the designers' family names: S. E. Rashkov, V. E. Shentsov, and S. S. Rozanov. This cannon could also be fitted with a 45-mm barrel, but only the 57-mm barrel was tested on the Tu-2. The modification of Tu-2 No. 26146 from Z.23 was completed on 6 December 1946.

Factory flight tests were undertaken from 9 December 1946 until 28 February 1947 with a crew consisting of test pilot V. P. Marunov, lead armaments engineer A. Gorokhov, and armaments engineer M. L. Bazhenov. After the completion of the factory tests, state tests were conducted from 21 April 1947 to 30 May 1947. It is not clear if this version retained the ability to mount bombs in the bomb bay (because of the presence of the large cannon), though presumably it could still carry bombs on the wing root racks. Although the tests seemed to have been generally positive, with no especial difficulties in piloting the aircraft or firing the cannon being noted, no production of this version was forthcoming, as the efficiency of a large aerial cannon was found to be low. Other ground-attack versions are described further on.

Tu-2S-2ASh-83

On 20 July 1944, the NKAP through Order No. 444 directed the Tupolev OKB to test the experimental high-altitude ASh-83 engines fitted to a Tu-2. The Tu-2 chosen for this was the first Tu-2S (aircraft No. 716), which was fitted in 1945 with this engine of 1,900 hp driving a four-bladed propeller. Although the engine installation was very similar to that used with the ASh-82FN, it differed in having a long air intake over the cowling (similar to that used on the La-5FN fighter). The installation also featured seven individual exhausts per side, like the La-7 fighter, and not the single exhausts per side as featured on the production Tu-2s.

The aircraft first flew on 18 May 1945 with A. D. Perelyot as the pilot. The aircraft was tested from August 1945 until May 1946, when the engines were worked on. The aircraft was tested again by the NII VVS from 22 August to 21 November 1946. The range was a disappointing 1,030 miles (1,660 km), but the maximum speed was an impressive 395 mph (635 kph) at 23,294 feet (7,100 metres). Despite the excellent speed, development was not proceeded with as the ASh-83 remained an experimental engine and never went into large-scale production. This aircraft is sometimes referred to as the Tu-2M, which is an apparently erroneous designation not used by the Soviets at the time.

The Tu-2RShR with the RShR 57-mm cannon in the nose. (*Viktor Kulikov's Collection*)

Above: A front view of the Tu-2RShR. Notice how the cannon is offset to port. (*Viktor Kulikov's Collection*)

Below: The ASh-83 engine installation on the Tu-2S-2ASh-83. (*G. F. Petrov Photo Archive*)

Tu-2Sh Ground-Attack Bomber

Several different variants of a *shturmovik* or ground-attack version of the Tu-2 were built after the war, differing mainly in their fixed armament (the Tu-2RShR-57, with its 57-mm cannon, is described previously).

The first version was equipped with no fewer than eighty-eight (eleven rows of eight guns) Shpagin PPSh-41 sub-machine guns fitted into the bomb bay, to fire downwards and forwards at an angle of 30 degrees depression. Each gun carried seventy-one rounds. The decision to test this system on two Tu-2S was made on 10 October 1944 at a meeting with head of the Red Air Force, Marshal A. A. Novikov. This system was called the 'Battery PPSh'. It was intended to be used against enemy infantry. Although the firepower was devastating, it would have been of short duration and it would have been difficult (or impossible) to rearm the guns in flight, so the idea was abandoned. The effectiveness of more conventional anti-personnel weapons such as fragmentation bombs also made this version redundant.

Other *shturmovik* versions resorted to more conventional type armament, with large cannon in the nose (such as the previously mentioned Tu-2RShR-57). A version tested in 1944 had a 75-mm cannon that was loaded by the navigator and fired

Above left: A Tu-2Sh with PPSh-41 sub-machine guns in February 1946. (*Viktor Kulikov's Collection*)

Above right: A Tu-2Sh with PPSH-41 guns now mounted in the bomb bay. (*Viktor Kulikov's Collection*)

through the nose. This version was intended to be a train-buster. It was tested at a shooting range (it apparently was not test fired in the air), but this version was unsuccessful because of the stress put on the airframe by the firing of this large and powerful cannon.

A version tested in 1946 had two NS-37 37-mm and two NS-45 45-mm cannon in the nose, along with the two ShVAK 20-mm cannon fitted in the wing roots on most Tu-2s. This would have proved a devastating armament against both unarmoured and armoured ground targets. One machine gun was kept for defensive purposes. Despite the heavy armament, it was faster than the normal Tu-2S bomber version, with a top speed of 357 mph (575 kph) at 19,029 feet (5,800 metres).

Although all were powerfully armed, none of the ground-attack variants of the Tu-2 went into production; the post-war Soviet Air Force continued to rely upon the single-engined Il-10 *shturmovik* for its ground support.

Tu-2T Torpedo Bomber

After the war, the AVMF continued to use obsolescent aircraft such as the Il-4 and A-20 Boston (or DB-7S as it appears in some references) for torpedo bombers; therefore, there was a need for a Tu-2 torpedo bomber to give that force a more up-to-date aircraft. Even before the end of the war, development of a torpedo-carrying version of the Tu-2 had commenced in 1944, with the issuance of a request from the AVMF in September 1944, with two aircraft being modified. Tupolev had actually started work on a torpedo-carrying version of the Tu-2 in June 1944, before the AVMF had even issued its request.

These aircraft differed from the 62T experimental torpedo bomber in featuring the standard nose of a Tu-2S. The Tu-2T had provision for two 45-36-AN torpedoes, equipped with TsAGI stabilisers suspended under the wing roots from DER-4-44 locks, with the aircraft's flaps cut away to accommodate the torpedoes. A BL-4 winch was used to lift each torpedo to the underwing racks. Each torpedo weighed 2,130 lb (966 kg). As befitted its maritime role, the Tu-2T was equipped with a life raft and survival equipment, including food and clothing. In addition, it featured a special aiming sight for the torpedoes, the PTN-5. The tests done in February 1945 were considered good, and the Tu-2T ('T' for *Torpedonets*, or 'Torpedo Carrier') was tested in total from 13 February 1945 until 5 April 1945.

In 1947–48, several regiments of the Soviet Navy were equipped with the Tu-2T. By the early 1950s, there were three Tu-2T-equipped regiments: the 5th MTAP (Mine and Torpedo Aerial Regiment) of the Black Sea Fleet, the 567th MTAP of the Pacific Fleet, and the 66th MTAP of the Baltic Fleet.

The last regiment to re-equip with the Tu-2T did not do so until 1952, by which time the jet-powered Tu-14T Bosun was already in production and the Soviet Navy were already receiving them. As a consequence of only a relatively small number of Tu-2Ts being produced (the exact number is not recorded), they were not able to completely replace the Il-4 and Boston torpedo bombers. These older aircraft

The Tu-2T during joint tests in 1945. (*Viktor Kulikov's Collection*)

A front view of the Tu-2T during joint tests in 1945. (*Viktor Kulikov's Collection*)

A Tu-2T in service with the Black Sea Fleet in 1949. (*Viktor Kulikov's Collection*)

therefore operated alongside the Tu-2T for some time, until these earlier bombers were replaced by either the Tu-14T Bosun or the Il-28T version of the Beagle (the Il-28T also replaced the Tu-2T). The Tu-2T operated in Soviet service until the mid-1950s, when it was replaced by jet-engined aircraft. It thus had the distinction of being the last piston-engined torpedo bomber operated by the Soviet Union.

The Soviet AVMF were not the only user of the Tu-2T as the Bulgarians equipped one regiment with it, the 25th MTAP, which was equipped with the Tu-2Ts from 1947.

Tu-6 (Tu-2R) Post-War Reconnaissance Version

Although used for reconnaissance during the war, with a specialised version being tested in very late 1942 to early 1943 (work having started as early as 1942), a post-war reconnaissance variant of the Tu-2, called the Tu-2R ('R' for *Razvedchik*, Russian for 'Reconnaissance') or the Tu-6, was tested. It began as Tu-2 No. 1/36 from Z.23, which was converted at the end of 1945. Instead of bombs in the bomb bay, this variant carried a diverse fit of cameras, ranging up to 100 mm in focal length. The cameras tested were the AFA-33s/20, the AFA-33s/33, the AFA-33s/50, the AFA-33s/75, and the AFA-33s/100, with the 100 mm focal length. This camera was so large that it protruded from the bomb bay and was fitted with a fairing to make the installation more streamlined. In addition to the cameras, and in place of an extra fuel tank in the bomb bay, FOTAB 35 or FOTAB 50 flash bombs could be carried for night photography, mounted in a PKD2 cassette. An NAFA-3s camera could be fitted for night photography.

In January and February 1946, Z.23 undertook ground and flight tests. The aircraft was improved from March to December 1946. From 26 December 1946 to 9 April 1947, the state tests were conducted. On 22 August 1947, a Council of Ministers Order No. 2941-957 authorised the production of the Tu-6 at *Zavodi* 23 and 39.

The Tu-2R (Tu-6). (*Viktor Kulikov's Collection*)

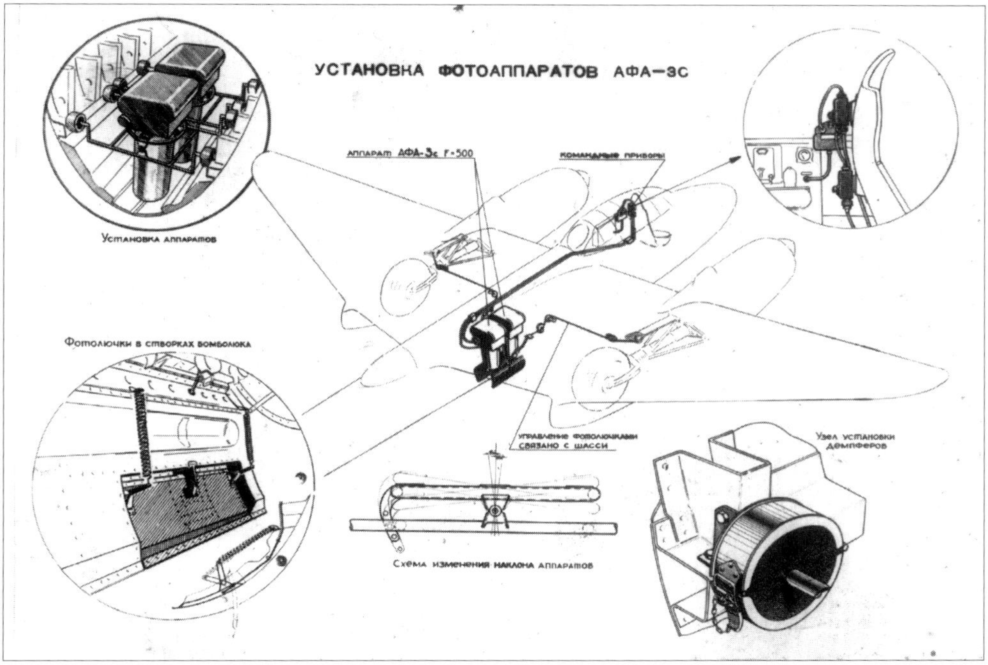

A diagram of the camera installation of AFA-3s cameras on a Tu-2R. (*Viktor Kulikov's Collection*)

An unknown number of the Tu-6s were produced and it is unclear from the record how long they served operationally, and one source states that two were even provided to Romania.

An interesting system for night illumination was tested on the Tu-6, called the 'Yavor-2'. It was mounted on Tu-2 No. 33/54. The system consisted of a pulsed high-voltage electrical system. It was to be used in conjunction with NAFA-3s night cameras. The GSK-1500 generator was replaced with a more powerful GSN-3000 generator. Z.23 in 1948 produced five aircraft with this system. One of them was tested from 16 November 1948 until 8 January 1949 in state tests. Unfortunately, the powerful shaft of light that was produced by the Yavor-2 was considered too apt to attract anti-aircraft fire, so the system proved impractical.

Tu-8 (69) Long-Range Bomber

The last of the Tu-2 long-range bomber developments to be built was essentially a development of the Tu-2D, incorporating that version's lengthened wings. In addition, the nose section was changed once again, with the navigator now sitting upright in a seat in a lengthened nose section, and a co-pilot seated next to the pilot instead of behind him, which necessitated widening the cockpit. The landing gear was moved forward to improve the landing characteristics. To preserve stability with the longer fuselage, the vertical tail planes were increased in size. The size of the ailerons and the outer wings were also increased in chord, becoming broader, although the wingspan remained the same as with the earlier long-range Tu-2s. The aircraft was equipped with the de-icing system introduced on the post-war Tu-2S. The navigator was equipped with the OPB-4s, which was based on the wartime American Norden bombsight. The aircraft could not only be used as a long-range level bomber, but with the appropriate equipment could also be used as a torpedo bomber.

In addition to these changes, 2,100-hp ASh-82Ms (a development of the standard ASh-82FN) and AV-9K-22A four-bladed propellers were to power the 69. These propellers did not have the square tips that characterised the four-bladed propellers used on later production Tu-2S, and instead had rounded tips, like the earlier three-bladed units. It had been intended to fit the new M-93 engines, but there were delays with this engine, so the ASh-82Ms were to be fitted instead. By Order of the Council of Ministers of the USSR 493-192, issued on 11 March 1947, the aircraft was to be built. It was given the service designation of Tu-8, with the OKB designation of '69', using the 62T airframe as a basis for the modification, and it was suitably modified in May 1947.

Additionally, the defensive armament was also changed, with a fully enclosed position for the rear dorsal gunner's position, mounting an MV-11 electrically powered turret with a Berezin B-20 20-mm cannon and a remote-controlled turret replacing the ventral gunner's position, carrying one Berezin B-20 20-mm cannon. These cannons replaced the UBT 12.7-mm (.50-calibre) machine guns. The remote-control turret was guided by looking through recessed blisters on either side of the fuselage, a feature that would also be seen in the later 73 jet bomber (this feature would even find its way onto the Tu-80, an experimental development of the Tu-4). In addition to these changes, both the gunners now had seats. The pilot operated a B-20 cannon on the starboard side of the fuselage, giving a total of four B-20 cannon. The feature of a pilot-operated cannon on the fuselage starboard side found its way onto the later Tu-16 Badger bomber. The bombload was increased to a maximum of 9,921 lb (4,500 kg), which was the heaviest load carried by any of the Tu-2 variants. At 31,416 lb (14,250 kg) it was also the heaviest of all the piston-engined Tu-2 variants (only the jet-engined Tu-12 (the 77) at 34,657 lb (15,750 kg) was heavier).

The Tu-8 was completed in May 1947. The aircraft was first flown in May 1947 with the standard ASh-82FNs, as it was decided not to fit the ASh-82Ms to the first example, and only one Tu-8 was ever built. The OKB tests were conducted from 24 May 1947 to 20 April 1948. As recorded in these factory tests, the maximum speed was 320 mph (515 kph) and the range was 2,265 miles (3,645 km).

The Tu-8 had a larger bombload and a longer range than the standard Tu-2S; indeed, it had the second longest range (after the 67) and the largest bombload of any of the Tu-2 variants. However, there were problems with its weak electrical system (including the electrically operated remote-controlled lower turret), it suffered from longitudinal instability, weak landing gear, and its performance overall was disappointing. In addition, problems with the de-icing and the cockpit lighting compromised its ability to operate in bad weather or at night. As a consequence of these problems, it was decided not to proceed with further development. As recorded in the state tests, the

The Tu-8 (69) during official tests in 1948. (*Viktor Kulikov's Collection*)

A side view of the Tu-8. Note the prominent sighting blisters for the ventral gunner. (*Viktor Kulikov's Collection*)

A front view of the Tu-8. The widened front fuselage, to allow side-by-side seating for the pilot and co-pilot, can be seen in this image. The cannon on the starboard side of the nose can also be made out. (*Viktor Kulikov's Collection*)

A cutaway of the Tu-8. (*Viktor Kulikov's Collection*)

maximum speed was 315 mph (507 kph) at 18,701 feet (5,700 metres) and its range was 2,548 miles (4,100 km). By the time that tests were concluded on the Tu-8, it was realised that the age of the piston-engined tactical bomber had passed. Another of the factors in the decision not to proceed with development of long-range versions of the Tu-2, such as the 65, 67 and the Tu-8 (69), was the urgent need for the Tupolev OKB to concentrate on its development of the Tu-4 Bull, the reverse-engineered Soviet copy of the B-29, which potentially had much greater range and capability.

In an effort to keep the Tu-8 programme alive, Tupolev even suggested two variants of the Tu-8, the Tu-8B, with AM-42 engines (the engine used by the Il-10 *shturmovik*), and a version with the ACh-30B diesels, possibly with the designation of Tu-8S; however, these projects were not proceeded with. Tu-2 development had finally come to an end.

Tu-10 (68) Improved Tactical Bomber

This was basically the Tu-2S with Mikulin AM-39FNV inline engines of 1,850 hp replacing the radial ASh-82FN engines of the same horsepower, with some other modifications and improvements. It was modified from a standard Tu-2S from Z.23. It was first flown by A. D. Perelyot on 19 May 1945. The AM-39FNV engines drove AV-5LV-22A three-bladed propellers. These were then changed to AV-5L-166B, then AV-9K-22A four-bladed propellers. These last propellers were used with the AM-39F-2 engine of 1,870 hp (one source has this engine as being the AM-40, an engine that is otherwise unknown to the author). These new propellers and engines were fitted after the end of the state tests.

Other changes besides the different engines were made to the basic Tu-2S airframe. The cockpit canopy was widened and the number of fuel tanks was reduced from fourteen to nine. This decreased the fuel capacity from 713 gallons (2,700 litres)

The Tu-10 (68) during factory tests in 1945. Other than the inline-engines, the aircraft appears very similar to a standard Tu-2S. (*Viktor Kulikov's Collection*)`

A side view of the Tu-10. Note the enlarged tail planes. (*Viktor Kulikov's Collection*)

The Tu-10 rebuilt after a crash, being tested in February 1946. (*Viktor Kulikov's Collection*)

The Tu-10 with AM-39FN-2 engines during official tests in September 1946. Four-bladed propellers have been fitted to this aircraft. (*Viktor Kulikov's Collection*)

to 581 gallons (2,200 litres). Additionally, after the state tests had been concluded, the vertical tail planes were increased in area and a larger tail wheel was fitted. The horizontal stabiliser's incidence was adjustable, as it had been with the early Tu-2s (and with the 65). The inner wings' leading edges were provided with ports that led into the water radiators for the engines. The radio operator's gun mount was changed from a VUB-2M to a VUB-65, while the navigator's gun mount was changed from the BUSh-1 blister mount to a VUS-1. The maximum bombload was also increased to 8,818 lb (4,000 kg) from the Tu-2S's maximum of 6,614 lb (3,000 kg).

The prototype Tu-10, which was created by modifying a production Tu-2S airframe, aircraft no. 16120, was completed by 1 May 1945 (the Great Patriotic War ended on 9 May 1945). It flew for the first time on 19 May 1945 with A. D. Perelyot at the helm. The OKB tests began 6 June 1945, with the state trials running from 28 June 1945 to 30 July 1945. The aircraft was damaged in a wheels-up landing on 30 July (or possibly June) 1945 and was repaired, which took until 16 November 1945 to complete. A second series of state tests started on 17 November 1945 and lasted until 8 March 1946.

After the second state trials had ended, the aircraft was modified at Z.156, the modifications being completed on 24 May 1946; in this modified form, it first took to the air on 28 May 1946, being flown by A. D. Perelyot. The OKB tests went on until 10 August 1946. On 16 September 1946, the state trials began and they ended on 20 November 1946. During these tests, the Tu-10 showed an impressive maximum speed of 393 mph (634 kph) at 24,750 feet (7,550 metres) (one source has 395 mph (635 kph) at 23,294 feet (7,100 metres)). The range was a somewhat less than impressive 1,031 miles (1,660 km), no doubt due to the decrease in the fuel capacity resulting from the removal of several fuel tanks. At one point, the aircraft was designated the

Tu-4, but this was changed to the Tu-10 after the Tu-4 designation was assigned to the Soviet-built B-29.

A few (apparently ten) were produced with three-bladed propellers, perhaps to keep the line going at Z.166 in Omsk (although one source has it being produced at Z.82, at Tushino, near Moscow, and another has it being produced at Z.1 in Kuibyshev). However, it did not go into large-scale production as the AM-39 engines themselves did not go into large-scale production. Additionally, it was felt that the time of the piston-engined bomber was passing (although given the long post-war service of the Tu-2S and its American equivalent, the Douglas A/B-26 Invader, this last sentiment may have been premature). No service units evidently used the production examples, which probably spent their remaining days in various tests.

Izdeliye 71

Mention is made in one source of a project with the *Izdeliye* number of '71'. This project was designed in 1946 and was to feature the M-93 engines with a redesigned front fuselage. Another variant of the 71 was considered, this version having M-45 liquid-cooled engines, with a take-off power of 2,500 hp. Neither of these designs were proceeded with.

Izdeliye 72

The first attempt to fit jet engines to the Tu-2 involved the 72 project, which grew out of a project to power a Tu-2 derivative with two ASh-2TK engines and a jet in the tail. The ASh-2TK was essentially two ASh-82 engines mounted on a common crankshaft, which was to have produced 3,300 hp. In addition to the new engines, it would have had power-driven turrets, a tricycle landing gear, and a fuselage based upon that of the Tu-8 (69). This project was cancelled in January 1947 while still a paper project, to be replaced by a design that featured two jet engines. This was the 72.

The 72 was to utilise essentially the same fuselage as the Tu-8 (69), with the wings and tail planes being basically the same, but with the wings suitably modified to fit a jet engine under each wing. The jet engines to be used were the Rolls-Royce Nene engines, the same engine that was used on the MiG-15. The landing gear was to be of the tricycle type. The maximum bombload was to be 8,818 lb (4,000 kg). The top speed was estimated to be 450 mph to 466 mph (725 kph to 750 kph), with an estimated range of 1,243 miles (2,000 km). In the event, the 72 was never completed.

Izdeliye 74

A high-altitude, pressurised reconnaissance version of the 72. It appears that this design never went beyond the project stage.

Tu-12: The Tu-2 Gets Its Jets (77)

It soon became apparent to the Red Air Force that gas turbine-powered aircraft were the wave of the future, and that bombers would need jet engines to stand any chance of outrunning jet-powered interceptors (or keeping up with their own jet-powered fighter escorts).

Although based on the Tu-2S airframe, the conversion of the Tu-2 into the Tu-12 was not simply a matter of the piston engines being replaced by jet engines (two 5,000-lb st (static-thrust) Rolls-Royce Nenes), and considerable additional changes were made. Notable among these was the replacement of the traditional tail wheel landing gear with a more modern tricycle landing gear (although it still retained a small retractable tail skid to deal with over rotation on take-off). The side profile of the fuselage was changed, with the top of the fuselage continuing in a smooth line from the top of the cockpit canopy to the aft gunner's position. The nose position was similar to that of the Tu-8 (69), with the navigator being seated in the nose. Both the aft gunner and ventral gunner's positions accommodated a single hand-held 12.7-mm (.50-calibre) UBT machine gun as with the Tu-2, and there was a single Nudelman-Suranov NS-23 23-mm cannon mounted on the starboard side of the nose for use by the pilot. The maximum bombload of the Tu-2S, 6,614 lb (3,000 kg), was unchanged.

The prototype first took to the air on 27 July 1947, flown by A. D. Perelyot. The maximum speed was 487 mph (783 kph) at 13,123 feet (4,000 metres) and the range was 1,367 miles (2,200 km).

There was never a serious possibility of the Tu-12 entering mass production, but six Tu-12s were produced (including the prototype), apparently at the insistence of Josef Stalin; after completing their NII VVS testing in October 1947, they were used to familiarise bomber pilots with flying jet aircraft and were also used as flying laboratories. One was used to test the RD-550 subsonic ramjet, which was actually mounted above the fuselage.

The Tu-12 (77). (*Viktor Kulikov's Collection*)

The Tu-12 from the starboard side. Note the semi-external cannon mounted on the side of the nose. Note also the small retractable tail skid under the rear fuselage. (*Viktor Kulikov's Collection*)

The UTB: The Trainer

Since the Tu-2 was still a front-line aircraft after the war, it was felt that a trainer version of the Tu-2 would be useful, and the job of converting the Tu-2 into a trainer was given to Pavel Osipovich Sukhoi's (1896–1975) OKB (whose bureau would later become famous for its jet fighters). The task was given to Pavel Sukhoi because Andrey Tupolev was busy with the design of the Tu-4. A serial production Tu-2S was received on 8 March 1946 for conversion into the trainer version. The conversion was completed in early June 1946.

The resulting design, which first flew on 14 June 1946, was similar in basic design to the standard bomber version, differing most notably in having low-powered ASh-21 air-cooled radial engines (designed by V. S. Nitchenko, this was basically a seven-cylinder version of the fourteen-cylinder twin-row ASh-82 with around 700 hp at take-off), driving two-bladed VISh-111V metal propellers. The propellers had a diameter of 11.15 feet (3.4 metres). The aircraft was called the UTB (which stood for *Uchebno Trenirovochniy Bombardirovshchik*, Russian for 'Learning Training Bomber') and was sometimes also called the UTB-2 (although the '2' may have referred to the number of engines and not been an official designation). The initial tests ended on 1 July 1946, with the flights totalling fifteen hours and ten minutes. The tests confirmed that the aircraft could be transferred to the GK NII VVS for state tests.

In addition to the new low-power engines, it featured a widened cockpit to accommodate side-by-side seating for an instructor and trainee (or cadet) pilot, with provision for either one or two navigators/radio operators seated behind. Evidently the navigator/radio operator could also man the rear dorsal machine gun position, with access to the aft fuselage being provided through the former bomb bay. In addition, its design and construction were simplified, its ailerons and flaps were redesigned, the oil system was redesigned, several of the fuel tanks were removed, and the cockpit gunner and ventral gunner positions were deleted, although the rear dorsal position was retained for gunnery practice.

The trainer version of the Tu-2—the UTB. (*Viktor Kulikov's Collection*)

A front view of the UTB. Note the two-bladed propellers and the dive brakes. (*Viktor Kulikov's Collection*)

Another view of the UTB. (*Viktor Kulikov's Collection*)

Due to the much less powerful engines and the drag of the wider front fuselage, despite a lower structural weight, it was considerably slower than the bomber version—it had a top speed of 236 mph as compared to 340 mph for the Tu-2S (380 kph as compared to 547 kph). It also had a much lower service ceiling, 19,685 feet (6,000 metres) compared to 31,168 feet (9,500 metres) for the Tu-2S, again due to the low-powered ASh-21 engines. Otherwise, its flight characteristics were similar to the ASh-82 powered Tu-2s.

The aircraft was supposed to be available for state tests from July 1946, but modifications to eliminate defects delayed the beginning of the state tests at the GK NII VVS until 14 August 1946, when test pilot Captain G. A. Tinyakov and engineer-pilot Major E. V. Zyuskevich started the trials. A total of 125 flights, tallying fifty-one hours and forty-seven minutes, were carried out, with the tests ending on 30 September 1946. In early December 1946, MAP (the former NKAP) decided to put the UTB into production at Z.381 in Moscow.

By May 1947, the first production UTB, c/n 3810001 was completed. It differed from the experimental UTB in having an improved oil system, the engines were positioned forward by 0.49 feet (150 mm), and the fuselage was increased in length by 0.98 feet (300 mm). From 7 May 1947, factory tests were conducted and the production aircraft was found to satisfy the air force requirements. The tests were completed in November 1947.

A dive bomber trainer version was also tested. Apparently, even without dive brakes, a UTB had better diving performance than the standard Tu-2 bomber. Testing on dive bombing training on the UTB started on 16 November 1947, with pilot N. D. Fikson making the first flight. The testing was completed on 25 December 1947. The aircraft made a total of eight flights with a flying time of six hours and thirty minutes. There were problems with the oil system operating during the dive, and a decision in June 1948 to curtail expenditures on experimental work spelled doom for this version of the UTB and work was stopped. The Sukhoi OKB, which had worked on the UTB, was itself dissolved, although it would later reappear and become one of the premier Soviet/Russian OKBs, with its fighters and fighter-bombers still serving around the world.

It would appear from the record that all the UTBs were produced by the conversion of combat Tu-2s and were not built as new airframes. One source even indicates that eighteen of the early series Tu-2s were converted into UTBs, although it is somewhat hard to believe that eighteen of these aircraft would have survived until 1947 (it may be that these were early series Tu-2S). Some aircraft were apparently supplied directly as new aircraft from Z.23 for conversion, while other aircraft were taken out of combat units for conversion. For example, by May 1948, a total of 102 machines had been provided for conversion, with Z.23 providing thirty-six Tu-2s, air force combat units supplying fifty-two examples, and naval units supplying fourteen. On 20 May 1948, the UTB was formally accepted for service and sixty-one were sent to various units, including the Soviet Navy. Although 520 UTBs were to have been produced, only 176 were in fact built (or more precisely, converted) from 1947–49 at Z.381. To make up for this less-than-anticipated number, some 'regular' unconverted Tu-2s were equipped with dual controls for use as trainers.

For use as a gunnery and bomber trainer, the UTB had a provision for one UBT machine gun with sixty rounds for use by the radio operator on a VUB-68 gun mount and could carry up to four FAB-100 bombs on external bomb racks for bombing practice, as the internal bomb bay was removed. It could carry either 110-lb (50-kg) or 220-lb (100-kg) bombs on these racks, for a total of 882 lb (400 kg) (some sources indicate it could only carry 441 lb (200 kg) of bombs).

Despite the relatively small numbers made, the UTB apparently continued in Soviet service even after the front-line versions of the Tu-2 had been retired. In addition to its Soviet use, it was operated by Poland and China in small numbers, with it continuing in Chinese service until 1965, making the Chinese the last user of this type.

Izdeliye 104

This derivative of the Tu-2 was designed as an all-weather radar-equipped interceptor. The '104' designation was derived from its serial (construction) number. It was based on a production Tu-2, unlike the Tu-1 (63P), which was based on the experimental SDB-2, but with the addition of radar and two VYa-23 23-mm cannon mounted under the nose. It also had variable incidence tail planes. It was flown by A. D. Perelyot on 18 July 1944. At first, no radar was fitted, just ballast, but the PNB-4 radar was installed in 1945. Official tests began in June 1945 and the tests were concluded in February 1946, after which it was converted into a UTB trainer. No production was forthcoming as piston-engined interceptors in what was fast becoming the jet age were considered obsolete.

Tu-18

This was to be a jet-engined version of the Tu-8. It was proposed in 1947, but it was apparently never built. Another source has this as being one of the designations for the Tu-12 (77).

Tu-28

Yet another proposed version of the Tu-8, this was to be a photo-reconnaissance variant carrying the latest photographic equipment and an extra fuel tank in the bomb bay. It was to be equipped with one fixed NS-23 23-mm cannon for use by the pilot; for defensive purposes, it had two B-20E 20-mm cannon on the dorsal (mid-upper) installation and one B-20E, apparently in a bottom turret as with the Tu-8. Among the cameras to be fitted were an AFA-30/200 and an AFA-IM. However, the project was not proceeded with.

Other Experimental Uses

The Tu-2 was used as a towing aircraft, as ordered by a Resolution of the Council of Ministers of the USSR, No. 796 252, dated 1 April 1947, and a MAP Order No. 190, dated 9 April 1947. The towing speed was to be 180 mph (290 kph). The aircraft was to be delivered for state tests by July 1947. However, it is not clear from the record exactly what the Tu-2 was supposed to be towing, but, given the slow stipulated towing speed, it must have been substantial.

One of the interesting uses to which the load-carrying ability of the Tu-2 lent itself was that of a vehicle-carrying transport. Although the fuselage was far too small for a vehicle to be loaded conventionally, it could accommodate a small jeep-like vehicle, the GAZ-67B, partially enclosed in the cut-out bomb bay. In this condition, a Tu-2S

A Tu-2 fitted with a GAZ-67 car/jeep under the fuselage for testing during July 1949. (*Viktor Kulikov's Collection*)

Above: A side view of this Tu-2 with the GAZ-67. Note that the aircraft still has its defensive armament fitted. It also has the four-bladed propellers and larger vertical tails of a late post-war Tu-2S. (*Viktor Kulikov's Collection*)

Below: Two Tu-2s practising in-flight refueling in 1949. (*Viktor Kulikov's Collection*)

with four-bladed AV-9VF-21K propellers was tested in July 1949 and flew a top speed of 235 mph (378 kph) at 16,303 feet (5,000 metres) while carrying the GAZ-67B. It was suggested that some sort of fairing in front of the vehicle being carried was needed to improve the performance. This would have improved the streamlining. Although the Tu-2 was not used operationally for carrying large external loads this way, these tests led the way for large loads to be carried externally by the Tu-4.

Post-war, the Tu-2 was used in some of the first Soviet tests with air-to-air (in-flight) refuelling, from February to July 1949. The results of these tests were successful enough for it to be tested on the Tu-4, then adopted operationally for the Tu-4 and then the Tu-16 Badger jet bomber.

Specification Table of Tu-2 Experimental Versions (data from various sources)

Type	No. 716 (Tu-2S Prototype)	Tu-1 (63P)	Tu-2D (62)	62T	63 (SDB) No.
Year	1943	1947	1944	1946	1944
Maximum Speed (mph (kph))	340 (547)	398 (641)	329.9 (531)	311 (501)	397.6 (640)
Range (miles (km))	1,304 (2,100)	1,400 (2,250)	1,733 (2,790)	2,360 (3,800)	950 (1,530)
Service Ceiling (feet (metres))	31,168 (9,500)	36,090 (11,000)	32,480 (9,900)	25,250 (7,700)	32,480 (9,900
Offensive Armament	2 × ShVAK 20-mm cannon	2 × NS-45 45-mm cannon, 2 × NS-23 23-mm cannon	2 × ShVAK 20-mm cannon	2 × ShVAK 20-mm cannon	2 × ShVAK 20-n cannon
Defensive Armament	3 × Berezin UBT 12.7-mm machine guns	2 × Berezin UBT 12.7-mm machine guns	3 × Berezin UBT 12.7-mm machine guns	3 × Berezin UBT 12.7-mm machine guns	2 × Berezin UE 12.7-mm machi guns
Maximum Bombload (lb (kg))	6,614 (3,000)	2,205 (1,000)	8,818 (4,000)	6,614 (3,000)	8,818 (4,000)
Empty Weight (lb (kg))	16,477 (7,474)	20,885 (9,460)	18,333 (8,316)	N/A	18,253 (8,280
All-up Weight (lb (kg))	22,839 (10,360)	28,119 (12,755)	27,094 (12,290)	29,761 (13,500)	24,085 (10,92
Maximum Weight (lb (kg))	N/A	31,878 (14,460)	29,409 (13,340)	N/A	30,093 (13,65
Engines and take-off hp	2 × Shvetsov ASh-82FN (M-82FN) 1,850	2 × Mikulin AM-43VS 1,950	2 × Shvetsov ASh-82FN (M-82FN) 1,850	2 × Shvetsov ASh-82FN (M-82FN) 1,850	2 × Mikulin AM-39F 1,87
Crew	4	3	5	3	3
Length (feet (metres))	45.28 feet (13.8)	44 feet 7½ inches (13.6)	47.25 feet (14.42)	47.25 feet (14.42)	44.58 feet (13.3
Wingspan (feet (metres))	61.88 feet (18.86)	61.88 feet (18.86)	72 feet 4½ inches (22.06)	72 feet 4½ inches (22.06)	60.76 feet (18.5 or 61.83 feet (18.85)

65 (Tu-2DB)	67	Tu-2R (Tu-6)	Tu-8 (69)	Tu-10 (68)	Tu-12 (77)
1946	1946	1946	1947	1945	1947
360 (579)	316 (509)	338.6 (545)	320 (515)	398.3 (641)	487 (783)
1,597 (2,570)	3,107 (5,000)	1,727 (2,780)	2,264 (3,645) or 2,548 (4,100)	1,081 (1,740)	1,367 (2,200)
36,090 (11,000)	29,000 (8,850)	29,700 (9,050)	25,100 (7,650)	34,300 (10,450)	37,305 (11,370)
2 × ShVAK 20-mm cannon	2 × ShVAK 20-mm cannon	2 × ShVAK 20-mm cannon	1 × Berezin B-20E 20-mm cannon	2 × ShVAK 20-mm cannon	1 × NS-23 23-mm cannon
3 × Berezin UBT 12.7-mm machine guns	3 × Berezin UBT 12.7-mm machine guns	3 × Berezin UBT 12.7-mm machine guns	3 × Berezin B-20E 20-mm cannon	3 × Berezin UBT 12.7-mm machine guns	2 × Berezin UBT 12.7-mm machine guns
8,818 (4,000)	8,818 (4,000)	N/A	9,920 (4,500)	8,818 (4,000)	N/A
21,376 (9,696)	18,349 (8,323)	18,068 (8,205)	22,270 (10,100)	19,554 (8,870)	19,826 (8,993)
24,317 (11,030)	30,040 (13,626)	23,335 (10,585)	31,415 (14,250)	25,683 (11,650)	34,657 (15,720)
35,190 (15,962)	33,543 (15,215)	N/A	36,927 (16,750)	N/A	N/A
× Mikulin AM-44TK 2,200	2 × Charomskiy ACh-30BF 1,900	2 × Shvetsov ASh-82FN (M-82FN) 1,850	2 × Shvetsov ASh-82FN (M-82FN) 1,850	2 × Mikulin AM-39FN2 1,850	2 × Rolls-Royce Nene I 5,000-lb thrust
5?	5	4	5	4	5
47.25 feet (14.42)	47.25 feet (14.42)	45.28 feet (13.8)	47 feet 11 inches (14.61)	45.28 feet (13.8)	53 feet 11½ inches (16.45)
72 feet 4½ inches (22.06)	72 feet 4½ inches (22.06)	61.88 feet (18.86)	72 feet 4½ inches (22.06)	61.88 feet (18.86)	61.88 feet (18.86)

8

The Jet Successors to the Tu-2

Izdeliye 73

The 73 can trace its ancestry all the way back to the Tu-2, by way of the 72, which was based on the 69 (or Tu-8), itself a development of the Tu-2D, the long-range version of the Tu-2. What was initially started as a scaled-up version of the 72 and 69 bomber turned into a new design, with three jet engines, two under the wings and one mounted in the tail. As the tail was occupied with a jet engine, there was no tail gunner, but instead the aircraft was equipped with two remote-controlled turrets, one behind the cockpit and one under the rear fuselage, both equipped with two NS-23 23-mm cannon and two 23-mm cannon for the pilot. It made its first flight on 29 December 1947, being flown by test pilot F. F. Opadchiy. Factory tests ended in mid-June 1948. During a test flight in August 1948, the aeroplane allegedly achieved 572 mph (920 kph) in a dive, although there is some doubt that the aircraft actually achieved (or could achieve) this speed. Nonetheless, tests showed the aircraft to be stable and easy to fly. It looked like it might indeed enter into production. However, Tupolev was not ready for production and the smaller, simpler Il-28 Beagle had already flown on 8 July 1948; it was this aircraft that was ultimately chosen for the VVS tactical bomber role.

The aircraft was fairly conventional in layout, having two engine nacelles under the straight wings and a tricycle landing gear, standard for jet-engined aircraft; the only unusual features were the swept horizontal tail surfaces combined with the un-swept vertical tail surfaces and the third smaller jet engine in the tail. Although a new design, with a thinner profile, the straight wings were similar in shape to the Tu-2's. Tupolev designed this aircraft to the same Soviet Air Force specification that led to the Il-28 and was a competitor against it for service use. With the replacement of the rear jet engine with a tail gunner, and a redesign of the armament (which included deletion of the remote-controlled turrets), this aeroplane was developed (via the 81) into what became the production Tu-14 Bosun.

The 73. Note the jet engine in the tail and that the remote-controlled turrets are armed. (*Viktor Kulikov's Collection*)

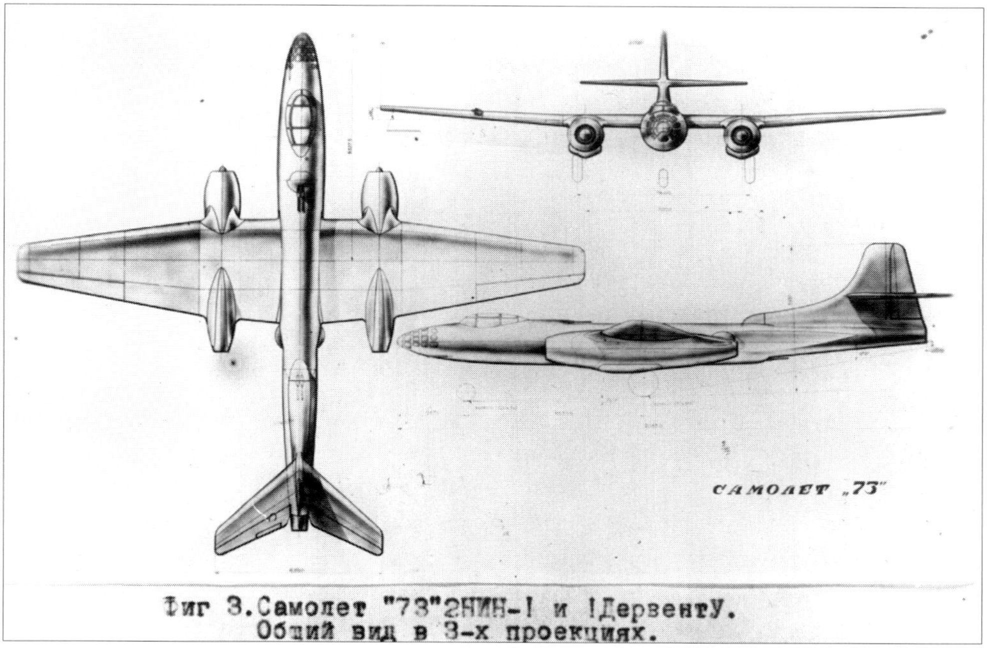

A plan view of the 73. (*Viktor Kulikov's collection*)

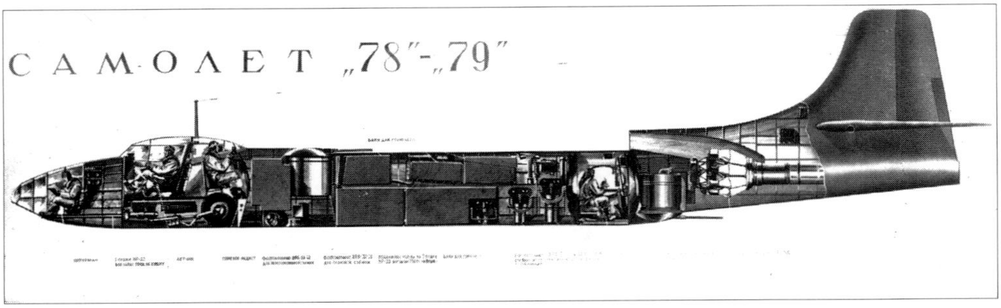

A 73 cutaway (the drawing says '78–79', but this is the 73 as can be seen by the tail-mounted jet engine and twin remote-controlled turrets). (*Viktor Kulikov's Collection*)

Izdeliye 78

This variant of the 73 was powered by two RD-45s, the Soviet-built version of the Rolls-Royce Nene. It first flew on 17 April 1948, but production was not proceeded with. It apparently was given the service designation of Tu-20.

Izdeliye 79

A long-range reconnaissance variant of the 73, this aircraft was never built and remained a project only. It was to have been powered by two VK-1 jet engines. One source has the service designation Tu-22 set aside for this aircraft (not the last time by far this designation would be used).

Izdeliye 81

This was basically the 73 with the rear engine removed, replaced by a tail turret. The crew was reduced from four to three. The rear engine was no longer needed as two of the more powerful Klimov VK-1 engines (which were developed from the Nenes) replaced the Nene engines (5,952-lb thrust compared to 5,000-lb thrust). The two remote-controlled turrets were also removed. The tail turret installation was not optimal as the 23-mm cannon were somewhat limited in their traverse, so further development on this aeroplane led to the 89, which became the production Tu-14.

Izdeliye 82

In what was perhaps the ultimate expression of the Tu-2 design, the 82, or Tu-82 was developed. It was a thorough modernisation of the 73, and featured fully swept surfaces. As built, it was a smaller aeroplane than the 73. The 82 may have been

The 81 (the immediate precursor of the Tu-14 Bosun). In the 81, the remote-controlled turrets have been deleted and a manned tail turret has replaced the tail engine of the 73. (*Viktor Kulikov's Collection*)

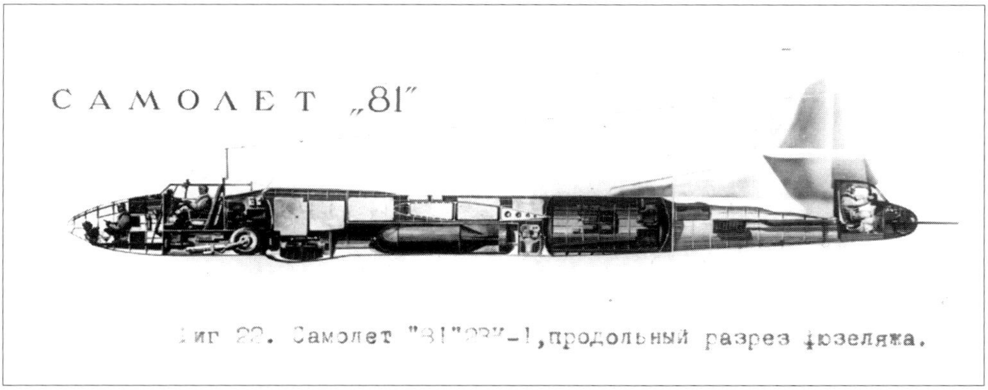

A cutaway drawing of the 81. (*Viktor Kulikov's Collection*)

provisionally given the service designation of Tu-22 (which was certainly used on the much later Tu-22 Blinder). It was given the NATO reporting name of 'Butcher', but did not go into production.

Development of the design did not stop with the Tu-82 prototype, and further developments were the unbuilt 83, 84, and the 87 projects. It was the 87 that evolved into the 88, which became the Tu-16 Badger. As improbable as it may seem, by many steps, projects, and prototypes, it appears that the long-serving Badger (which is still in service with mainland China) can trace its ancestry all the way back to the Tu-2.

Tu-14 Bosun (89)

The 81 was modified into the 89, with a new tail turret, the KDU-81 with better coverage, mounting two B-20E 20-mm cannon instead of the 81's NR-23 23-mm cannon. Compared to the Il-28, although it had better range, it was inferior in maximum speed, service ceiling, and in take-off and landing characteristics (it needed longer runways than the Il-28). The Il-28, as noted previously, was chosen by the VVS for the tactical bomber role.

With the rebuff of the Tu-14 by the VVS, Tupolev now turned to the AVMF, the Naval Air Forces. In this instance, the larger bomb bay of the Tu-14 allowed it to accommodate large torpedoes. Tests were conducted by the AVMF in January 1951. By August 1951, the Secretary of the Navy, Vice-Admiral Kuznetsov, recommended that the Tu-14 enter service with the navy. This aircraft saw service with the AVMF as the Tu-14T, and was given the NATO nickname of 'Bosun'. This aircraft partially replaced the Tu-2Ts in service. Eighty-seven were produced (one source indicates 150) as torpedo bombers and the type served with the Soviet Navy from 1952 to 1962 (from 1959 in reserve units), until they were replaced by the Il-28T version of the 'Beagle' (the NATO designation of the Il-28), the aircraft the 73 and the Tu-14 had lost out to in the Soviet Air Force competition for a light tactical bomber. Fifty surplus examples were supplied to China.

Il-28 Beagle

The Tupolev OKB's successor to the Tu-2, tracing its ancestry all the way back to the Tu-2 itself, was the Tu-14, described previously. However, the Tu-14 only served in relatively small numbers as a torpedo bomber with the Soviet Navy. As far as widespread use, length of service, and mass production, the real successor to the Tu-2 in terms of a versatile Soviet Air Force tactical bomber was the Il-28, designed by the Ilyushin Bureau.

First flown on 8 July 1948, by the time it entered service in the late 1940s, the jet-engined Beagle was considered a light bomber, but it continued on with the tradition of a fast, well-armed tactical bomber like the Tu-2. It was a rather conventional design, with two engine nacelles mounted under the wings, like the Tu-14, but was unusual in having swept tail surfaces combined with a straight wing. Like the Tu-14, it incorporated a rather large manned turret in the tail, with two NR-23 23-mm cannon. The pilot had control over two 23-mm cannon that were mounted in the forward fuselage. The torpedo-carrying version was called the Il-28T.

It was designed by the Ilyushin OKB and enjoyed a long career with a number of air forces, including the Chinese, who produced it as the Harbin H-5 and used them into the present millennium; the Czechoslovakian Air Force also used the Il-28 alongside their locally produced Avia B-228s and CB-228s (trainer versions, Il-28Us in Soviet parlance). The Beagle saw action in several wars, including the wars in the Middle East (it was used by Egypt), the Vietnam War (where it was used by North Vietnam in small numbers), and the Soviet war in Afghanistan. It directly replaced the Tu-2 in Soviet service and in some of the countries that had been supplied with the Tu-2. In total, the Il-28 ended up serving with around two dozen different air forces around the world, mainly in Africa and Asia, and over 6,000 were produced. As of the time of writing (2016), amazingly a few are apparently still in service with North Korea. There is a colour photograph of the Harbin H-5 Chinese-built version in the colour plates section.

The Tu-14 Bosun. Note that the manned tail turret is different than that on the 81—this was the main external difference between the two. (*Viktor Kulikov's Collection*)

The Tu-14 Bosun from the back, showing a closer view of the rather large manned turret. (*Viktor Kulikov's Collection*)

Specification Table of Jet Successors to the Tu-2 (data from various sources)

Type	Tu-12 (77)	73	78
Year	1947	1947	1948
Maximum Speed (mph (kph))	487 (783)	542 (872)	542 (872)
Range (miles (km))	1,367 (2,200)	1,746 (2,810)	1,746 (2,810)
Service Ceiling (feet (metres))	37,305 (11,370)	37,730 (11,500)	37,730 (11,500)
Offensive Armament	1 × NS-23 23-mm cannon	N/A	N/A
Defensive Armament	2 × Berezin UBT 12.7-mm machine guns	4 × NR-23 23-mm cannon	4 × NR-23 23-mm cannon
Maximum Bombload (lb (kg))	6,614 (3,000)	N/A	N/A
Empty Weight (lb (kg))	19,826 (8,993)	31,614 (14,340)	31,505 (14,290)
All-up Weight (lb (kg))	34,657 (15,720)	46,517 (21,100)	N/A
Maximum Weight (lb (kg))	N/A	53,351 (24,200)	52,447 (23,790)
Engines and take-off lb thrust	2 × Rolls-Royce Nene I 5,000-lb thrust	2 × Rolls-Royce Nene I 5,000-lb thrust	2 × RD-45 5,000-lb thrust
Crew	5	4	4
Length (feet (metres))	53 feet 11½ inches (16.45) or 51 feet 8 inches (15.75)	66 feet 8 inches (20.32)	67 feet 7¾ inches (20.62)
Wingspan (feet (metres))	61.88 feet (18.86)	71 feet 2¾ inches (21.71)	71 feet 2¾ inches (21.71)

81	82	Tu-14 (89)	Il-28
1950	1949	1951	1948
535 (861)	580 (934)	525 (845)	560 (902)
1,960 (3,150)	1,488 (2,395)	1,783 (2,870)	1,355 (2,180)
37,730 (11,500)	37,402 (11,400)	36,745 (11,200)	40,350 (12,300)
1 × NR-23 23-mm cannon	1 × NR-23 23-mm cannon	2 × NR-23 23-mm cannon	2 × NR-23 23-mm cannon
2 × NR-23 23-mm cannon	2 × NR-23 23-mm cannon	2 × B-20E 20-mm cannon	2 × NR-23 23-mm cannon
N/A	N/A	6,614 (3,000)	6,614 (3,000)
31,812 (14,430)	24,749 (11,266)	32,914 (14,930)	28,417 (12,890)
46,296 (21,000)	32,891 (14,919)	46,297 (21,000)	40,565 (18,400)
54,233 (24,600)	40,431 (18,339)	56,886 (25,350)	46,738 (21,200)
2 × Klimov VK-1 5,952-lb thrust	2 × Klimov RD-45F 5,004-lb thrust	2 × Klimov VK-1 5,952-lb thrust	2 × Klimov VK-1A 5,952-lb thrust
4	3	3	3
70 feet 2½ inches (21.4)	58 feet 8 inches (17.57)	72 feet 1¾ inches (21.95)	57 feet 11 inches (17.65)
71 feet 2¾ inches (21.71)	58 feet 5 inches (17.81)	71 feet 2 inches (21.69)	70 feet 4½ inches (21.45)

9

Post-war Service

Soviet Use

Military Use

Not only did the Tu-2 continue in production until 1951 (or even 1952), but it also continued in Soviet use well into the 1950s, until at least 1955 for the combat versions, and even longer for the trainer version (the UTB). One Russian author reports seeing a trainer in use as late as 1963. The NATO reporting name or nickname was the 'Bat'. In post-war service, the Tu-2 replaced such wartime bombers as the Pe-2, the Il-4, and the American lend-lease A-20 Boston.

Civilian Use

Some Tu-2s were converted for use by the Soviet civilian air carrier Aeroflot as freighters and, with the military equipment removed, could transport up to 4,409 lb (2,000 kg) internally. Some sources refer to this variant as the Tu-2G, although it is not clear if this was an official designation or what the 'G' stood for.

Bulgaria

Although this communist state was provided with second-hand Tu-2s from the Soviet Union, the record is not very informative on their use. They were apparently supplied second-hand from the Soviet Union soon after the war and were possibly retired by 1954. The Bulgarians also received some Tu-2T torpedo bombers in addition to the standard tactical bomber version. One Bulgarian Air Force Tu-2 has been preserved in Plovdiv, Bulgaria, and is on outside display.

Two Tu-2s flying in 1947. (*Viktor Kulikov's Collection*)

The crew and maintenance crew of an AVMF Black Sea Fleet Tu-2 in 1949. The de-icing boots on the leading edge of the tail fins can be seen. (*Viktor Kulikov's Collection*)

China

The Communist Chinese were first supplied by the Soviet Union with Tu-2s while the Chinese Civil War (1945–49) against the Nationalist Chinese was still raging. The mainland Chinese may not have retired their Tu-2s until as late as 1982, making them by far the last users of the Tu-2. One source has the last thirty Tu-2s being retired in 1982. This source also states that the Chinese received some UTB trainers, with these being retired in 1965, although it is a bit curious that the trainers would have been retired so long before the other versions were.

In addition to receiving an unknown number of second-hand Tu-2s from the Soviet Union, one source indicates that the Chinese put the Tu-2 into production, although it is not clear from the record how many were produced (if at all). It does appear that some Tu-2s were re-engined in the 1960s with Chinese-built Dongan HS-8 engines, copies of the original ASh-82FN Soviet engines.

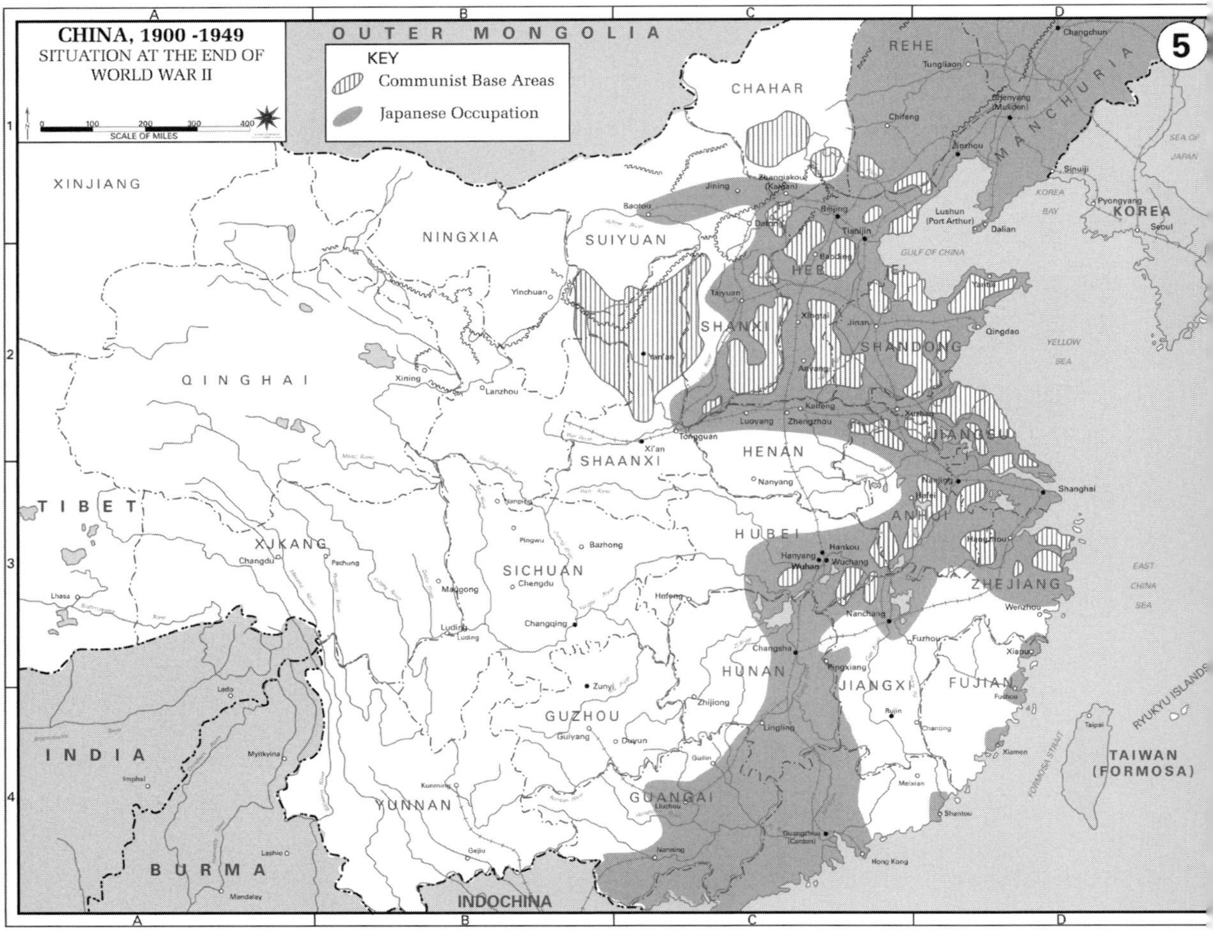

The Chinese Civil War, situation in 1945. (*History Department of the United States Military Academy*)

The Tu-2 first saw use by Communist China against the Nationalist Chinese while the Chinese Civil War was being fought. The Tu-2 was also used by the Chinese in both Korea in the early 1950s, during the Korean War, and against the Tibetans in the late 1950s and early 1960s. Although it is known that they were used in combat, there is little information about their actual combat use, especially in Tibet.

Korean War

Chinese Tu-2s were used in the Korean War in support of North Korean and Chinese forces against the United Nations forces. Missions were planned to strike islands off of the western shore of Korea, which housed UN installations. Apparently, the first mission met with little opposition, but on the second mission the Chinese Tu-2s were intercepted by USAF North American F-86 Sabre jet fighters and a number of Tu-2s were downed. The third mission was therefore moved to night-time, but this was also met by UN aircraft, this time in the form of American night fighters that were able to disperse the Tu-2s, which then returned to China.

Tibetan Uprising

The Tu-2 was used against the Tibetans in the late 1950s and early 1960s during Tibet's unsuccessful attempt to break free from Chinese control. The revolt involved not only Tibet, but nearby provinces such as Gansu, Sichuan, and Qinghai. The Tu-2s were used for ground attack, reconnaissance, and even liaison duties, but little else is known of their service in this somewhat murky conflict. As noted previously, there is very little information about their combat use—as long as the Communist Party stays in power in mainland China and in control of Tibet, this is not likely to change. This is something of a pity for the historian, as it may have seen extensive service.

Hungary

Hungary is mentioned as a country that utilised Soviet-supplied Tu-2s post-war, but little else is known of their use.

Indonesia

Little is known of these Tu-2s, although given Indonesia's one-time close relationship with Communist China, these were most probably machines supplied by China from its own Tu-2 stocks, not directly by the Soviet Union. As with much of the Communist-supplied equipment provided during the 1950s from the Chinese, they probably ended their days in storage, before being scrapped.

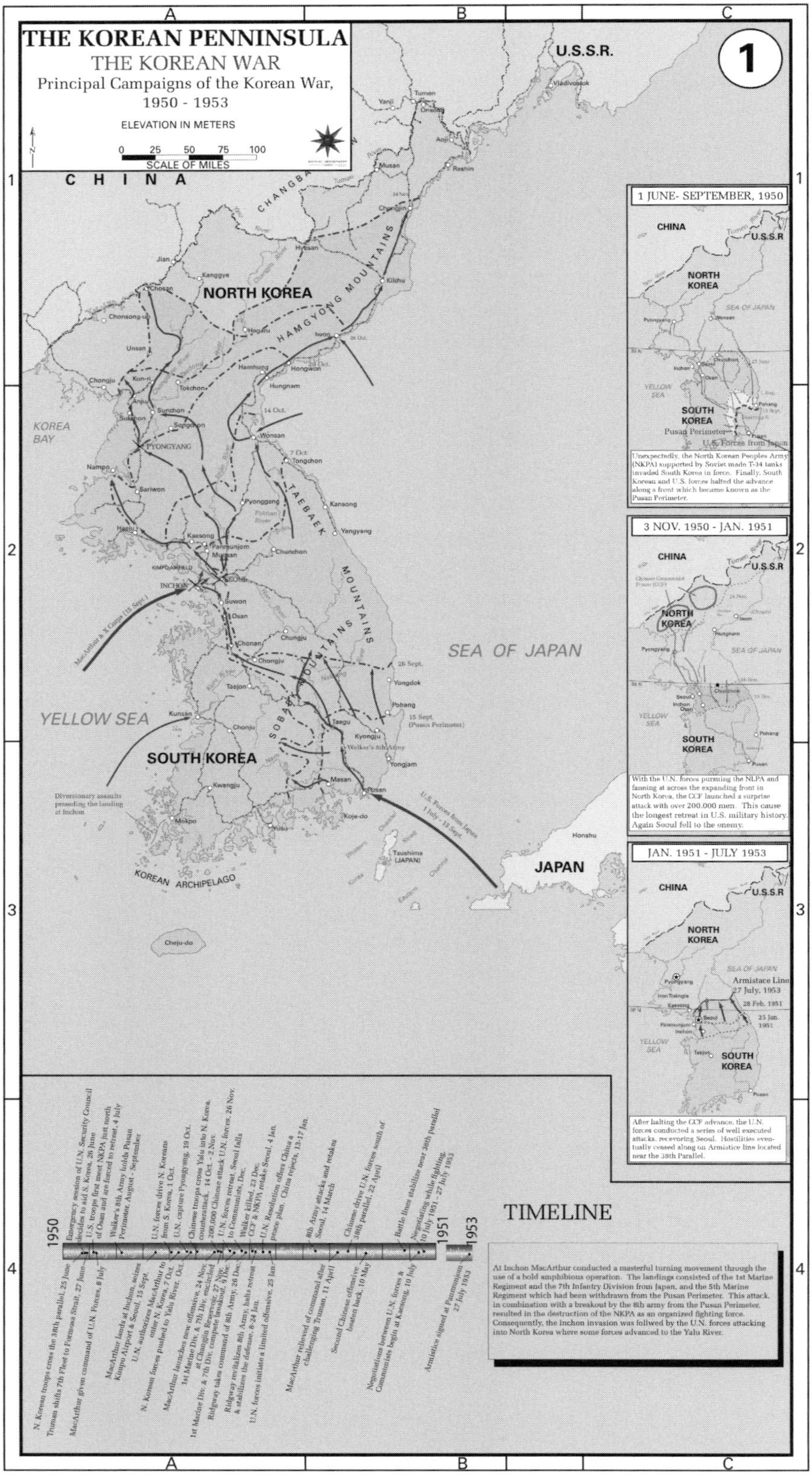

The Korean War. (*History Department of the United States Military Academy*)

North Korea

The North Koreans also used Tu-2s; in this case, second-hand Soviet aircraft from Chinese stocks. It is not clear when they were retired from service. North Korean Tu-2s were used in the Korean War against the UN forces. Due to the UN's aerial superiority, they suffered heavy losses, but there is otherwise little record of their actual use.

Poland

One source mentions that the Polish Air Force used the Tu-2 from 1949 to the early 1960s. In addition to the Tu-2, Poland also received examples of the dedicated trainer version, the UTB. Two Polish Tu-2s have been preserved, one exhibited inside a museum in Krakow and one exhibited outside in Warsaw. As was definitely the case with the Il-2, the Tu-2 may have been used against Ukrainian separatists in the south-eastern corner of Poland, but the record is unfortunately silent on this.

Romania

One source has the Romanian Air Force receiving six aircraft in 1950—two Tu-2s, two Tu-2 trainers (possibly UTBs), and two of the Tu-6 reconnaissance variant.

10
The Tu-2 in Detail

This description is for a Tu-2S from Z.23 in Moscow. Where changes were made during the production run, these will be noted by the series number, where available. The description covers both aircraft produced during the Second World War and those produced after the war, when the majority of Tu-2s were actually produced.

General Description

The Tu-2 was a mainly metal, shoulder-winged, twin-engined cantilever monoplane with fully retractable main landing gear and a fully retractable tail wheel. The pilot and navigator sat in a fully enclosed cockpit and the two gunners sat in the rear fuselage, where they were also protected by canopies. The tail unit was composed of twin vertical tails mounted on the ends of the horizontal tail planes.

Fuselage

The oval-section fuselage was made out of a mostly metal (or was all-metal for post-war Tu-2s) semi-monocoque construction, although most Great Patriotic War Tu-2s had a wooden nose and tail cone in an effort to save on scarce aluminium supplies. This wooden nose was replaced by a metal nose on Tu-2s from the series 20 onwards according to one source. The wooden nose was covered in 0.24-inch (6-mm) plywood. It appears that the post-war Tu-2s were equipped with the metal nose. The early Tu-2s had a clear conical cover at the very tip of the wooden nose, probably made out of Plexiglas. The Tu-2S had a semi-conical clear tip to its nose, with the top half of the tip being either wooden or metal according to the construction of the rest of the nose. The tail cone was also wooden on the Great Patriotic War Tu-2s. The tail cone was apparently made out of metal from the series 44 onwards.

The fuselage was constructed out of three main sections: the nose (wooden during most of the Great Patriotic War), the centre section (which housed the bomb bay and the wing attachments), and the tail section (which the horizontal tail planes were attached to, including the wooden tail cone during the Great Patriotic War).

The upper part of the nose section, before the series 20 Tu-2s, was made of plywood up to the third frame, and the lower part was made of Plexiglas panels 0.24 inches (6 mm) thick. This enabled the pilot to observe the ground while bombing and would also enable him to spot any fighters coming from below and to the front of the aircraft. From the 57 series onwards (one source states from the series 48 onwards), the area of the Plexiglas was extended by 20 inches (0.5 metres) to the rear on the starboard side back to the bomb bay, as the pilot's lower view, especially during dive bombing, was considered inadequate. This improved view also helped the pilot to see landmarks and targets on the ground while in level flight.

The pilot sat under the slightly bulged cockpit canopy 4.72 inches (120 mm) to the left of the centre-line of the fuselage. The pilot's seat, made out of stamped steel armour plate, was adjustable, being able to move vertically up or down 3.15 inches (80 mm) and horizontally 9.84 inches (250 mm—from the 50 series onwards). The navigator sat behind the pilot on a folding seat and could turn around to operate a rearward-facing UBT 12.7-mm machine gun for defence. The windscreen was made out of armour glass or what the Soviets called transparent armour. The canopy frames were made out of welded steel tubing. The top of the cockpit canopy, consisting of three panels, opened to the port where it was held open by a strut, while the starboard side of the canopy, consisting of five panels, swung down to allow access to the cockpit for the pilot and the navigator. A radio mast, which also incorporated a pitot tube, was mounted offset to the port side above the armoured windscreen. From the series 48 onwards, the top of the cockpit canopy was made flat. It was perhaps at this time that the pilot tube was moved to just underneath the top of the antenna mast (it had been mounted lower down in previous versions of the Tu-2).

The central part of the fuselage housed the bomb bay, which started at frame ten and ended with frame twenty-two. The centre section itself started at frame ten and ended at frame twenty-three, so it can be seen that the rather capacious bomb bay occupied almost the entire centre section. The frames ten, twelve, thirteen, fifteen, seventeen, and nineteen were reinforced to handle the weight of the bombs hanging in the bomb bay. The rear of the bomb bay had two small windows that enabled the radio operator to inspect the status of the bomb bay in flight. There were two bulkheads composed of sealed metal and impregnated fabric that kept exhaust gasses from entering the cockpit, improved the aerodynamic qualities of the aircraft, and helped to prevent the spread of fire.

The aft fuselage was located from frame twenty-three to frame forty. A camera was located between frames twenty-four and twenty-six, and consisted either of an AFA-IM or of an NAFA-19 camera for night bombing. The radio operator/gunner was located between frames twenty-four and twenty-nine. The ventral gunner from the series 20 to the series 43 was equipped with three enlarged windows (larger than the earlier windows) to give better lighting for his position. The windows were located at frames thirty-three, thirty-four, and thirty-five, and the glass was 0.12 inches (3 mm) thick. From the series 44 onwards, the three windows were replaced by one

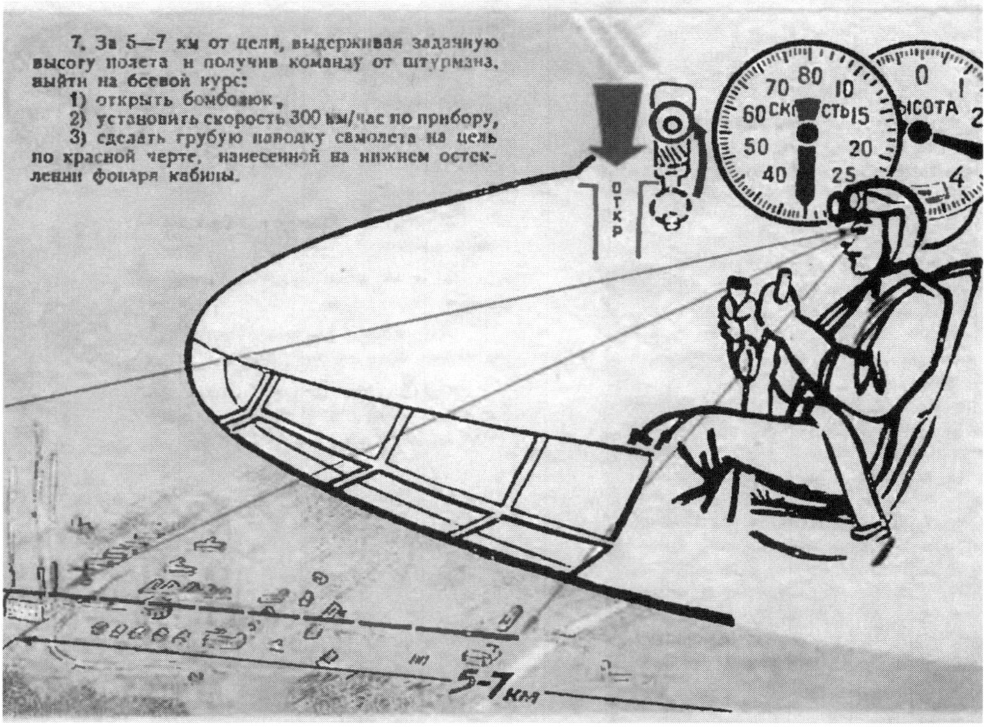

A drawing of the pilot's position and the nose glazing. (*Drawing from the 1945 Tu-2 Flight Manual*)

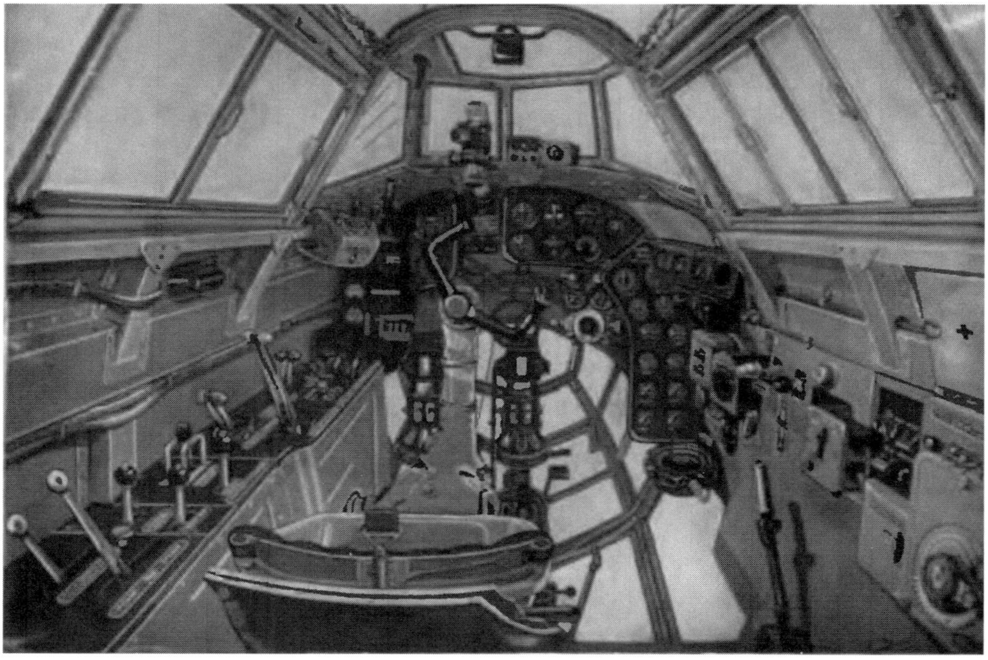

The forward cabin (cockpit). (*Drawing from the 1945 Tu-2 Flight Manual*)

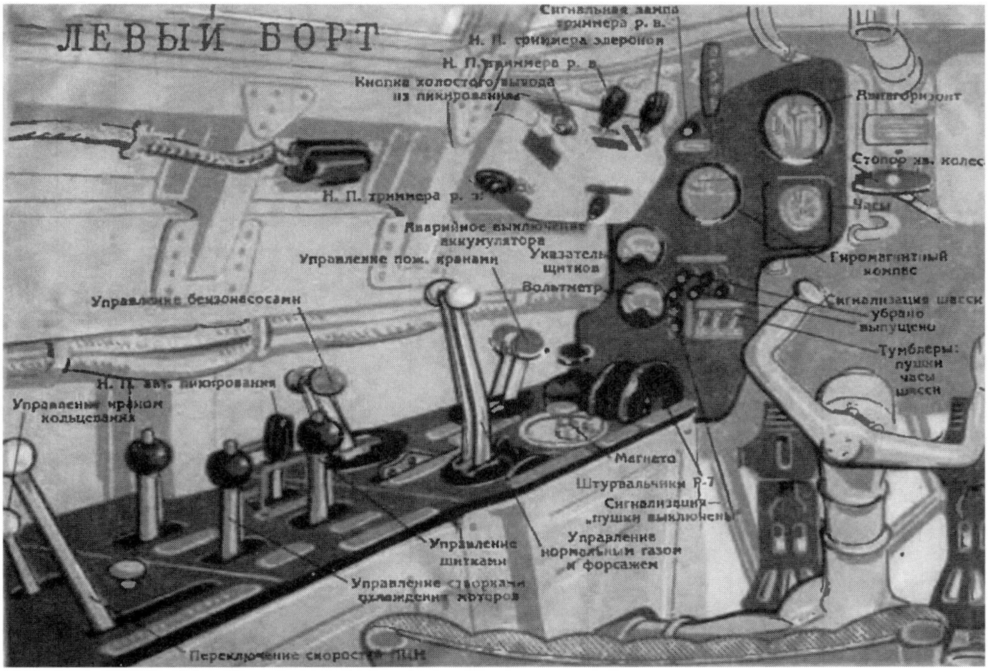

The port side of cockpit. (*Drawing from the 1945 Tu-2 Flight Manual*)

The starboard side of cockpit. (*Drawing from the 1945 Tu-2 Flight Manual*)

The 103U under construction at *Zavod* 156 (TsKB-29) in 1940. Note the inline engines.

A drawing of the opened cockpit canopy. (*Drawing from the 1945 Tu-2 Flight Manual*)

large window on each side. Between frames thirty and thirty-three there was a ventral hatch for the evacuation of the radio operator and the ventral gunner. The ventral gun position was located between frames thirty-three and thirty-six, the ventral gunner laying down to operate his UBT machine gun. He was protected from below and the back by armour.

The wooden tail cone, as used in the Great Patriotic War Tu-2s, consisted of a structure of three wooden frames with stringers, covered by a wooden, probably plywood veneer. From the series 44 or 45 onwards, it was replaced by a metal cone.

Armour Protection

One change that was made to the Tu-2S over the early version of the Tu-2 was the provision of more armour for the crew. The total weight of the armour on the Tu-2S was 538 lb (244.2 kg). The pilot had a seat made out of 0.59-inch (15-mm) thick armour and he was also protected on the port side by a sheet of armour 0.59 inches (15 mm) thick. The navigator was protected on the underside by a sheet of armour that was 0.31 inches (8 mm) thick, on the starboard side by 0.24-inch (6-mm) thick armour, and from the back by 0.59-inch (15-mm) thick armour. The radio operator/gunner was protected by a 0.24-inch (6-mm) thick plate of armour on the underside and had a plate of 0.47-inch (12-mm) thick armour protecting him on the back. The ventral gunner was protected by a sheet of armour that was composed of two layers—one 0.79 inches (20 mm) thick and another layer 0.06 inches (1.5 mm) thick to protect the gunner from shrapnel.

Wings

The wings were cantilever, shoulder-mounted, and were of two-spar all-metal construction, except for the wingtips, which were of wooden construction on the Great Patriotic War Tu-2s. Metal wingtips from the series 52 onwards replaced the wooden wingtips. The engines and the main landing gear were attached to the front spar. In combination with corrugated skin panels (covered by smooth dural panels), the two wing spars formed a torsion box for the wing centre section, which was very strong and could bear up to 95 per cent of the torsional loads. This centre section also featured ten ribs. In addition to the two main spars, the flaps were attached to a rear auxiliary spar. From the series 59 onwards, the leading edges were fitted with de-icing boots that worked by pulsating the rubber edges. The starboard wing had a landing light that could extend out from under the outer part of the wing and could retract back in. The wings were initially covered with a dural skin of 0.03 inches (0.8 mm) and 0.05 inches (1.2 mm), which was later changed to a thicker skinning of 0.04 inches (1.5 mm) and 0.08 inches (2 mm). The leading edges of the wing were smooth, with no air inlets, as there were no water radiators to cool them; the engines on the Tu-2S were air-cooled radials.

Tail Planes

The tail planes consisted of two fins and rudders, attached to the ends of the cantilever horizontal stabilisers (which were themselves attached to the fuselage by four bolts), with the vertical tail planes being perpendicular to the ground and parallel to each other. The construction of the tail planes was of metal, with the stabilisers having two metal spars, with a metal covering except for the rudders and elevators, which were of metal structure with fabric covering. Originally, the skin of the stabilisers was 0.03 inches (0.8 mm) thick, but this was changed to 0.04 inches (1.5 mm) later. The right rudder and both elevators had electrically controlled trim tabs. The fins (vertical stabilisers) consisted of two spars with eight ribs and were of all-metal construction. The elevator construction consisted of one spar and thirteen ribs with a fabric covering.

The horizontal stabilisers were mounted with a dihedral angle of 6 degrees 52 minutes and were of a 433 Gottingen profile. On the early version of the Tu-2, the incidence of the horizontal stabilisers could be adjusted, but with the Tu-2S the stabilisers were fixed as part of the simplification and lightening programme that characterised the Tu-2S. From the series 59 onwards, the leading edges were fitted with de-icing boots, as with the wings and the vertical tail planes.

Control Surfaces

The ailerons, twin rudders, and elevators were all made of a dural (aluminium alloy) structure, covered by fabric. The Schrenk-type flaps (a Schrenk-type flap was a flap that was lowered from the bottom only, with the top being a fixed integral part of the wing) were all-metal, split to allow clearance for the engine nacelles and hydraulically operated. These were capable of opening up to 45 degrees for landing (one source states that they could open up to 55 degrees) and were set to 15 degrees for take-off. The flaps were attached to a rear auxiliary wing spar. The Frise-type ailerons (a Frise-type aileron was an aileron having a nose portion projecting ahead of the hinge axis and a lower surface in line with the lower surface of the wing) were split into three sections, with the inner section of the starboard aileron having a trim tab that could be moved up or down 15 degrees and the two outboard sections for both ailerons had fixed-metal trim tabs that could be bent up or down on the ground. The ailerons themselves could be moved up 25 degrees and down 15 degrees. The moveable aileron trim tab was electrically operated. This moveable trim tab was on the starboard wing only; the port wing only featured the two ground-adjustable fixed tabs.

The rudders could be moved only 2 degrees to the left or right, while the rudder trim tab, present only on the starboard rudder, could be moved 15 degrees in either direction. The elevators could be moved up 35 degrees and down 20 degrees. The elevator trim tabs could be moved 6 degrees up only. The trim tabs were all electrically operated (except of course for the fixed ground-adjustable tabs on both of the ailerons).

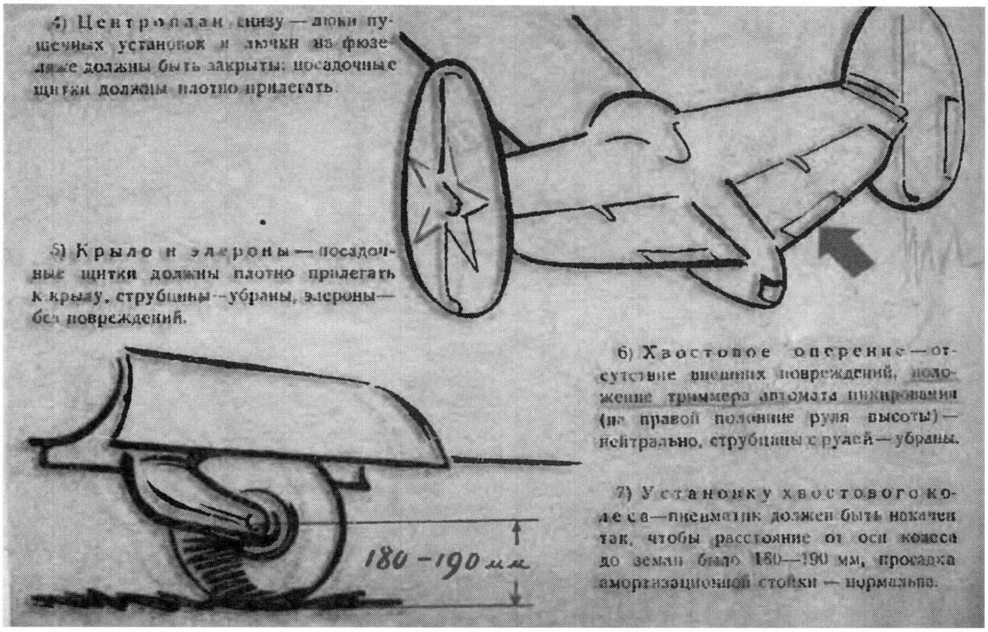

A drawing of the tail wheel and the tail surfaces. Notice the doors for the tail wheel and that only the starboard rudder and not the port rudder has a trim tab. Both elevators have trim tabs. (*Drawing from the 1945 Tu-2 Flight Manual*)

Engine

The basic engine for all production variants of the Tu-2 bombers was the M-82 fourteen-cylinder, twin-row, air-cooled, four-stroke radial engine, with a two-speed supercharger, also known as the ASh-82 from 1 April 1944, after its designer Arkadiy Dmitrievich Shvetsov (1892–1953). One of the features of this engine was that it had a short stroke, which decreased the diameter of the engine from what it would have been. This in turn allowed the engine to be housed in a smaller diameter cowling, which decreased drag. In fact, the Tu-2 had a well-designed, close-fitting cowling that, combined with the large propeller spinner, gave it good streamlining for a radial-engined aircraft. This engine had been developed from the M-62 nine-cylinder, single-row engine (its cylinders were based on the M-62 cylinder design), itself a development of the M-25, a license-built version of the famous American R-1820 Wright Cyclone nine-cylinder, single-row radial engine, which powered the B-17 Flying Fortress and some of the Douglas DC-3s, among other famous aeroplanes. The Tu-2s carried two of the ASh-82 engines. The engines could be started mechanically by Hucks starter dogs on the front of the spinners, fitted by shafts to starter trucks, but were normally started pneumatically from compressed air from the AK-50M compressor, which was mounted on the right engine's gearbox. An oil tank of 13.21 gallons (50 litres) was located behind the engine's firewall. From the series 15 onwards, there was a system for warming the engines—a very useful feature indeed in a central Russian winter.

An interesting feature of the engines was that the engine assemblies were interchangeable between the port and starboard sides, with an easily removed front assembly or 'power-egg'. This made the replacement of engines relatively easy from a maintenance standpoint and added to the general ease of maintaining the Tu-2. Some twin-engined aircraft were 'handed' with engines that swung propellers in opposite directions, such as the American Lockheed P-38 Lightning fighter. This eliminated torque, but the engines were slightly different, which made maintenance more difficult and made using the engines for either side impossible. In contrast, the Tu-2 was built for easy maintenance.

Although the eighty early version Tu-2s built in 1942 had the un-boosted M-82A engine, the variant fitted to the vast majority of the Tu-2s was the ASh-82FN (M-82FN), with boosting and direct fuel injection. This was the same engine fitted to the La-5FN and La-7 fighters. In the ASh-82FN version, the engine was capable of 1,850 hp at take-off. As with the La-5FN and La-7, there were louvres fitted to the front of the engine that could be opened and closed to control the flow of air over the engine cylinders. The louvres were different from those used on the Lavochkin fighters in that they were iris-like, instead of being two sets of discs with fixed blades, and could be controlled either automatically or manually by the pilot.

A small air inlet over the engine fed the supercharger (as with the La-5 fighter) and there was a broad and shallow intake under the engine for the oil cooler. The inlets over the engine were enlarged and equipped with dust filters from the series 61 onwards. The exhaust was collected from the fourteen cylinders on each engine to exit via one exhaust on each side of the engine, with seven of the cylinders feeding into the one exhaust, protruding through the cowling. At some point during production, apparently after the war, the external exhaust pipe was shortened. The engine installations were attached to the front wing spar via welded steel trusses.

The engine drove a constant-speed three-bladed AV-5V-167A metal propeller with rounded tips for the Tu-2S, but this was changed after the war from the series 59 onwards to a constant-speed AV-9VF-21K four-bladed propeller with blunt tips. The three-bladed propeller had a diameter of 12.47 feet (3.8 metres), while the four-bladed unit had a diameter of 11.81 feet (3.6 metres). The three-bladed unit had an R-7E speed regulator, while the four-bladed unit had an R-9SMI speed regulator. A large conical spinner usually covered the propeller. At least two of the preserved Chinese Tu-2s feature non-standard (at least for Soviet Tu-2s) four-bladed propellers with rounded tips and without spinners. It is not known if this was a modification done while they were still in service. These propellers actually resemble American propellers; perhaps they were taken from Chinese Tu-4 Bulls (the Soviet B-29, which were supplied by the Soviet Union to the Chinese and which used propellers based on the original American units).

The engines were installed in close-fitting cowlings that resembled those fitted to the radial-engined Lavochkin fighters (the La-5 and La-7), which also utilised the ASh-82 engine. From the series 20 onwards, the cowlings were made even more close-fitting, which required small fairings being fitted to cover the rocker heads on the engine cylinders. Single panels on either side of the engine opened up to allow easy access for maintenance, as can be seen in two of the photographs further on. Three latches on the bottom kept the cowling panels locked together. These latches can be seen clearly

An engine with opened cowling panels on a post-war AVMF Tu-2. (*G. F. Petrov Photo Archive*)

The ASh-82FN engine on a Tu-2S. (*Viktor Kulikov's Collection*)

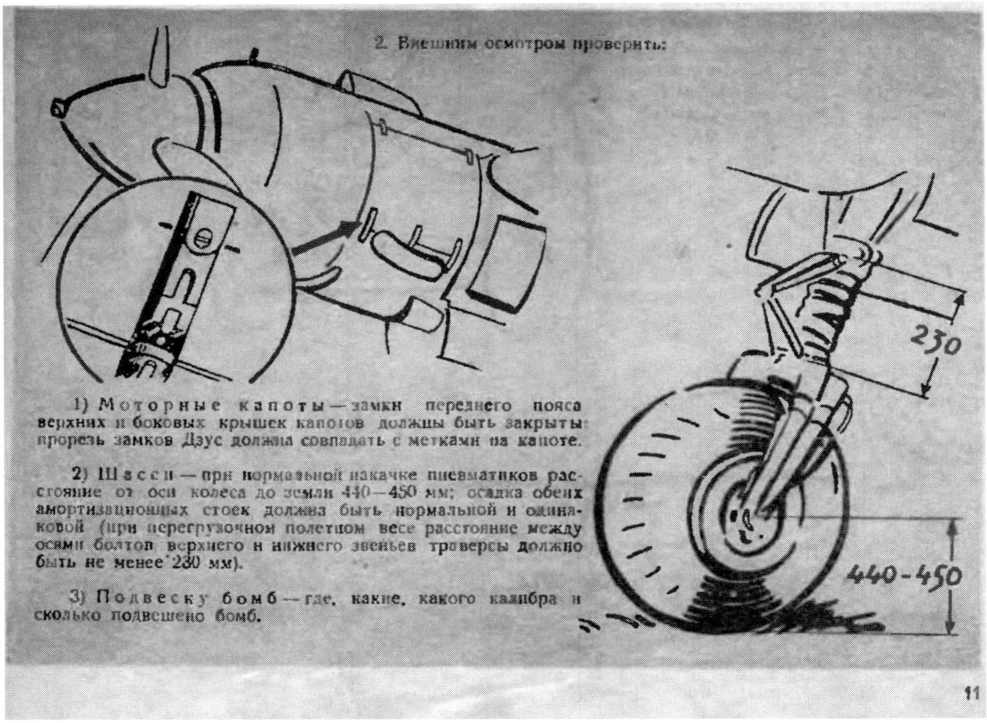

A drawing showing the latch mechanism for the engine cowling. The main landing gear is also shown. (*Drawing from the 1945 Tu-2 Flight Manual*)

in one of the photographs. A preserved ASh-82FN engine can be seen in the colour plates section.

Landing Gear

Both the main landing gear and the tail wheel were retractable, retracting aft, and were completely enclosed by doors when retracted. The main landing gear consisted of a single large oleo strut that was symmetrically forked to attach to the wheel on either side. The tail wheel was similarly forked. The main wheels were equipped with hydraulic drum brakes and had oleo-pneumatic shock absorbers. All the units were hydraulically operated, with a compressed air backup system. The main wheel tyre size was 1,100 × 425 mm (two sources state 400 mm—this may have been for the earlier Tu-2 variant); from the series 51 onwards, this was 1,100 × 395 mm, using a higher air pressure. The tail wheel tyre size was 470 × 210 mm, which from the series 51 onwards was increased to 530 × 230 mm, probably to deal with the greater all-up weight. The tail wheel strut could be locked in place, which assisted in take-offs and landings. The freely-moving, unlockable tail wheel of the early version of the Tu-2 had caused slewing, which led to some accidents.

Electrical System

The electrical system powered the cockpit lights, the radio equipment, and the heating. The cockpit used ultraviolet lighting for night flying. The electrical power was supplied by a GS-1000V generator, with a GSK-1500V from the series 52 onwards. The Tu-2s built at Z.166 after the war featured a GSN-3000V generator.

Fuel System

The fuel system consisted of nine fuel tanks. The main fuel tank was housed in the fuselage above the bomb bay, between the two wing spars. The wing tanks consisted of two inner and two outer fuel tanks in each wing, housed between the two spars. The total capacity was 616 gallons (2,800 litres) (one source says 761 gallons (2,880 litres) and another says 793 gallons (3,000 litres); the fuel capacity may well have varied from series to series). The tanks were of welded steel sheet construction of 1–1.2-mm thickness, with self-sealing rubber seals, and featured the normal Soviet fire-suppression system of neutral gasses being pumped into the fuel tanks as they were emptied, so that an explosive fuel vapour-air mix would not build up—the gas displaced this dangerous mixture. The neutral gasses were supplied to the fuel tanks from the exhaust of the starboard engine, after cooling and being passed through a filter.

Tu-2s built at Z.23 after the war may have had fourteen fuel tanks, and Tu-2s from Z.166 built post-war may have had twelve.

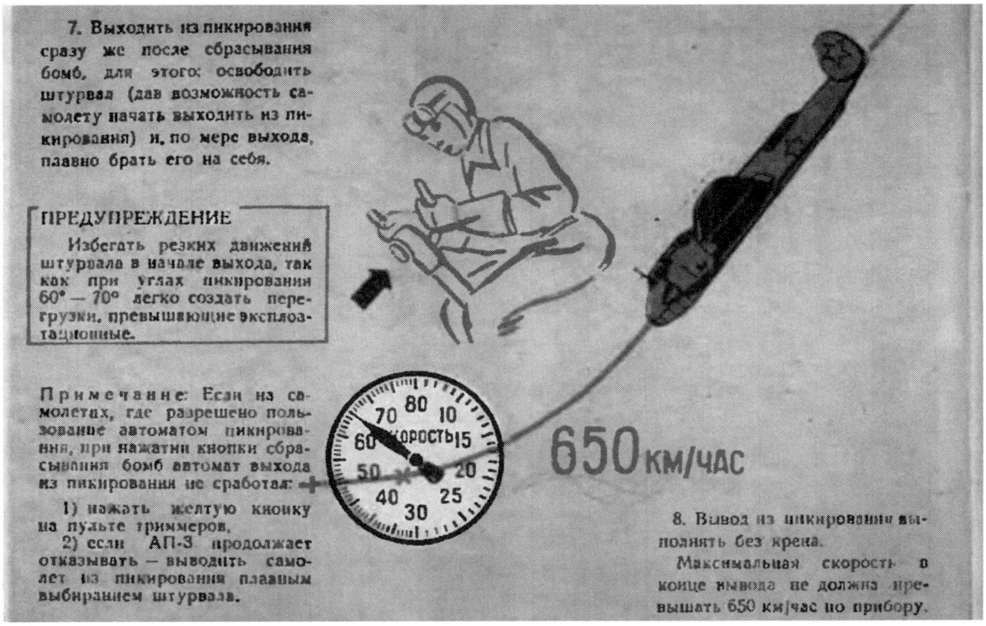

This drawing shows the Tu-2 diving at its maximum speed. (*Drawing from the 1945 Tu-2 Flight Manual*)

Hydraulic System

The hydraulic system was used to power the landing gear, the wheel brakes, the wing flaps, radiator flaps, and the bomb bay doors. The total volume was 8.72 gallons (33 litres).

Oil System

The oil system contained 72.91 gallons (276 litres) of oil, housed in two tanks, the pumps, oil lines, and the radiators.

Oxygen/Pneumatic System

The Tu-2 was equipped with eight 1.06-gallon (4-litre) oxygen canisters that were mounted on brackets in the aft fuselage and provided oxygen to the crew. The ShVAK 20-mm cannon in the wing roots were reloaded pneumatically. The backup retraction system for the landing gear was pneumatically operated by compressed air.

Electronic Equipment

The Tu-2S was initially fitted with the RSB-3bis radio. This was replaced by the RSI-6 from the series 51 onwards (the 1947 Standard Tu-2 had carried an RSI-5 radio). An SPU-4 intercom was used for on-board communication between the crew. At least some of the Tu-2s used an RPK-7 radio compass, while others used the RPKO-10M radio compass. Later still, an RPK-2B radio compass was used; this was used from the series 50 until the series 63 aircraft. From the series 63 aircraft onwards, blind flying equipment in the form of an RV-2 radio altimeter, an ARK-5 radio compass, and an MRP-48 bearing receiver was fitted. From the series 35 onwards, an 'identification friend or foe' (IFF) SCh-3 UHF system was fitted. The electronic equipment was continuously changed and upgraded on the Tu-2S during production, so there was no standard set of equipment, except for a specific series.

Fixed Armament

The fixed armament consisted of two Shpitalniy-Vladimirov ShVAK 20-mm cannon in the wing roots on all production Tu-2s, which could be used for ground-attack strafing or to discourage head-on attacks from enemy fighters. They were located between the first and third wing ribs. The pilot, using a fighter-type reflector gun sight, the PBP-1, which could also be used for dive bombing, aimed these cannon. Each cannon was equipped with 150 rounds and was cooled by air.

The guns were fired electrically and the reloading was done using compressed air. The spent cartridges and links were ejected from chutes under the wings. The firing button was located on the pilot's steering wheel. These two cannon gave the Tu-2S the very same forward firing armament as the La-5 and La-7 fighters. The early version of the Tu-2 also featured two ShKAS machine guns mounted on either side of the nose that were fired by the pilot. These were deleted from the Tu-2S as being unnecessary.

Moveable Armament

The moveable armament consisted for the Tu-2S of three Berezin UBT 12.7-mm (.50-calibre) heavy machine guns on flexible mounts (the earlier version had the smaller ShKAS 7.62-mm (30-calibre) machine guns on at least some of the mounts). K-8T reflector gun sights were used to aim the guns. The rear portion of the radio operator's canopy could be slid forward (to the front of the aeroplane) over the radio operator's head to allow the use of his machine gun. When not in use, this portion of the canopy slid back, to fully enclose the radio operator's cabin, with a small slot in the bottom of the canopy to clear the machine gun when it was stowed.

With the continuing development of the Tu-2, the gun mounts were changed. With the series 48 Tu-2S, the navigator received a new gun position, the VUS-1, which replaced the BUSh-1 blister-type installation, and the gun now had 170 rounds (the gun on the BUSh-1 had 190 rounds) and a K-8T gun sight with an OMP-6 stabiliser. It appears that, from the series 44 onwards, the radio operator/dorsal gunner's mount was changed from the VUB-2B to the VUB-68 mount, with 250 rounds, with the K-8T or K-20T gun sight, with the OMP-6 or OMP-7 stabiliser. From the series 50 onwards, the radio operator had a fixed canopy over his gun mount, replacing the moveable canopy. From the series 46, the ventral gunner was equipped with the LU-68 gun mount, with 350 rounds (or 300 rounds according to one source), replacing his earlier LU/Pe-2 mount that had 300 rounds (it was called the 'LU/Pe-2' mount because it was based on the Pe-2's ventral gun installation). The guns were equipped with bags that caught the spent shell cartridges and links. On some late Tu-2s, the UBT for the rear dorsal gunner was replaced by a Berezin B-20E 20-mm cannon, perhaps from the series 50, when the fixed gunner's canopy was apparently introduced. There are photographs that show what looks to be a 20-mm cannon in the rear dorsal position, under the fixed canopy.

The field of the fire for the navigator's gun was 45 degrees to the right and left, 90 degrees up, and 10 degrees down. For the radio operator's gun, the field of fire was 110 degrees to the right and 105 degrees to the left, 65 to 70 degrees upwards, and 15 degrees downwards. The ventral gunner had a field of fire of only 23 degrees to the right and left, 45 degrees down, and 1 degree up. This field of fire for the three defensive machine guns gave good protection from most angles, especially to the rear.

From the 52 series onwards, the moveable guns had a PAU-22 gun camera to record the shooting results; from the 57 series, the pilot also had a gun camera.

The starboard ShVAK 20-mm cannon. (*Viktor Kulikov's Collection*)

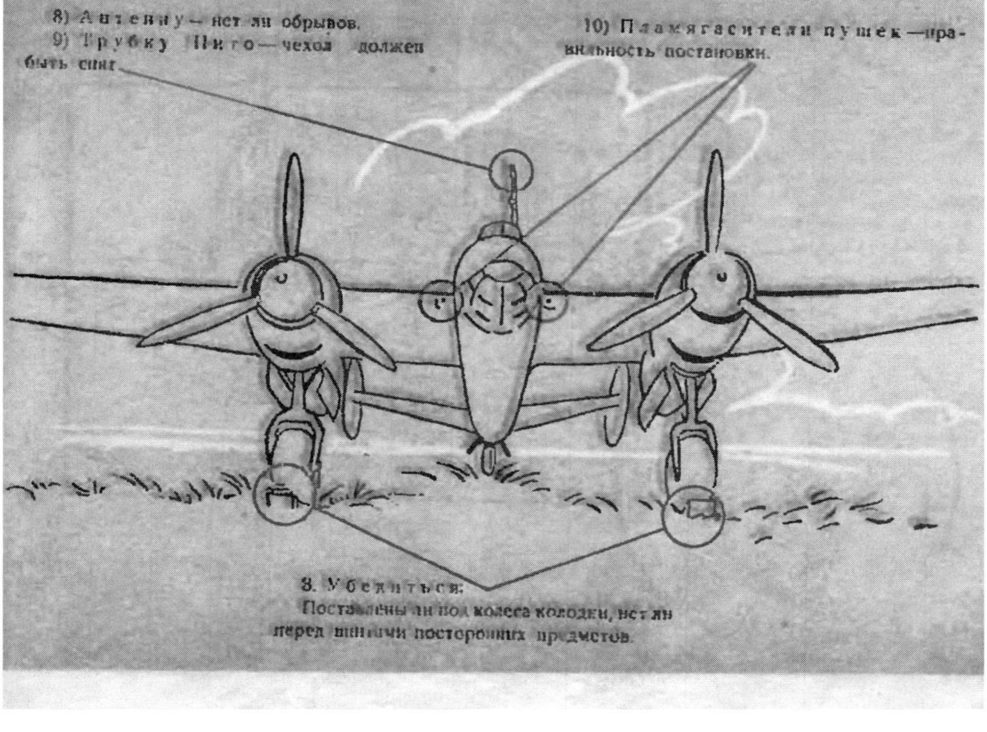

This drawing shows the ShVAK 20-mm cannon mounted in the wing roots and the offset antenna mast (offset to port). (*Drawing from the 1945 Tu-2 Flight Manual*)

3) прицел ПБП-1 перевести в боевое положение, потянув его за головку-хомут доотказа на себя (до щелчка стопора);

4) индексы шкал прицела поставить на нуль.

Right: A drawing showing the pilot's PBP-1 gun sight. (*Drawing from the 1945 Tu-2 Flight Manual*)

Below: The BUSh-1 blister mount for the navigator's UBT 12.7-mm machine gun. (*Viktor Kulikov's Collection*)

The rear dorsal position for the radio-operator's UBT 12.7-mm machine gun. Notice how the sliding portion of the canopy has been moved to the front to allow the gun to be used. (*Viktor Kulikov's Collection*)

Disposable Armament

One of the most important features of the Tu-2 was its capacious bomb bay and excellent bombload, up to 8,818 lb (4,000 kg) in some post-war versions. With this amount of bombs, some of them had to be mounted on the underwing bomb racks, located near the wing roots, with one on each side. The bomb bay itself was large and could accommodate a single 4,409-lb (2,000-kg) bomb, one of the biggest bombs in the Soviet inventory. This ability for a medium bomber to carry such a large bomb was considered a definite plus for the Tu-2. A more normal bombload would have consisted of smaller bombs in the bomb bay. Normally, the bombload did not exceed 6,614 lb (3,000 kg), consisting of three 2,205-lb (1,000-kg) bombs, with one in the bomb bay and two under the wings, but this heavy load was used only on short-range missions, with a more normal bombload being 2,205 lb (1,000 kg) or 4,409 lb (2,000 kg). As an alternate to the 1,000-kg bombs, four FAB-250 551-lb (250-kg) bombs could be mounted, two in the bomb bay and two under the wings on the wing-root bomb racks, for a total of 2,205 lb (1,000 kg). If the smaller FAB-100 220-lb (100-kg) bombs were carried, up to nine could be accommodated internally in the bomb bay for a total of 1,984 lb (900 kg) if no other bombs were carried. Besides carrying the FAB high-explosive bombs, the Tu-2 could also carry the BRAB armour-piercing bombs, PTAB anti-tank bomblets, and fragmentation bombs.

The bombs were aimed by the navigator for level bombing, using the OPB-1R sight (or OPB-1D from the series 24). For dive bombing, the PBP-1 sight could be used.

Above left: The bomb bay closed, with two bombs mounted on the wing racks. (*Viktor Kulikov's Collection*)

Above right: The bomb bay opened, showing mounted FAB-250 bombs. (*Viktor Kulikov's Collection*)

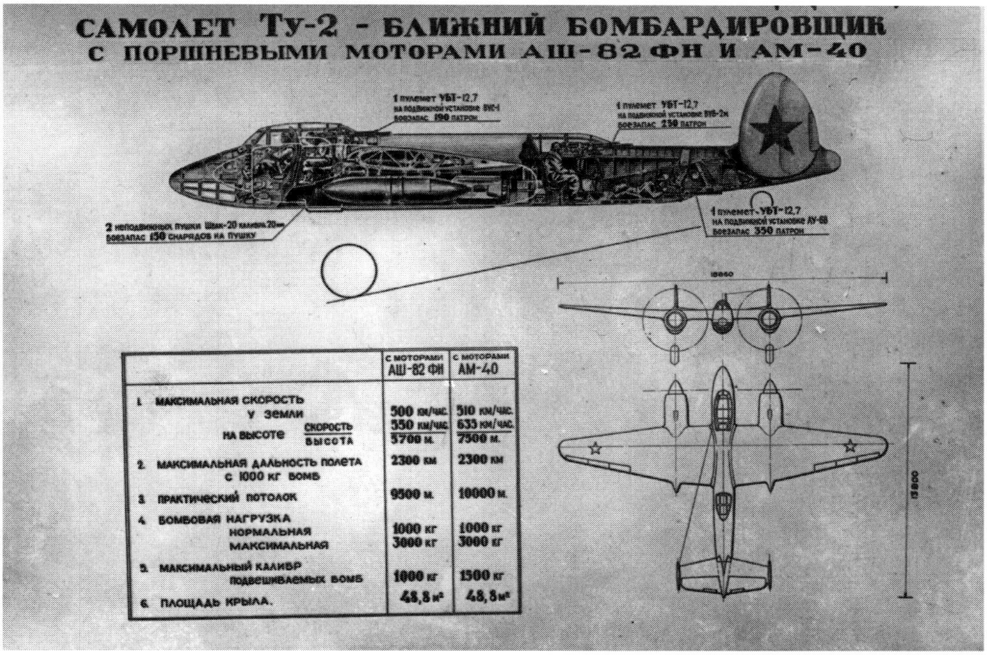

A cutaway and plan of the Tu-2S. (*Viktor Kulikov's Collection*)

APPENDIX I

Tu-2 Specifications

Tu-2 Prototypes and Production Variants Specification Table (data from various sources)

Type	103	103U	103V (Tu-2 Prototype)	Tu-2 (Z.166)
Year	1941	1941	1941	1942
Maximum Speed (mph (kph))	395 (635)	379 (610)	323 (521) or 328 (528)	324 (521)
Range (miles (km))	1,180 (1,900)	1,180 (1,900)	1,242 (2,000)	1,255 (2,020)
Service Ceiling (feet (metres))	34,780 (10,600)	34,449 (10,500)	29,528 (9,000)	29,528 (9,000)
Offensive Armament	2 × ShVAK 20-mm cannon, 2 × ShKAS 7.62-mm machine guns	2 × ShVAK 20-mm cannon, 2 × ShKAS 7.62-mm machine guns	2 × ShVAK 20-mm cannon, 2 × ShKAS 7.62-mm machine guns	2 × ShVAK 20-mm cannon, 2 × ShKAS 7.62-mm machine guns
Defensive Armament	2 × ShKAS 7.62-mm machine guns	3 × ShKAS 7.62-mm machine guns	2 × Berezin UBT 12.7-mm machine guns, 1 × ShKAS 7.62-mm machine gun	2 × Berezin UBT 12.7-mm machine guns, 1 × ShKAS 7.62-mm machine gun

No. 716 (Tu-2S Prototype)	Tu-2S (Z.23)	Tu-2S (Z.166)	Tu-2S (Z.39)	Tu-2S (Z.166)	UTB
1943	1944	1947	1948	1949	1946
340 (547)	340 (547)	342 (550)	342 (550)	348 (560)	236 (380)
1,305 (2,100)	1,305 (2,100)	1,628 (2,620)	1,243 (2,000)	1,274 (2,050)	N/A
31,168 (9,500)	31,168 (9,500)	30,184 (9,200)	29,856 (9,100)	29,528 (9,000)	19,685 (6,000)
2 × ShVAK 20-mm cannon	2 × ShVAK 20-mm cannon	2 × ShVAK 20-mm cannon	2 × ShVAK 20-mm cannon	2 × ShVAK 20-mm cannon	N/A
3 × Berezin UBT 12.7-mm machine guns	3 × Berezin UBT 12.7-mm machine guns	3 × Berezin UBT 12.7-mm machine guns	3 × Berezin UBT 12.7-mm machine guns	3 × Berezin UBT 12.7-mm machine guns	1 × Berezin UBT 12.7-mm machine gun

Type	103	103U	103V (Tu-2 Prototype)	Tu-2 (Z.166)
Rocket Armament	N/A	10 × RS-132 132-mm rockets?	10 × RS-132 132-mm rockets	10 × RS-132 132-mm rockets
Maximum Bombload (lb (kg))	4,409 (2,000)	4,409 (2,000)	6,614 (3,000)	6,614 (3,000)
Empty Weight (lb (kg))	16,812 (7,626)	17,246 (7,823)	16,171 (7,335)	16,757 (7,601) or 16,347 (7,415)
All-up Weight (lb (kg))	21,936 (9,950)	23,005 (10,435)	22,802 (10,343)	23,232 (10,538)
Maximum Weight (lb (kg))	24,233 (10,992)	25,302 (11,477)	25,955 (11,773)	25,942 (11,767)
Engines and take-off hp	2 × Mikulin AM-37 1,380	2 × Mikulin AM-37 1,400	2 × Shvetsov M-82A 1,700	2 × Shvetsov M-82A 1,700
Crew	3	4	4	4
Length (feet (metres))	43 feet 3⅝ inches (13.2)	45.28 feet (13.8)	45.28 feet (13.8) or 44 feet 11¾ inches (13.71)	45.28 feet (13.8)
Wingspan (feet (metres))	61.88 feet (18.86)	61 feet 8¼ inches (18.8)	61 feet 8¼ inches (18.8)	61.88 feet (18.86)

No. 716 (Tu-2S Prototype)	Tu-2S (Z.23)	Tu-2S (Z.166)	Tu-2S (Z.39)	Tu-2S (Z.166)	UTB
N/A	N/A	N/A	N/A	N/A	N/A
6,614 (3,000)	6,614 (3,000)	6,614 (3,000)	6,614 (3,000)	6,614 (3,000)	882 lb (400 kg)
16,477 (7,474)	16,477 (7,474)	N/A	N/A	N/A	11,770 (5,339)
22,839 (10,360)	22,839 (10,360)	24,317 (11,030)	25,133 (11,400)	N/A	14,431 (6,546)
25,944 (11,768)	25,044 (11,360)	N/A	N/A	N/A	N/A
2 × Shvetsov ASh-82FN (M-82FN) 1,850	2 × Shvetsov ASh-82FN (M-82FN) 1,850	2 × Shvetsov ASh-82FN (M-82FN) 1,850	2 × Shvetsov ASh-82FN (M-82FN) 1,850	2 × Shvetsov ASh-82FN (M-82FN) 1,850	2 × Shvetsov ASh-21 700
4	4	4	4	4	3
45.28 feet (13.8)	45.28 feet (13.8)	45.28 feet (13.8)	45.28 feet (13.8)	45.28 feet (13.8)	44.88feet (13.68)
61.88 feet (18.86)	61.88 feet (18.86)	60.76 feet (18.52)	60.76 feet (18.52)	60.76 feet (18.52)	61.88feet (18.86)

APPENDIX II
Survivors

Due to its sturdy all-metal construction (in the post-war versions), and usage into at least the 1970s and very possibly the early 1980s, there may be more than a dozen examples of the Tu-2 existing to this day (or at least their component parts). As far as I know, there are no flyable examples, although at least one museum in the United States may be restoring a Tu-2 to flyable status as of the time of writing (2016).

Bulgaria

There is a Tu-2 on outside display at the Bulgarian Museum of Aviation in Plovdiv. It is complete, but not in the best of conditions, as is common with aircraft displayed outdoors. A photograph of this aeroplane can be seen in the colour plates section.

China

Not surprisingly, since mainland China was the last user of the Tu-2, using them until perhaps as late as 1982, a few Tu-2s have been preserved at the Chinese Aviation Museum, near Beijing (Datangshan), and at the Military Museum of the Chinese People's Revolution in Beijing. The Tu-2s on outside exhibit could certainly be in better condition and, not surprisingly, the Tu-2s exhibited inside are in a better state. One source mentions that a dozen have been preserved or perhaps just their component parts, although it appears that some of these parts may now have found their way to the United States. Some photographs of these Tu-2s can be seen in the colour plates section.

Poland

Poland has one Tu-2S on outside exhibit in Warsaw alongside other Soviet aircraft, such as the Il-2 and the Pe-2, at the Polish Museum of the Army. This Tu-2S was used by the 7th Independent Dive Bomber Regiment. Being outside, it is unsurprisingly showing a bit of wear and tear. Another Tu-2S is in an inside exhibit in Krakow at the Polish Aviation Museum and it appears to be in a far better condition than the example housed outside. The example at Krakow had been used for testing ejection seats and it has the rear dorsal gunner position open as with one of the analogous Soviet Tu-2Ks. Photographs of these Tu-2s can be seen in the colour plates section.

Russia

There is one Tu-2, with the post-war four-bladed propellers, preserved at Monino, Russia, at the Central Air Force Museum located outside of Moscow. Once exhibited outside, thankfully this aircraft has been moved into a hangar, where it is now protected from the weather. Surprisingly, this is apparently the only Tu-2 preserved in Russia. It survived only because it had been used as a trainer near Moscow. However, with the possible closure or down-sizing of the Central Air Force Museum at Monino, its fate is uncertain. It may end up at the new Patriot Park (scheduled to be completed by 2017) at Kubinka near Moscow. Several photographs of this aircraft at Monino can be seen in the colour plates section.

No doubt there are some wrecked Tu-2s lurking elsewhere in the former Soviet Union, but I know of none that have been found, yet.

United States

At least one Tu-2 is currently undergoing restoration in the United States of America, at the War Eagles Air Museum in Santa Teresa, New Mexico. This is a preserved Chinese Tu-2 that may be restored to airworthy status. GossHawk Unlimited in Casa Grande, Arizona, at one time owned four Tu-2s for potential restoration (these probably came from Chinese stocks). As of the time of writing (2016), it is unclear what has happened to these airframes.

APPENDIX III

Production Figures

Production at all *Zavodi* (Official Numbers from MAP—Post-War Ministry of the Aircraft Industry)

Zavod	1941	1942	1943	1944	1945	1946	1947	1948	1949	1950	1951	1952	Total
23 (Tu-2S)			16	378	742								2,028
39 (Tu-2S)							5	48	161	4			218
82 (Tu-10)											19	6	25
166 (Tu-2/Tu-2S)	1	79	1			2	48	62	110				81/222
381 (UTB)—apparently all converted aircraft							35	117	25				176
												Grand Total	2,750 (2,574 excluding the UTBs)

A production line at a Tu-2 factory, probably Z.23 in Moscow. (*G. F. Petrov Photo Archive*)

Production Notes

Up to the end of the war, 1,013 Tu-2s were built (one source states that 1,111 Tu-2s were delivered by the end of the war, another source states 1,100 were, yet another states that 1,216 were produced from 1942–45). The source that states 1,216 Tu-2s were built during the war also records that 764 were transferred to the VVS. Presumably the aircraft that were not handed over to the VVS were given to the AVMF, kept by Tupolev, lost in transit, or lost in test flights at the factory. Apparently, the 1,216 number also includes those aircraft built between 9 May 1945 (the official end of the Great Patriotic War) and the end of 1945. The 764 aircraft appear to be those that were actually handed over to the air force by the end of the Great Patriotic War. According to the official totals from the MAP, a total of 2,750 Tu-2s were built overall (if you include the UTB conversions; without these conversions, the number is 2,574), including post-war examples (another source indicates 2,527 were produced and another that 2,649 were produced).

It is uncertain why the production figures vary from one source to the other; it may be that some include prototypes, or the UTBs (which were apparently all conversions of existing aircraft), or it may be due to the semi-secretive nature of the Tu-2. However, whichever figure is accepted, it can be seen that more Tu-2s were built after the war than during it. This would almost certainly not have been the case if Josef Stalin had not made the mistake of stopping production of the early version of the Tu-2 in 1942. If that unfortunate decision had not been made, many thousands of this very useful aircraft would no doubt have been produced during the Great Patriotic War.

Z.1

This plant, based at Kuibyshev (now Samara) on the middle Volga River, produced thousands of Il-2s during the Great Patriotic War. According to one source, this *zavod* built six reconnaissance Tu-2s (possibly Tu-6s) in 1946. According to another source, in 1947, it produced ten of the Tu-10s (68). However, another source says Z.82 produced these Tu-10s.

Z.18

At one time, in 1941, it was planned for the early version of the Tu-2 to be produced at this plant, at that time located in Voronezh, on the Don River. The onset of the Great Patriotic War and the German advance forced the evacuation of the plant to Kuibyshev and, instead of producing Tu-2s, the plant became the main Il-2 plant and produced a plurality of the thousands of Il-2s built during the war.

Z.22

This *zavod* in Kazan (on the middle Volga River) was slated to produce the Tu-2S, but it never produced a single one. This may be the same factory noted as Z.124 in one source.

Z.23

Based in Moscow (Fili), this *zavod* was responsible for producing the Tu-2S during the Great Patriotic War and continued to produce them post-war until as late as May 1949, although at least one source states that production was ended in 1948. Prior to producing the Tu-2, it had produced Il-4 medium bombers. In addition to the standard Tu-2S tactical bomber version, this factory apparently also produced the Tu-6, the post-war photo-reconnaissance version that was produced in small numbers. Andrey Tupolev was assigned the factory on 17 July 1943 and it went on to produce more than half of all the Tu-2s.

Z.39

This factory, located at Irkutsk in Siberia, produced the Tu-2S from 1947 to 1950, with a total of 218 being produced. These modernised versions had the four-bladed propellers and improved avionics. This *zavod* may have also produced the Tu-6 (Tu-2R) photo-reconnaissance variant after the war.

Z.82

This *zavod*, located near Moscow at Tushino, may have produced the Tu-10s (68) according to at least two sources and to the production table from the MAP. The MAP production list has this *zavod* producing twenty-five aircraft in 1951 and 1952, which is more than the ten Tu-10s that were supposedly produced. It may be that these twenty-five aircraft were not all Tu-10s, but they may have included some of the 'modernised' Tu-2s.

Z.125

One source states that this plant produced 218 Tu-2s from 1947–50, in order to replace aircraft lost through attrition (according to other sources, production of the Tu-2 continued until 1951 or even 1952). This source mentions that these Tu-2s had modernised avionics and were driven by a more powerful version of the ASh-82, the ASh-82IR, which produced 2,100 hp and drove four-bladed AV-9VF-21K propellers. The plant was located at Irkutsk, Siberia. The *zavod* is not listed in the MAP production figures for the Tu-2. This plant appears to be the same one listed as Z.39 in the previous table.

Z.156

Based near Moscow, this was the original home of the Tu-2, where much of its design and development took place, initially under the supervision of the NKVD. It produced prototypes and made modifications to create experimental Tu-2 variants, but no large-scale production of the Tu-2 occurred here.

Z.166

Located in Omsk, Siberia, far out of the range of Luftwaffe bombers during the Great Patriotic War, this *zavod* produced the early version of the Tu-2, some eighty production aircraft in total. After the war, beginning in 1946, it also produced some 222 (or 225) of the Tu-2S. The following table shows the aircraft (by series) that were produced during the Great Patriotic War at this *zavod*.

Great Patriotic War Production at Zavod 166 (Omsk)

Series Number	Number Produced	Construction No. (c/n)	Date (1942)
1	5	101–105	March–April
2	5	201–205	April–May
3	10	301–310	May–June
4	10	401–410	June–July
5	10	501–510	July–August
6	20	601–620	August–September
7	20	701–720	September–October
Total	80		

Z.381

This plant, located at Moscow, was responsible for the conversion of combat Tu-2s into the trainer version, the UTB. It was active from 1947–49, during which time it converted 176 UTBs. From 1949, it started producing MiG-15 jet fighters.

APPENDIX IV

Plastic Scale Model Kits

For such a good aircraft, with such a long operational history (and considering that quite a few preserved examples are still extant), the Tu-2 has been rather poorly served in terms of scale models. Regarding injection-moulded plastic, there are none in 1/32nd scale (perhaps not that surprising considering its considerable size), one mould in 1/48th scale (although it is available in three different versions), and three different mouldings in 1/72nd scale. This is rather meagre coverage even by the unfortunately low standards of Soviet Great Patriotic War and early post-war aircraft subjects.

1/32nd Scale

The Tu-2 kits in this scale are very easy to describe—none.

1/48th Scale

Pend Oreille: A resin kit of the Tu-2. I cannot determine which exact version of the Tu-2 this kit represents. This kit is probably redundant with the release of the very nice Xuntong plastic kits, unless you like constructing resin kits or wish to have one as a collectible.

Xuntong: Until this Chinese manufacturer released their kit of the Tu-2T, there were no plastic injection-moulded models of the Tu-2 available in the scale of which I am aware. In addition to the Tu-2T, they have also released the same basic kit as the Great Patriotic War Tu-2VS (the early version of the Tu-2) and the later Great Patriotic War version, the Tu-2S. The kit appears to be very nicely moulded, with good detail. In 1/48th scale, it should be a good-sized model.

1/72nd Scale

Aviatrak: This Ukrainian company has come out with a kit based upon the ICM mould (see entry further on), but with parts of the torpedo carrying version, and has some photo-etched parts and Bulgarian markings.

Encore: This appears to be a rebranding of the ICM kit with decals for a Great Patriotic War Soviet version, a post-war Soviet version, and a post-war Polish version. The same comments regarding the ICM kit apply.

Flugzeug-Modellbaukasten: this kit is probably the same kit as the VEB/Plasticart kit, so see that entry further on for comment description.

Hobby Bossy: Something of the opposite of the ICM kit, this is a very simple to build kit, from the Hobby Boss Easy Assembly range, with relatively few parts, but without the detail that the ICM kit provides, especially in the interior. However, the moulding is very good, the surface detail is quite nice, with cleanly engraved panel lines, and there is little, if any, flash on the parts. It is missing the tail wheel doors, but these should not be hard to replicate for any reasonably experienced modeller using sheet plastic. Another peculiarity is that it has the rudder trim tab on the port rudder, while it should be on the starboard rudder. This should not prove to be a difficult fix. If you also replace the rather poor toy-like representations of the UBT machine guns (which you definitely should), this model can be built into a nice-looking representation of a Great Patriotic War Tu-2S. Note that the paint schemes are for the early version of the Tu-2 with the green and black camouflage; this kit should be done in the three-colour scheme, as it represents the later wartime Tu-2 (Tu-2S)—it has the cowlings with small bumps, but also has the three-bladed propellers, indicating that it represents a Great Patriotic War Tu-2S. You can use the profiles in this book for a couple of examples of Tu-2s with the proper schemes.

ICM: A nicely detailed kit, with excellent and delicate surface detail, and accurate in shape and outline, this kit is nonetheless over-engineered and appears to be rather complicated to build, with some fit problems. I have seen it built up, however, so I know that with care it can be built into a fine-looking model. Although sometimes packaged with the Yak-9M as a Korean War duo (the Tu-2 being in Communist Chinese markings), this kit represents the Great Patriotic War Tu-2S; it has the three-bladed propellers (it is unclear if these were used in the Korean War), as opposed to the post-war version with four-bladed propellers. However, a three-bladed Chinese Tu-2 is presently preserved so they apparently did use the version with the three-bladed propellers at some point, perhaps even during the Korean War.

Modelist: This Russian manufacturer has a kit of the Tu-2, apparently using the ICM mould. In that case, the same comments regarding the ICM kit apply.

VEB/Plasticart: A fairly crude Soviet-era East German kit, it represents the post-war version with the four-bladed propellers. Long out of production, this kit can still be found if you search online sites such as eBay, but it is probably only useful as a collectible.

Bibliography

Internet Resources

vvs.hobbyvista.com: Modelling the Aircraft of the Soviet VVS—this was a useful site for making VVS models. It contains some useful information, although its articles on colour are controversial and should not be taken for gospel. This site is now moribund and the forum portion is no longer functioning, but the reference articles are still up as of the time of writing (2016).

www.airwar.ru: An excellent Russian-language resource for aviation-related material of all eras. It has much textual information on Great Patriotic War and post-war aircraft, including the Tu-2, and also has many plans and drawings, again, including the Tu-2.

www.arcforums.com: Not specifically for the VVS, but contains threads and posts regarding VVS aircraft and colours.

www.aviapress.com: A good site for Soviet aircraft kits, accessories, and books. The prices are not cheap, however.

www.britmodeller.com: A good site for modelling in general, containing some threads and posts concerning Soviet aircraft and VVS colours, some from this very author.

www.hannants.co.uk: An excellent British online ordering house. They have Tu-2 kits and accessories.

www.hobbyterra.com: A good site for Soviet/Russian aviation subjects; it includes some Tu-2 kits and accessories.

www.iremember.ru: A site that has interviews with veterans of the Great Patriotic War. The interviews are available in both Russian and English. Unfortunately, there are at present no interviews with Tu-2 pilots, or at least none that mention the Tu-2, but nonetheless recommended not just for aviation historians, but also for anyone interested in the experiences of Soviet military men and women during the Great Patriotic War.

www.lindenhillimports.com: A good internet store for all things concerning Soviet/Russian aviation, including VVS subjects.

www.modelism.airforce.ru: An excellent site that describes and reviews various aircraft models and accessories. In Russian, but with plenty of helpful photographs.
www.redbanner.co.uk: The successor site to Modelling the Aircraft of the Soviet VVS. The same comments about the old site generally apply to this site.
www.ScaleModels.ru: A very good site for reference material on VVS aircraft, including the Tu-2 bomber and its kits. In Russian with automatic English translation available (with all the interesting translation artefacts and peculiarities that entails).
www.sovietwarplanes.com: An excellent website for all things VVS and run by the illustrator of my books on the Il-2 Shturmovik and wartime Lavochkin fighters, Massimo Tessitori. Highly recommended for all those interested in Soviet Great Patriotic War aircraft and has accurate representations of the colour schemes that they wore. This site should also be of great interest for the plastic modeller of VVS aeroplanes. It now includes low-resolution versions of the colour profiles in this book.
www.squadron.com: A very good online ordering house with a good selection of aeroplane kits, including VVS subjects such as the Tu-2. They offer quick delivery in the United States.
www.tupolev.ru/en/aircrafts: Tupolev's own site; it has some interesting information about the Tu-2.

Further Reading

Note on literature: Although I have attempted to be as comprehensive as possible regarding good literature on the Tu-2, I may have missed some worthy titles. Nevertheless, if you are able to obtain and read at least some of the following books and magazines, then you will have gained an even better understanding of the history and development of the Tu-2 than can be contained in any one volume, even one as comprehensive as this book. In addition, since the Red Air Force was such an important part of all the major Soviet battles and operations, I have also added some books that give more background on these battles, as my coverage of these actions has been somewhat cursory, this being a general reference work on the Tu-2 and not a war history. These war histories are books that I have personally read and found to be both interesting and informative, and I hope that you will also find them so should you choose to read them. Please remember that these books are general military histories, not aviation histories, but for those who are interested in learning more about the battles that the Tu-2 took part in (or even Eastern Front battles in general), these books can be recommended.

Note for modellers: An important item to remember is that much of the literature mentioned further on that have Tu-2 profiles have colour inaccuracies in their profiles. Typically they have profiles with the fictitious colour scheme of green and brown, which should either be green and black, or dark grey, green, and tan, depending on the time period (mid-1941 to mid- to late 1943 for the black and green scheme, and mid- to late

1943–1945 for the dark grey, green, and tan scheme). Sometimes they will also feature the equally spurious scheme of green and dark green, or overall green for a Great Patriotic War Tu-2. It is also not clear from the record when or if the Tu-2 received the two-grey 'fighter' scheme. You should never rely only on profiles for your paint schemes unless you have no photographs or other references. You will have to interpret whether to use the black with the green scheme, the dark grey, green, and tan scheme, or the single overall topside colour schemes used post-war, depending on the time period of your Tu-2, if the profiles show any of the spurious schemes mentioned previously.

Air War Over Kursk: Turning Point in the East, by Dmitriy B. Khazanov. Besides containing a good account of the air war, which had an important impact on the ground fighting, this book contains many good colour profiles and tables of statistics dealing with the different units and aircraft that fought on both sides. Even though the early version of the Tu-2 took part in the battle, perhaps a bit surprisingly (or perhaps not, given the small numbers involved), the Tu-2 is not mentioned in this book. Despite this omission, this is still a good book on the air battle over Kursk.

Aviakollektsia: Soviet VVS Colours 1941-1945, by Mikhail Orlov. Contains colour profiles, photographs, and NKAP templates. To date, this is the definitive work on Great Patriotic War VVS colours. Highly recommended. In Russian.

Battleground Prussia: The Assault on Germany's Eastern Front 1944-45, by Prit Buttar. An excellent account of the Soviet invasion of East Prussia and the terrible retribution that the Red Army exacted on the German soldiers and civilians there.

Colours of the Falcons, by Jiri Hornat and Bob Migliardi. The best reference work for VVS colours in English. Recommended, although it does contain some inaccuracies, such as the spurious 'Southern Front' schemes. Note that this book only covers fighters, but the early black/green scheme is discussed, which was used on both fighters and bombers, such as the early version of the Tu-2.

Finland's War of Choice: The Troubled German-Finnish Coalition in World War II, by Henrik O. Lunde. This book gives a good and balanced insight into the complex relationship between the democratic Finns and Nazi Germany, including their sometimes joint, but more often disjointed actions against the Soviet Union.

Tu-2 Flight Manual. This is the original flight manual for the Tu-2S, published in 1945. Recommended for its drawings and historical value. In Russian.

Ivan's War: Life and Death in the Red Army, 1939-1945, by Catherine Merridale. This book tells the story of the common soldier in the Red Army. This book seems free of the prejudices and misconceptions, both flattering and unflattering, so common to popular accounts of the Red Army soldier. Highly recommended if you wish to know what it was like to be one small cog in the huge Soviet war machine during the Great Patriotic War.

Kiev 1941: Hitler's Battle for Supremacy in the East, by David Stahel. A book that explores an often overlooked chapter of the war in 1941—the Battle for Kiev and how it derailed the German advance on Moscow. This book gives a fairly convincing argument that this battle was crucial in the failure of Operation Barbarossa, at least in its failure to capture the Soviet capital before the end of 1941 and possibly knock the Soviet Union out of the war.

Red Phoenix Rising, by Von Hardesty and Ilya Grinberg. A general history of the VVS during the Great Patriotic War. Although not specifically about VVS bombers, it is the best reference in English of the VVS during the Great Patriotic War. Highly recommended if you wish to gain an overall understanding of the VVS and its strategy and tactics as used during the Great Patriotic War.

Soviet Air Power in World War 2, by Yefim Gordon. As the title suggests, this is a comprehensive reference book covering Soviet aircraft in general during the Second World War. It does contain a good section on the Tu-2 and its variants.

Soviet Combat Aircraft of the Second World War: Volume Two – Twin-Engined Fighters, Attack Aircraft, and Bombers, by Yefim Gordon and Dmitry Khazanov, with Alexander Medved'. Although not devoted just to the Tu-2, it contains a good section describing it and its many derivatives.

Stalingrad: How the Red Army Triumphed, by Michael K. Jones. An excellent and balanced look at what I believe to be the pivotal battle of not just the Great Patriotic War, but of the war in Europe.

The 900 Days: The Siege of Leningrad, by Harrison E. Salisbury. A fascinating book on the most deadly siege of all times.

The Battle of the Tanks: Kursk, 1943, by Lloyd Clark. Although at times seeming a bit too trusting of the inflated tank kill claims of the Germans, still a good and detailed overview of this important battle.

The Fall of Berlin 1945, by Antony Beevor. A thorough and balanced account of the last great battle of the Great Patriotic War.

The Retreat: Hitler's First Retreat, by Michael Jones. A good account of the Battle of Moscow, in what was, after Stalingrad, the most important battle of the Great Patriotic War. Although the Tu-2 did not feature in this battle, this is still a good book about the early part of the Great Patriotic War.

The Soviet Air Force in World War II, The Official History, Translated by Leland Fetzer, Edited and Annotated by Ray Wagner. Originally published in the 1970s in the Soviet Union, this book is as propagandistic as one might expect from a Soviet-era book on the Great Patriotic War. Nonetheless, if one can look past the propaganda, there is interesting and generally accurate information about the evolution of the Red Air Force during the Second World War. Recommended if you can stand a fair helping of Soviet propaganda ('Socialist Heroes of the Motherland versus the Fascist Invaders', etc.).

Tupolev Aircraft Since 1922, by Bill Gunston. Although not specifically about the Tu-2, it does contain some good information about the Tu-2 and its derivatives.

Tupolev: The Man and His Aircraft, by Paul Duffy and Andrei Kandalov. Another book that is not specifically about the Tu-2, but does contain some information about this aircraft.

Books

Duffy, P., and Kandalov, A., *Tupolev: The Man and His Aircraft*, (Warrendale: SAE International, 1996)

Gordon, Y., and Khazanov, D., with Medved', A., *Soviet Combat Aircraft of the Second World War – Volume Two – Twin-Engined Fighters, Attack Aircraft, and Bombers*, (The Hollow: Midland Publishing, 1999)

Gordon, Y., and Rigmant, V., *OKB Tupolev: A History of the Design Bureau and its Aircraft*, (Hinckley: Midland Publishing, 2005)

Gordon, Y., *Soviet Air Power in World War 2*, (Hinckley: Ian Allen Publishing Ltd, 2008)

Gunston, B., *Tupolev Aircraft Since 1922*, (Naval Institute Press, 1995)

Hardesty, V., and Grinburg, I., *Red Phoenix Rising: The Soviet Air Force in World War II*, (Lawrence: University Press of Kansas, 2012)

Kulikov, V., *Monografie Lotnicze 77: Tupolew Tu-2, Tu-1, Tu-6, Tu-8, Tu-10*, (Gdansk; AJ-Press, 2001)

Moore, J. N., *Il-2 Shturmovik: Red Avenger*, (Stroud: Fonthill Media, 2015)

Moore, J. N., *Lavochkin Fighters of the Second World War*, (Stroud: Fonthill Media, 2016)

Rigmant, V., *Bomber Tu-2*, (Moscow: Aviatsiya i Kosmonavtika, 2015)

Saukke, M. B., and Kotel'nikov, V. R., *Bomber Tu-2: Part 1* (Moscow: Modelist-Konstructor, 2008)

Saukke, M. B., and Kotel'nikov, V. R., *Bomber Tu-2: Part 2* (Moscow: Modelist-Konstructor, 2008)

Tu-2 Flight Manual (Leningrad; Leningrad Military Aviation Academy of the Red Army, 1945)

Yakubovich, N., *Our Aviation and the Battle for Berlin: Victory 'Stalin's Falcons'* (Moscow: 'Yauza', 'EKSMO', 2015)

Yakubovich, N., *Tu-2: Light Bomber: Patriotic War* (Moscow: 'Yauza', 'EKSMO', 2010)

Magazines

Voiyna V Vozdukhe Magazine, Vol. 66, Tu-2

Voiyna V Vozdukhe Magazine, Vol. 67, Tu-2

Index

AA (anti-aircraft (artillery)), *see flak*
ACh-30 engine 25, 95, 108, 121
Air Army (VA) 10, 57, 60, 63, 66-67
airfields
  targets of VVS 48-49, 67
Air Fleet (German) 60
AM-35 engine 27, 32-33
AM-37 engine 30, 32-33, 36-37, 43, 91, 156
AM-38 engine 32, 37
AM-39 engine 86, 91, 108, 110-111, 120-121
AM-42 engine 108
AM-43 engine 86-87, 120
AM-44 engine 93, 121
Army Fronts (Soviet)
  1st Byelorussian 63
  Kalinin 43-45, 46, 49
  Southwestern 45-46, 49, 58
  Trans-Baikal 66-67
Army Groups (German)
  Centre 18, 47, 58-60
  South 47
ASh-83 engine 99-100

B-20 20-mm cannon 72-73, 93, 96, 106, 117, 121, 125, 129, 149
Bagration, Operation 18, 58-60, 73
Baltic Sea operations 12, 46, 60, 63, 67
Baltic States
  Latvia, operations in 60, 68
  Lithuania, operations in 60
Barbarossa, Operation 10, 13, 21-22, 36, 41, 60, 169
Beria, Lavrentiy 17, 29, 32, 36
Berlin, Battle of 18, 20, 47, 57, 63-66, 170-171
Bf 109 45
bombs, effectiveness
  FAB-100 45, 48
  FAB-1000 46, 67
bridges, attacks on 67
Byelorussia, operations in 6, 58-60

camouflage schemes, Tu-2
  1941 camouflage (black/green) 50, 53, 166, 168-169
  1943 camouflage (three-colour) 40, 72-74, 166, 168-169
  mythical brown/green scheme 50, 168
  post-war 74, 168-169
Churchill, Winston 62
Citadel, Operation, *see Kursk, Battle of*
close air support (CAS) 10-11

DB-3, *see Il-4*

fighter escort 12, 15, 44-45, 58, 68, 77, 112
  Tu-2 to be used as 85-87
Finland
  Winter War 21-23
  Continuation War 58, 169
  end of war with the Soviet Union 58
First World War (Great War) 19
flak (AA) 10-11, 28, 44, 57, 60, 63, 65
  Tu-2 losses to 44, 58, 68
Fleets
  Black Sea Fleet (CMF) 11, 67, 102-103, 131

Red Banner (Baltic) Fleet (KBF) 12, 67, 102
Northern Fleet (SMF) 14
Frontal Aviation 11
fuel, Axis lack of 57, 60
Fw 190 45-46

German Army (*Heer*), *see Wehrmacht*
Great Patriotic War (GPW) 5-7, 74
definition 11
Great War, the, *see First World War*
ground attack 11-12, 14-15, 19-20, 24-25, 37, 42, 76, 78-80, 99, 101-102, 133, 148

Heer, *see Wehrmacht*
Hero of the Soviet Union (HSU) 11
Hitler, Adolf 169-170
death 65
HSU, *see Hero of the Soviet Union*

Il-2 11, 14-16, 25, 32, 37, 41, 49-50, 74, 135, 158, 162, 168, 171
Il-4 21, 23, 27, 66, 76-79, 81, 83, 102-104, 130, 162
Il-10 102, 108
Il-28 12, 104, 122, 125-126, 129
Ilyushin, Sergey Vladimirovich 13, 23, 77
designer of Il-2 14

Khalkhin Gol, Battle of (Nomonhan Incident) 21-23
Kharkov, Battle of, *see von Manstein, Erich*
Kiev, First Battle of 169
Kriegsmarine 12, 15
Kursk, Battle of 5, 22, 24, 46-48, 169-170

lend-lease 14, 79, 81, 130
Leningrad 5, 12, 58, 60, 66, 170-171
Luftwaffe 12, 15, 28, 34, 36, 57, 65, 76, 163
near disappearance from the Eastern Front 60

M-105 engine 25, 27, 29, 83
M-82 (ASh-82) engine 26, 37, 39, 43, 45, 49, 52, 54, 82, 120-121, 143-146, 156, 157
Manchurian Campaign (Manchurian Strategic Offensive Operation) 11-12, 18, 66-67, 78
markings, aircraft 50, 72-74, 166
Moscow, Battle of 5, 170
Murmansk 14

NII VVS 12, 34-35, 38, 41-42, 54, 71, 89, 93, 99, 112-113, 115
NKVD 5, 7, 13-14, 17, 24, 29, 30-32, 36, 39, 41, 163
Novikov, Aleksandr Aleksandrovich (head of VVS during GPW) 15, 57-58, 63, 101

Oder River 62-63
Overlord, Operation 60

PTAB 152
effectiveness 67
Pe-2 14, 21, 23-25, 27, 31, 44-45, 47-48, 50, 63, 68, 78, 83, 130, 149, 158
petroleum products, *see fuel, Axis lack of*
Poland 14, 25, 78, 116, 135, 158-159
polk definition of 14

railways, railroads, stations, and trains, attacks on 47-48, 58, 60, 67, 101-102
Red Air Force, *see VVS*
Red Army 6, 11-12, 14-15, 28, 47, 60, 63, 65, 87, 169-171
rockets
RS-132 39, 42, 156
Rokossovskiy, Konstantin Konstantinovich 47
Roosevelt, Franklin Delano 66
Russia, as distinct from the Soviet Union 6-7, 15
Russian, as distinct from Soviet 6-7, 15
Russo-German War, *see Great Patriotic War*

ShKAS 7.62-mm machine gun 27-29, 33, 39, 42, 51, 54, 77, 83, 149, 154
ShVAK 20-mm cannon 26-27, 39, 42, 54, 82, 86-87, 91, 93, 96, 102, 120-121, 148, 150, 154-155
Sevastopol
base of Black Sea Fleet 11
sharashka 13-14, 30-31
Shturmovik, *see Il-2*
Soviet Air Force, *see VVS*
Soviet Army, *see Red Army*
Soviet Union
definition of 6-7, 15
triumph over Germany 65
Stalin, Josef Vissarionvich 5-6, 17, 30-31, 36, 49-51, 57-58, 62-63, 66, 112, 161, 171
Stalingrad, Battle of 5, 46, 170

Tu-2
analogous aeroplanes to the Tu-2 75-84
armament 148-153
armour 141

bombs used 152-153
combat assessment (early version) 49
combat assessment (Tu-2S) 68
combat losses 44-45, 49, 58, 68, 135
combat tactics 67-68
development of early version of Tu-2 28-41
development of Tu-2S 51-56
engines used, *see ACh-30, AM-37, AM-39, AM-42, ASh-83 or M-82*
experimental versions 85-102, 104-113, 116-121
first combat action (early version) 43-44
first combat action (Tu-2S) 57
fit and finish 13
foreign service 130-135
gunners 149-152
introduction into service (early version) 43-45
introduction into services (Tu-2S) 56-57
performance of different versions 120-121, 154-157
plastic models of 165-166, 168
post-war Soviet service 130
predecessors 21-27
production 160-164
production, cancellation of 49-50
proportion of in VVS 68
radios 43, 72, 137, 147-148
successors 122-129
surviving examples 158-159
wooden components 43, 70, 136-137, 141
Tu-2R (Tu-6) 104-105
Tu-2T 102-104
Tu-14 102, 104, 122, 124-127, 129
Tupolev, Andrey Nikolayevich 5, 7, 13-17, 21-24, 28-33, 36, 41, 50-52, 54, 69-70, 85-87, 93, 102, 108, 113, 122, 126, 162, 170-171
Tupolev SB 21, 23-24, 27, 45, 76, 78
UBT (Berezin) 12.7-mm machine gun 26-27, 39, 42, 72-73, 77, 79, 82-83, 87, 89, 91-93, 96, 106, 112, 116, 120-121, 128, 137, 141, 149, 151-152, 154-155, 166
UTB (Tu-2 Trainer) 113-116
Ukraine, the
civilian casualties in 6
operations in 60

VVS (Red Air Force, Soviet Air Force) 7, 10, 12-15, 17, 21, 23-24, 28-30, 32, 36, 43, 46, 49, 51, 54, 56-58, 60, 63, 68-69, 72, 80, 101-102, 112, 122, 126, 161, 167-171
Vistula to Oder Operation 62-63
Volga River 41, 162
von Manstein, Erich
Kharkov, Battle of 46
Kursk, Battle of 47

Wehrmacht 11-12, 15, 47, 60

zavod (factory) 6, 14-16
evacuation of 41, 162
production figures 160
Zavod 1 111, 162
Zavod 18 41, 162
Zavod 19 37
Zavod 22 56, 162
Zavod 23 54-56, 70, 96, 99, 104-105, 108, 116, 136, 147, 155, 157, 160-162
Zavod 39 72-73, 155, 157, 160, 162-163
Zavod 82 111, 160, 162-163
Zavod 125 163
Zavod 156 14, 31-33, 37, 41, 54, 86, 89, 91, 110, 163
Zavod 166 37-41, 45-46, 49-50, 54, 69-70, 93, 111, 147, 154-157, 160, 163-164
Zavod 381 115-116, 160, 164
Zhukov, Georgy Konstantinovich 63